E O T H L ᴚ

By

A. W. KINGLAKE

WITH AN INTRODUCTION AND NOTES

By ANON

WITH A FRONTISPIECE

FROM A PAINTING

By THE AUTHOR

LONDON

METHUEN & CO.

36 ESSEX STREET, W.C.

MDCCCC

Πρὸς ἠῶ τε καὶ ἡλίου ἀνατολὰς ἐποιέετο τὴν ὁδόν. —HEROD. vii. 58.

CONTENTS

CONTENTS

INTRODUCTION

I

EOTHEN is the earliest work of Alexander William Kinglake, best known as the historian of the Crimean War. It is an account of a tour— or rather of selected adventures which occurred during a tour—undertaken in the Levant in 1834, but was not published until ten years later. The biographical notices of the Author are somewhat meagre, as by his dying directions all his papers were destroyed. He was born near Taunton in 1809, and educated at Eton and Trinity College, Cambridge, at which latter he is said to have been the friend of Thackeray and Tennyson. On leaving college he started on his Oriental tour with Lord Pollington (the Methley of *Eothen*), and on returning to England was called to the Bar at Lincoln's Inn, and obtained a lucrative practice. But the life was too tame to suit his taste. In 1845 he visited Algeria, and went through a campaign with the flying column of St. Arnaud; and in 1854 went to the Crimea with Lord Raglan, and was present at the battle of Alma. On returning to England he decided to go into politics, and was elected for Bridgewater in 1857 in the Liberal interest. He seems to have been a poor speaker, and to have exercised little parliamentary influence; but we are told that in 1859 he was strongly opposed to the Conspiracy Bill, which was introduced after Orsini's attempt to murder Napoleon III., and that in 1860 he denounced the cession of Nice and Savoy to France. In both cases he was apparently actuated by his personal dislike of Napoleon, which is evident in his historical works. In 1868 he was again returned for Bridgewater, but unseated on petition, for bribery. One might have supposed that he had acquired this habit in the East, but his biographers assert that he knew nothing of the irregularities which were committed by his agents. But the chief business of his later life was the composition of the *History of the War in the Crimea*, of which the first two volumes appeared in 1863, and the seventh and eighth (completing the work) in 1887. He died in 1891.

II

His earlier and less ambitious, though perhaps more charming, book was rejected by several publishers, but proved an immense success. It caught the popular fancy at once, and after the lapse of more than fifty years still maintains an honourable position. In the year after its first appearance it passed through three editions, containing several variations from the *editio princeps* which have attracted the attention of those who are interested in bibliography. It is only fair to reprint the book with these corrections, which seem mostly due to the author's laudable desire for greater accuracy. For instance, he was apparently seized with qualms as to his assertion (end of chap. xiii.) that when he emerged from the Dead Sea after bathing therein his "skin was thickly encrusted with sulphate of magnesia," and cautiously substituted "salts" for the more chemical expression. Yet I observe that the most recent Encyclopædia states that "the water of the Dead Sea is characterised by the presence of a large quantity of magnesian salts," so perhaps his first statement was not so wrong after all. He also found that he had talked of Jove when he should have said Neptune in his account of the Troad, and, conceiving a mistrust of the former deity, removed his name not only from this passage but also from chap. xviii., in which he altered "That touch was worthy of Jove" into "In that touch was true hospitality." I confess that I think this regard for truth might have moved him to expunge his account of the advances made to him by the young ladies of Bethlehem (end of chap. xvi.); I cannot believe that narrative to be even probable, but anyone may retort that my scepticism is due to the absence of those attractive qualities which Kinglake possessed.

In chap. xvi. he says that shrouds are dipped in the holy water of the Jordan and "preserved as a burial dress which shall inure" (later editions "enure") "for salvation in the realms of death." Some critical scholar of eminence should be called upon to emend or explain this mysterious passage. At least, if people are allowed to print such things in the nineteenth century what right have we to emend the classical authors when they choose to be unintelligible?

The truth is that *Eothen*, despite its great literary merits, is often comfortably slipshod. And very properly so, for if there is to be any correspondence between subject and style, it must be inappropriate for a traveller recounting confidentially his diversions and mishaps to adopt the phraseology of Gibbon. Matthew Arnold, in his "Essay on the Literary Influence of Academies," selected the *History of the Crimean War* as an example of what he called the Corinthian style. *Eothen* certainly presents specimens of this manner, but they are hardly characteristic; it is often "urbane," and has "the warm glow, blithe movement, and pliancy of life," which, according to the critic's definition, Corinthians lack. It is not devoid of unity, but it is many sided and kaleidoscopic. The author varies from the trivial to the solemn, from boisterous exuberance to careful austerity, from flippancy to rhapsody, and is perhaps never quite serious. One wonders whether one is reading a clever but somewhat slangy letter, or a long-meditated essay polished and repolished by incessant *labor limæ*. Perhaps between 1834 and 1844 he worked up and rearranged old spontaneous effusions, as indeed his preface suggests. He often writes like a schoolboy, and sometimes like a philosopher; he is at his best when he records what he has seen in phrases not without rhetoric and not without humour, but distinct and clear as his own impressions. "The foot falls noiseless in the crumbling soil of an Eastern city, and silence follows you still. Again and again you meet turbans, and faces of men, but they have nothing for you—no welcome—no wonder—no wrath—no scorn —they look upon you as we do upon a December's fall of snow—as a 'seasonable,' unaccountable, uncomfortable work of God, that may have been sent for some good purpose to be revealed hereafter." How vivid and how true!

But perhaps the reader may ask, as I ask myself, whether an introduction to *Eothen* is really necessary. The book is so simple and complete in itself that it seems to require no explanation or commentary. But for the benefit of those who are not acquainted with the Levant of to-day, it is well to explain that the sixty-four years which have elapsed since Kinglake made his Eastern tour have brought about important changes in the extent, and some few in the condition, of the Turkish Empire. The "unchanging East" is a popular phrase which is only true in a very limited sense. It has arisen chiefly from the habit of pious publishers of representing Abraham in the costume of a modern Bedouin Sheikh, and it is peculiarly audacious to apply it to regions like Constantinople and Egypt, which have witnessed exceptional vicissitudes and undergone remarkable changes,—political, religious, and linguistic. It is however just to say that the Turk is unchanging,—and it is to the presence of the Turk that are due the peculiar characteristics of the Levant, as the region visited by Kinglake may conveniently be termed ; like the Bourbons, he forgets nothing and learns nothing ; as he was on the day when he entered Europe, so he was in 1834 and so he is now. The boundaries of Turkey have changed ; there are now no Pashas at Belgrade, or even at Sofia ; and Ottoman territory is no longer plague-stricken. But whenever one crosses the Turkish frontier, one may find functionaries like the delightful potentate of Karagholookoldour, and be conscious of effecting within the space of a few hundred yards a change greater than can be experienced in any amount of travel in other European countries, including Russia. One passes from regions where people have roughly the same habits and ideas as ourselves—where they believe in political economy, get drunk in public, sit upon chairs, and do not feel there is anything indelicate in mentioning their wives—to a land where people do none of these things, where the naked desolation of the country at the side of the railway offers a startling contrast to the smug prosperity of the Balkan States, where people prefer to sit curled up on hard sofas, and where it is bad taste to condole with a man on his wife's death.

In 1834, the year of Kinglake's journey, Turkey in Europe was considerably more extensive than at the present day. Greece had already revolted and been recognised as an independent state. Wallachia and Moldavia were in process of securing their freedom. But the territories now known as Bulgaria, Bosnia, and Herzegovina were still integral portions of the Ottoman Empire; and though Servia (in which the scene of the opening chapters of *Eothen* is laid) had been constituted a principality under Milosh Obrenovich as prince, in 1830, several of the fortresses were still garrisoned by Ottoman troops, which accounts for the presence of the Pasha at Belgrade. It is interesting to observe that though our Author must have proceeded to Adrianople straight across Bulgaria, he never mentions the name of that country. This apparently strange omission is really quite natural. The Bulgarians, though in some ways the most vigorous element among the Balkan races, passed through greater trials than the Servians or Roumanians, and for a time lost their national consciousness more completely. They were nearer Constantinople, and therefore any political movement was more easily kept in check; while all the religious and educational establishments of the country were in the hands of Greek priests who practically proscribed the Bulgarian language. I have been informed by a gentleman who has resided forty years in Turkey, that when he first entered the Ottoman dominions every educated Bulgarian called himself a Greek, and would have been ashamed to employ his national designation, which was hardly in general use before the movement of 1860. Another striking omission of *Eothen* is that it contains hardly any allusion to the Sultan. At the present day the descendant of Osman, who claims to be also the successor of the Prophet, is a well-known figure to the British public. The *Pall Mall Gazette* familiarly calls him " The Shadow." [1] The friends of the Armenians hold him personally responsible for the massacres ; and a modern Kinglake, even if bent on avoiding " political disquisitions," would certainly describe the Selamlik or weekly visit of the Sovereign to the mosque. You cannot travel in Turkey without hearing the name of " Our Master " (Effendimiz) or " the Imperial Person " (Zat-i-Shahane) daily mentioned, and feeling that his wishes (which usually do not coincide with those of European travellers, and affect the minutest details) are the only real power in the country. This state of things is due almost entirely to the personal energy of the present occupant of the Ottoman throne, who for good or evil has succeeded in concentrating all power into his hands, and in displaying the greatest

---

[1] The title " Shadow of God," or " Divine Shadow," is really used comparatively rarely, and only in the Court language. Judged by a strict standard it is of doubtful orthodoxy.

example of practical autocracy ever seen. In 1834 Mahmoud was Sultan, one of the most vigorous of Ottoman princes, but then near his end, and doubtless wearied out by a reign of constant reverse and ineffectual efforts at reform.

The Armenian question, like the Bulgarian, is of recent date, and we consequently find that Kinglake says as little of the one as of the other; but he often speaks of the doings of Mehemet Ali and his son Ibrahim Pasha, which at this period formed one of the chief preoccupations of the Porte. Mehemet Ali was a native of Cavalla who held a military command in Egypt. In the troubles which succeeded the French occupation of that country, at the beginning of the century, he succeeded in making himself head of the popular party in Cairo, ousted the Turkish Governor, and established himself in his place. He was recognised by the Porte in 1805, and the Khediviate was subsequently made hereditary in his family. At this time the Mamluks (or descendants of the Turkish Guard instituted by the Sultans of Egypt in the thirteenth century) occupied a position somewhat similiar to that of the Janissaries at Constantinople. Mehemet Ali, like Sultan Mahmoud, felt that this military *imperium in imperio* rendered fixed Government impossible, and determined to consolidate his own rule by breaking the power of the Mamluks. He did so by inviting their leaders to a banquet, at which they were surprised and massacred. The Sultan, in return for his recognition of Mehemet Ali as ruler of Egypt, made use of him during some years to keep in order various rebellious provinces of the Empire. He was first ordered to quell the Wahabi insurrection in Arabia, and his campaign there is alluded to in chap. xviii. These people were a sort of Mohammedan Puritans [1] who had made themselves masters of the Holy Cities of Mecca and Medina. Mehemet Ali sent against them his son Tosun, who captured Mecca in 1813, but died, and was replaced by his younger brother Ibrahim Pasha, who is often mentioned in *Eothen*. He finally concluded the Wahabi war in 1818, and is next heard of fighting against Greece, which was beginning the struggle for independence. Mehemet Ali was again called upon to assist the Sultan in suppressing rebellion, and again sent his son to represent him. Ibrahim captured Missolonghi in 1825, but was defeated in 1827 by the united fleets at Navarino, under Sir Edward Codrington, and retired from Greece. In return for these services Mehemet Ali claimed that the Pashalik of Syria should be added to his dominions. The Sultan refused the request of his powerful vassal ; but the latter picked a quarrel with the Turkish governor of Syria, and sent Ibrahim to invade the province. Ibrahim not only made a triumphal entry into Damascus, but defeated the Turkish Army at Beilan and advanced into Asia

---

[1] It is hardly correct to call them the *Unitarians* of the Moslem world, as Kinglake does, for Unitarianism, that is Antitrinitarianism, is the essence of all Mohammedanism.

Minor, where he routed a second force, sent against him by the Sultan, near Konia, in December 1832. The defeated Turkish troops joined the Egyptians, Ibrahim advanced victoriously to Broussa, and had Constantinople at his mercy. The Sultan in his extremity called the Russians to his assistance. The Treaty of Unkiar Iskelesi was concluded in 1833; Ibrahim was obliged to retire, but the Pashaliks of Syria and Adana were given to Mehemet Ali, and treated with great rigour, as mentioned in chap. xv At the time of Kinglake's visit to Egypt the plague seems to have been the one absorbing pre-occupation of everyone in Cairo, and we learn little from him of the normal state of the country at this period. The most remarkable of his Egyptian sayings is the prophecy at the end of the chapter called " The Sphinx." " The Englishman leaning far over to hold his loved India will plant a firm foot on the banks of the Nile and sit in the seats of the faithful." To have made this prediction at a time when India was still under the Company, when we had no interests in North-East Africa or the Red Sea, before the Suez Canal was a serious project, perhaps before we had occupied Aden,[1] is indeed an example of no ordinary political foresight.

Such was the political condition of the lands

---

[1] Aden was occupied in 1839. *Eothen* must have been written between the tour in 1834 and its publication in 1844, but there seems to be no evidence as to the date of composition, and perhaps it was not all written at once.

b

which Kinglake visited, and of many aspects of
which he gives a most living picture. In his diverting
preface he disclaims all intention of being instructive,
of describing manners and customs, still less of dis-
cussing political and social questions. Perhaps his
narrative sometimes reminds the reader of his
statement (chap. viii.) that a story may be false
as a mere fact but perfectly true as an illustration. Some great writers impart durability to their
work by selecting from a mass of details such traits
as are important and characteristic, and passing
lightly over what is transitory. For instance, the
main impression left by Thackeray's novels is not
that the life there described is old-fashioned, but that
it is in essentials the life of to-day. So, too, in
Eothen a reader acquainted with the East hardly
notices anachronisms. Judged as a description of
the Levant of 1898, it is inaccurate, or rather
inadequate, almost exclusively on account of its
omissions. But the principal descriptions, inci-
dents, and portraits—the Mohammedan quarter at
Belgrade, the conversation between the Pasha and the
Dragoman, the meeting of the two Englishmen in
the desert, Dimitri and Mysseri—are, if considered
as types, as true to nature to-day as they were
sixty years ago, and doubtless will be sixty years
hence.

Kinglake treats the Levant in the only way it
ought to be treated if it is to be enjoyed—half-
seriously. Those whom business or philanthropy

oblige to devote to it any real exertion, sentiment, or interest, lay up for themselves nothing but disillusion and disappointment, for, whether they are fascinated by the picturesque and manly virtues of the Moslems, or roused to honourable indignation by the slaughter and oppression of their fellow-Christians, they will find in the end that, as Lord Salisbury once said, they have put their money on the wrong horse. In the Eastern Derby there are no winning horses. One after another they have all disappointed their backers ; the faults of Eastern Christendom brought about and still keep up the rule of the Turk, and few who have an adequate knowledge of the facts of the case believe either that the Christians are happy under that rule or that they furnish in themselves the elements of anything much better.

Yet this dreary tragedy — this daily round of oppression and misgovernment, varied by outbursts of interracial fury—has a brighter side. To the mere spectator, to the intelligent traveller with literary taste and a sense of humour, the surface of Levantine life is a stream of perpetual amusement, often broadening into comedy, and sometimes bursting all bounds and breaking into a screaming farce. The number and variety of races and languages afford infinite possibilities of misunderstanding and mistranslation (which it must be admitted are the basis of many good stories) ; the Orientalised European and the Europeanised Oriental are alike inexpressibly droll. Their very crimes have an element of the burlesque, which seems to disarm censure and remove the whole transaction to a non-moral sphere where ordinary rules of right and wrong do not apply. The Turk, if not precisely witty himself, is at least the cause of wit in others. Extreme Asiatic dignity amidst ludicrously undignified European surroundings, a mixture of pomp and homeliness, power and childishness, give rise to humorous anecdotes of a peculiar and very characteristic flavour, examples of which may be found in several works besides *Eothen*, notably Robert Curzon's *Monasteries of the Levant*. Another excellent illustration is supplied by Vazoff's *Under the Yoke*, a translation of which has been published in English. It is an historical novel, written by a Bulgarian burning with indignation against the Ottoman rule. Yet the Turkish Caimmakam, as drawn by a bitter enemy, is no bloody tyrant, but an exquisitely diverting old gentleman whose every appearance is hailed by the reader with impatient delight. As the violence of the Turk, so also the dishonesty and corruption of the Rayah seem to lose their enormity when viewed in this gentle, humorous light. The swindling is so palpable, and yet so gravely decorous in its external forms, that it ceases to shock ; it is so universal that in the end no one seems to have suffered much wrong. To vary the celebrated remark about the Scilly Islanders, one may say that these people gain a precarious livelihood by taking bribes from one another. Again the elaborate and ceremonious phraseology essential to all literary composition in the East enables a writer to make intrinsically preposterous assertions with a gravity which renders criticism impossible. What reply can be given to the officials who assert that Armenians commit suicide in order to throw suspicion on certain excellent Kurds residing in their neighbourhood? or who when called upon to explain why they have incarcerated a foreign traveller under circumstances of extreme indignity, blandly reply that "the said gentleman was indeed hospitably entertained in the Government buildings"?

This last instance shows that Oriental travelling must not be undertaken without due precautions. A certain retinue, and sufficient influence to secure the courtesy of the authorities (which Kinglake evidently had), are essential. With them the traveller acquires a feeling, often manifest in *Eothen*, that he is a sultan possessed of absolute authority over his surroundings. There is just enough hardship to make comparative comfort seem luxury, just enough danger to make it pleasant, when all is over, to hear from what perils one has escaped. Should, however, any reader be inclined to use *Eothen* as a practical manual, he must be cautious in following some of its precepts. Kinglake constantly insists that intimidation, haughtiness, and defiance of all regulations are the only means of impressing Orientals; and chronicles with great satisfaction his own exploits in this line, concluding with "the Surprise of Satalieh." What he says is true enough as long as the Oriental believes that the

traveller is a prince in his own country, and that any
interference with his mad whims will bring severe
punishment. But unfortunately the secret is out.
Enlightened officials are well aware that many
Englishmen are not cousins of the Queen, and have
a shrewd suspicion that hindrances placed in the way
of the prying European are not displeasing to the
Imperial Government. The "Lord of London,"
who fifty years ago obtained a firman which made
every provincial official bow before him, may now be
kept waiting days or weeks for a travelling passport;
and, unless he uses tact as well as bumptiousness, may
find himself in a position to write to the *Times* about
the interior of Turkish provincial prisons, and become
the subject of a Blue Book. Still even now, if
travellers will be cautious and polite in dealing with
people of whose language and customs they are
profoundly ignorant, and not bluster unless they know
very well what they are about (for I admit that
bluster has its uses), they will find travelling more
interesting, diverting, and enjoyable in the Levant
than in any other part of the world.

I write these lines as I sit in the hall of the largest
hotel in New York, a newly arrived stranger, somewhat dazed by the bustle and the glare. The whole
establishment is on a greater scale than anything else
in the world—except its own bills. Everything is
made of gold and marble, including, I fancy, the
food—at least this hypothesis plausibly reconciles
the quality and texture of the viands with the value

the vendors seem to attach to them. Enormous lifts shoot their living freights up into spheres unseen, or engulf them in abysmal chasms. All round people are ringing electric bells, telephoning, telegraphing, stenographing, polygraphing, and generally communicating their ideas about money to their fellow-creatures by any means rather than the voice which God put in the larynx for the purpose of quiet conversation. On one side an operatic concert is being performed, on the other porters and luggage jostle a brilliant throng of fashionably dressed people. It is as if someone had given an evening party at a railway station. "Whirr! whirr! all by wheels! whizz! whizz! all by steam!" and electricity, as the immortal Pasha of Karagholookoldour would have said. Now my mind (like the Pasha's) comprehends locomotives, and I am an enthusiast for progress, but amidst all the whizz and whirr and ringing of electric bells, my memory turns somewhat regretfully to a hotel where I resided not long ago in the "Exalted Country"—that fine old Stamboul's jargon is so much more soothing to the tongue than the strange abbreviations and initials they use over here—which was certainly more interesting, and not, I think, more uncomfortable than this Transatlantic Caravanserai. Perhaps I shall write an introduction congenial to the Shade of Kinglake (if indeed the Shades are interested in new editions of their works) if instead of instituting a comparison between the Levant of to-day and of 1834, I recount a journey to the town of Karakeui in the year of grace 1898, and describe the local hotel. Let not the reader in pursuit of that " sound learning " which Kinglake kept at arm's length rashly identify Karakeui with the first town he finds on the map bearing that name. The Turk has not a great variety of local designations. When possible he adopts one from some other language, treating it with the scant courtesy which longwinded, infidel polysyllables deserve (*e.g.* Edirné, Filibé, for Adrianople and Philippopoli) ; but when forced to have recourse to his own invention he calls most places Karakeui (or Blacktown), except those which are dubbed Oldtown, Newtown, or Whitetown.

It has been justly said that the East begins on the other side of Vienna, but, out of deference to the susceptibilities of the Magyars, who consider themselves in the van of civilisation, the Orient Express affects to be extremely European during its transit through Hungary. It bustles and shakes, and is very uncomfortable. In Servia it is more at its ease, though it still makes a pretence of thinking that time is money by only stopping ten minutes at every station. In Bulgaria it ceases to imitate Western ways, and becomes frankly Oriental, reposing for half an hour at spots where there are no passengers and no traffic. The part of the journey which lies on Turkish territory follows a singularly tortuous and corkscrew course, across a perfectly level plain which presents no obvious engineering difficulties. The Porte confided the construction of this line to an eminent Israelite at a remuneration of so much for every kilometre built. The eminent Israelite was straightway possessed by the spirit of his ancestors, and made a large fortune by laying the rails along a road as lengthy and complicated as that selected by Moses when he spent forty years in traversing a distance which anyone else can accomplish in a few days.

On arriving in Turkey we are at once seized by the representatives of the Board of Health. After all, times have indeed changed since *Eothen* was written. Instead of being put in quarantine by Europe, Turkey now puts Europe in quarantine. It is true that good Moslems still hold that men's souls leave their bodies when God calls them, and count it impious to suppose that neglect or precaution can hasten or delay the Divine summons. But though the Porte are not disposed to amend the sanitary condition of Mecca, they enforce quarantine regulations all round Constantinople with fanatical rigour. This is due partly to the fears of the Palace, and partly, I think, to a sense of humour. It is an excellent joke to apply a parody of European rules to Europeans in the name of sanitary science : to keep a set of fussy business people waiting a few days because they have come from a country which has not imposed quarantine on another country where there has been a doubtful case of cholera, or to detain a ship with a valuable cargo while embassies and merchants scream that thousands of pounds are being lost daily. On the present occasion we are told we must wait a day under inspection, to see if we develop the symptoms of any terrible malady, and are accordingly lodged in damp little wooden huts on a muddy plain, where we are certainly likely to fall ill even if hale and hearty on arriving. Turkish soldiers prevent us from crossing an imaginary line and contaminating the surrounding desert. The quarantine doctor, however, explains to me that he has a peculiar respect for my character, sanitary and general, and would like to take a walk with me outside the limits of the establishment. He has a remarkable pedigree. His father was a Bohemian monk who found convent life too narrow for his taste, and accordingly embraced Islam. Once within the true fold he made up for lost time by marrying as many wives as his new liberty allowed, and this is one of the results. He confides to me that his one ambition is to wear decorations, and that in return for his civilities strangers of distinction have procured for him the orders of their respective countries. The Siamese Minister, who recently passed through, made him a Commander of the Order of the White Elephant. Could I not obtain for him the Order of the Garter? Doubtless I possess it myself. With blushing mendacity I lead him to believe that I do, but explain that the distinction is only given to Englishmen and not to foreigners. I see that he does not believe me, and meditates revenge. Before we leave the quarantine station we have to be disinfected. The doctor attaches a garden hose to a reservoir filled with a fetid and corrosive fluid. The victims are led up one by one by the military authorities as if to execution, and the jet is turned upon them, causing their garments to burst out into leprous spots. I see by the doctor's eye that he means to make me pay for my unfriendliness in the matter of the decoration, and therefore, casting scruple to the winds, I assure him that if he will only treat me gently he shall have the Fourth Class of the Garter. He is at once all civility and consideration, and when I am led up in front of his infernal machine, directs an odoriferous douche to the right and left, leaving me unwetted in the middle.

Truly the way into Turkey is beset with as many difficulties as the road to paradise. After the quarantine comes the Custom House. The entry of most things is absolutely prohibited, and those which do enter pay a high duty. Books are treated with incredible severity. No work is allowed to pass the frontier which hints that the Turks were ever defeated, or that the Ottoman Government or the Mohammedan religion have any imperfections. Turkish officials having found by experience that very little European literature comes up to their high standard, simply confiscate as " seditious " every publication which mentions Turkey or the Moham-medan East. *Eothen*, even without the present highly seditious preface, is placed on the index, as are also Shakespeare, Byron, Dante, the *Encyclo-*

pædia Britannica, Baedeker, and Murray. In practice, of course, certain familiar *argumenta ad hominem* modify this Draconian system, but even the golden key sometimes fails to open the door. The officials watch one another, and know that they are much more likely to obtain a Turkish decoration by confiscating some infamous historian who is not ashamed to say that the Turks were once driven out of Hungary than they are to receive the Garter for letting his calumnies in. But there is an end to all troubles, even on the Turkish frontier, and at last we are allowed to proceed to Karakeui, where I ultimately alight at the hotel.

Karakeui lies on a plateau, under a range of snowy mountains which glitter with strange distinctness in the pure translucent air. A forest of minarets bears testimony to the piety of the place. It is the sacred month of Ramazan, and at sunset they will be festooned with lights and blaze like columns of fire, while in the mosque below myriads of little oil lamps will shed their soft glow on the bowing crowds, the plashing fountains, and the names of saints and prophets blazoned on the walls in green and red. In the streets is a motley throng of men and animals. Strings of camels and pack-horses, dogs, sheep, and turkeys are mixed up with the human crowd. Bulgarians and Servians quarrel in the bazaar, and denounce one another to the Turks. They each claim exclusive rights over the only Christian Church, and the Governor, to end the dispute, has shut it up altogether. A few Greeks are occupied in making large fortunes, and are ready to expatiate on the Hellenic Idea, and to explain how, from a certain peculiar point of view, the late war may be regarded as a victory for Greece. Albanians, armed with many weapons, and with moustaches as long as their own rifles, swagger through the crowd which respectfully makes way for them.

The hotel is kept by an Armenian, who left his native village on account of what are beautifully termed the " events " which occurred there. Having been inspired by these occurrences with a wholesome respect for the followers of the Prophet, he is a little apt to recoup himself at the expense of his coreligionists; but the local Ottoman authorities, to whose care I am duly recommended as being " one of those who wish well to the Sublime Government," have sternly informed him that I am not to be fleeced. (I wonder if the Governor of New York would address a similar warning to the proprietor of this hotel.) The establishment is constructed in the form of a quadrangle. The central space is a quagmire, wherein are embedded, and, so to speak, held as hostages for payment, the vehicles in which the travellers have arrived. The ground floor of the surrounding buildings is devoted to stabling. Outside the first floor, and above the aforesaid quagmire, runs a gallery, from which open a number of cells, bare and whitewashed, devoid of all furniture, but, contrary to what might be expected, scrupulously clean. A marble bath is not, as in New York, attached to each apartment, but in response to a suitable shout a boy brings a brass jug and basin, pours water over your hands and wipes them on an embroidered towel. There is no table and no bed. When you are disposed to sleep, a pile of rugs is spread on the floor. If you want to write, you naturally sit on your heels and hold your paper in your hand—an attitude which, at least in the case of Europeans, tends to restrain exuberance and keep literary composition within due limits. At meal times a little table like a high stool is brought in. The guests squat round it on their heels, and eat with their fingers out of a large saucer set on a broad tin tray. Turkish dinners consist of a quantity of dishes, generally at least seven or eight, and sometimes as many as twenty; but each is only tasted and rapidly removed. At first it looks somewhat mysterious when people apparently wrap up some pieces of string in brown paper and eat the parcel with avidity. But the string is cheese drawn out like very attenuated vermicelli, and the brown paper sheets of very thin bread which serve as a tablecloth and napkin as well as for food. During Ramazan no Moslem may eat, drink, or smoke between sunrise and sunset. The latter phenomenon is announced by a cannon, and some minutes before the gun fires a hungry crowd is gathered round the table waiting for the blessed sound. Then follows half an hour of rapid, silent nutrition, for Turks do not talk at table. Afterwards, an hour or more of prayer ; and then the earlier part of the night, until at least twelve or one, is devoted to visiting or attending the puppet show called Karagyöz.[1] Half an hour before dawn people go round the town beating drums, and the faithful hurriedly take a last meal before the morning cannon announces the dawn.

My neighbour in the room on the right is a spy appointed by the Imperial Government to watch over my doings. He is a charming companion, and I fancy has a very pretty talent for the composition of imaginative literature. My only regret is that I have never seen the daily reports which he draws up on my conduct. They are, I believe, replete with incident, and are excellent specimens of a new and interesting variety of fiction. The room on my left is occupied by the Christian Vice - Governor of the Province, who was appointed some months ago under immense pressure from the Powers, met by such resistance on the part of the Porte that one might have supposed his nomination was a deadly blow to the Turkish Empire. It is a wise plan of the Porte's never to make the most trivial concession without opposing a resistance, which is often successful, and always seems to enhance the importance of

[1] This is

"The moving row
Of magic shadow shapes which come and go,"

mentioned in Fitzgerald's version of *Omar Khayyam*.

the point in dispute. But the concession once made, means are soon discovered to deprive it of all its value, and the positions of victors and vanquished in the game prove to be reversed. In the present case the Christian Vice-Governor found that none of his co-religionists were disposed to let him lodgings ; and the local authorities, with a tender solicitude for his welfare, represented to him that these was a strong feeling against him in the town, and that he would be much more comfortable in the hotel ; predicting (like Kinglake's prophet, Damoor) that if he went out into the streets, or meddled in the administration, he would arouse that excitable sentiment known as Mussulman religious feeling. Like the Jews of Safet, the Christian Vice-Governor thought that the predictions of such practical men were not to be disregarded, and takes his ease in his inn with as good a grace as he can muster. Another interesting occupant of the hotel is the Turkish Inspector of Reforms. To rightly understand the duties of this functionary it must be remembered that the Turkish Government is divided into two parts, which have no connection with one another : *firstly*, the real Government, which is hard to comprehend, but of which one gets a dim idea by observation on the spot ; and *secondly*, the show Government, intended to impress Europe, and having as chief practical result the enrichment of telegraphic agencies. Two common manifestations of the show Government are circulars to the Powers, and commissions despatched to the

Provinces to rectify abuses. The present Commissioner has come to inspect reforms, and from the official language used respecting him it may be supposed that his mission is to tend and water the new institutions which are springing up like a luxuriant vegetation in a favourable climate, but at the same time to exercise a fatherly control, prevent the country from rushing into downright republicanism, and not permit the Christians to positively oppress their weaker Mohammedan brethren. He is a very affable man, with a broad, smiling face, and an amiable rotundity of person which causes his gorgeous uniform to burst its buttons and gape at critical points. He pays me long visits for the purpose of political discussion, being, as he calls it, *tout à fait dans les idées libérales,* and in order that this outpouring of radical views may not be interrupted, he brings a soldier to mount guard over the door. No tortures could make me disclose the Commissioner's confidences. I will merely observe that the long fasts of Ramazan are irksome to an enlightened mind, and that liberal theologians hold that a mixture of brandy and champagne does not fall under the Prophet's ban, inasmuch as it cannot accurately be described as either wine or spirits.

Very different is the room at the end of the passage. No guard is needed here. The door stands proudly open, and all the world may see that no crumb of bread or drop of water enters from sunrise to sunset. In the middle of a low sofa sits,

c

cross-legged, a Hodja, clad in striped silk. He is no ordinary country parson, but a noted preacher invited to tour in the provinces during Ramazan, and hold what in other countries would be called revival meetings. His thin nervous face shows that he is not a real Turk. Probably he is of Arab extraction, and in any case he burns with a Semitic indignation against those who " ascribe companions to God." Round him sit in a solemn circle the notables of the town,—stout, devout men of the churchwarden order, who, to judge from the heavy sighs and puffs which they occasionally emit, do not share the Hodja's fierce joy in trampling on the desires of the flesh. To-morrow he will preach in the Great Mosque with a sword in his hand, in token that the building was once a Christian Church and has been won from the infidel. I tell the Commissioner for Reforms that I think this dangerous and injudicious. He explains that the whole point of the ceremony lies in the fact that the sword is sheathed, as a token that religious discord is at an end, and that an era of mutual love and toleration has commenced. But when I think of that nervous, fanatical face, the green garments, the ample turban, the amulets and the sword, I cannot help suspecting that it is better to be a Christian traveller than a Christian resident at Karakeui.

Preface to the First Edition

Addressed by the

Author to One of His Friends

WHEN you first entertained the idea of travelling in the East you asked me to send you an outline of the tour which I had made, in order that you might the better be able to choose a route for yourself. In answer to this request I gave you a large French map, on which the course of my journeys had been carefully marked; but I did not conceal from myself that this was rather a dry mode for a man to adopt when he wished to impart the results of his experience to a dear and intimate friend. Now, long before the period of your planning an Oriental tour I had intended to write some account of my Eastern travels. I had, indeed, begun the task, and had failed; I had begun it a second time, and failing again, had abandoned my attempt with a sensation of utter distaste. I was unable to speak out, and chiefly, I think, for this reason, that I knew not to whom I was speaking. It might be you, or perhaps our Lady of Bitterness,[1] who would read my story, or it might be some member of the Royal

---

[1] ["Our Lady of Bitterness," said to have been a nickname of Mrs. Barry Cornwall, noted for her sharp tongue.]

Statistical Society, and how on earth was I to write in a way that would do for all three?

Well, your request for a sketch of my tour suggested to me the idea of complying with your wish by a revival of my twice-abandoned attempt. I tried; and the pleasure and confidence which I felt in speaking to you soon made my task so easy, and even amusing, that after a while (though not in time for your tour) I completed the scrawl from which this book was originally printed.

The very feeling, however, which enabled me to write thus freely, prevented me from robing my thoughts in that grave and decorous style which I should have maintained if I had professed to lecture the public. Whilst I feigned to myself that you, and you only, were listening, I could not by any possibility speak very solemnly. Heaven forbid that I should talk to my own genial friend as though he were a great and enlightened community, or any other respectable aggregate!

Yet I well understood that the mere fact of my professing to speak to you rather than to the public generally could not perfectly excuse me for printing a narrative too roughly worded, and accordingly, in revising the proof-sheets, I have struck out those phrases which seemed to be less fit for a published volume than for intimate conversation. It is hardly to be expected, however, that correction of this kind should be perfectly complete, or that the almost boisterous tone in which many parts of the book were originally written should be thoroughly subdued. I venture, therefore, to ask, that the familiarity of language still possibly apparent in the work may be laid to the account of our delightful intimacy, rather than to any presumptuous motive. I feel, as you know, much too timidly, too distantly, and too respectfully toward the public to be capable of seeking to put myself on terms of easy fellowship with strange and casual readers.

It is right to forewarn people (and I have tried to do this as well as I can, by my studiously unpromising title-page [1]) that the book is quite superficial in its character. I have endeavoured to discard from it all valuable matter derived from the works of others, and it appears to me that my efforts in this direction have been attended with great success. I believe I may truly acknowledge that from all details of geographical discovery, or antiquarian research— from all display of "sound learning and religious knowledge"— from all historical and scientific illustrations — from all useful statistics — from all political disquisitions — and from all good moral reflections, the volume is thoroughly free.

My excuse for the book is its truth. You and I know a man fond of hazarding elaborate jokes, who, whenever a story of his happens not to go down as wit, will evade the awkwardness of the failure by bravely maintaining that all he has said is pure fact. I can honestly take this decent though humble mode of escape. My narrative is not merely righteously exact in matters of fact (where fact is in question), but it is true in this larger sense—it conveys, not those impressions which *ought to have been* produced upon any "well-constituted mind," but those which were really and truly received at the time of his rambles by a headstrong and not very amiable traveller, whose prejudices in favour of other people's notions were then exceedingly slight. As I have

---

[1] "Eõthen" is, I hope, almost the only hard word to be found in the book ; it is written in Greek ἠῶθεν—(Atticè, with an aspirated ε instead of the η)—and signifies, "from the early dawn"—"from the East."—*Donn. Lex.* 4th edition.

felt, so I have written; and the result is, that there will often be found in my narrative a jarring discord between the associations properly belonging to interesting sites, and the tone in which I speak of them. This seemingly perverse mode of treating the subject is forced upon me by my plan of adhering to sentimental truth, and really does not result from any impertinent wish to tease or trifle with readers. I ought, for instance, to have felt as strongly in Judæa as in Galilee, but it was not so in fact. The religious sentiment (born in solitude) which had heated my brain in the sanctuary of Nazareth was rudely chilled at the foot of Zion by disenchanting scenes, and this change is accordingly disclosed by the perfectly worldly tone in which I speak of Jerusalem and Bethlehem.

My notion of dwelling precisely upon those matters which happened to interest me, and upon none other, would of course be intolerable in a regular book of travels. If I had been passing through countries not previously explored, it would have been sadly perverse to withhold careful descriptions of admirable objects merely because my own feelings of interest in them may have happened to flag; but where the countries which one visits have been thoroughly and ably described, and even artistically illustrated by others, one is fully at liberty to say as little (though not quite so much) as one chooses. Now a traveller is a creature not always looking at sights; he remembers (how often!) the happy land of his birth; he has, too, his moments of humble enthusiasm about fire and food, about shade and drink; and if he gives to these feelings anything like the prominence which really belonged to them at the time of his travelling, he will not seem a very good teacher. Once having determined to write the sheer truth concerning the things which chiefly have interested him, he must, and he will, sing a sadly long strain about self; he will talk for whole pages together about his bivouac fire, and ruin the ruins of Baalbec with eight or ten cold lines.

But it seems to me that this egotism of a traveller, however incessant, however shameless and obtrusive, must still convey some true ideas of the country through which he has passed. His very selfishness, his habit of referring the whole external world to his own sensations, compels him, as it were, in his writings to observe the laws of perspective;—he tells you of objects, not as he knows them to be, but as they seemed to him. The people and the things that most concern him personally, however mean and insignificant, take large proportions in his picture, because they stand so near to him. He shows you his dragoman, and the gaunt features of his Arabs—his tent, his kneeling camels, his baggage strewed upon the sand; but the proper wonders of the land —the cities, the mighty ruins and monuments of bygone ages, he throws back faintly in the distance. It is thus that he felt, and thus he strives to repeat the scenes of the Elder World. You may listen to him for ever without learning much in the way of statistics; but, perhaps, if you bear with him long enough, you may find yourself slowly and faintly impressed with the realities of Eastern travel.

My scheme of refusing to dwell upon matters which failed to interest my own feelings has been departed from in one instance—namely, in my detail of the late Lady Hester Stanhope's conversation on supernatural topics. The truth is, that I have been much questioned on this subject, and I thought that my best plan would be to write down at once all that I could ever have to say concerning the personage whose career has excited so much curiosity amongst

Englishwomen. The result is, that my account of
the lady goes to a length which is not justified either
by the importance of the subject, or by the extent to
which it interested the narrator.

You will see that I constantly speak of " my
People," " my Party," " my Arabs," and so on,
using terms which might possibly seem to imply that
I moved about with a pompous retinue. This of
course was not the case. I travelled with the
simplicity proper to my station, as one of the
industrious class, who was not flying from his
country because of ennui, but was strengthening his
will, and tempering the metal of his nature, for that
life of toil and conflict in which he is now engaged.
But an Englishman journeying in the East must
necessarily have with him dragomen capable of interpreting the Oriental languages ; the absence of wheeled
carriages obliges him to use several beasts of burthen for
his baggage, as well as for himself and his attendants ;
the owners of the horses, or camels, with *their* slaves
or servants, fall in as part of his train ; and altogether,
the cavalcade becomes rather numerous, without,
however, occasioning any proportionate increase of
expense. When a traveller speaks of all these followers in mass, he calls them his " people," or his
" troop," or his " party," without intending to make
you believe that he is therefore a Sovereign Prince.

You will see that I sometimes follow the custom
of the Scots in describing my fellow-countrymen by
the names of their paternal homes.

Of course all these explanations are meant for
casual readers. To you, without one syllable of
excuse or deprecation, and in all the confidence of a
friendship that never yet was clouded, I give the
long-promised volume, and add but this one " Good-
bye ! " for I dare not stand greeting you here.

EOTHEN

CHAPTER I

OVER THE BORDER

AT Semlin I still was encompassed by the scenes
and the sounds of familiar life; the din of a
busy world still vexed and cheered me; the unveiled
faces of women still shone in the light of day. Yet,
whenever I chose to look southward, I saw the
Osman's fortress—austere, and darkly impending
high over the vale of the Danube—historic Belgrade.
I had come, as it were, to the end of this wheel-
going Europe, and now my eyes would see the
splendour and havoc of the East.

The two frontier towns are less than a cannon-
shot distant, and yet their people hold no communion.[1]
The Hungarian on the north, and the Turk and
Servian on the southern side of the Save are as much
asunder as though there were fifty broad provinces
that lay in the path between them. Of the men

[1] [This is all changed now. There is constant communication beween the Servian and Hungarian banks, so
much so that Belgrade presents few national characteristics,
and looks quite as much a Hungarian as a Servian town.]

that bustled around me in the streets of Semlin there was not, perhaps, one who had ever gone down to look upon the stranger race dwelling under the walls of that opposite castle. It is the plague, and the dread of the plague, that divide the one people from the other. All coming and going stands forbidden by the terrors of the yellow flag. If you dare to break the laws of the quarantine, you will be tried with military haste; the court will scream out your sentence to you from a tribunal some fifty yards off; the priest, instead of gently whispering to you the sweet hopes of religion, will console you at duelling distance; and after that you will find yourself carefully shot, and carelessly buried in the ground of the lazaretto.

When all was in order for our departure we walked down to the precincts of the quarantine establishment, and here awaited us a "compromised"[1] officer of the Austrian Government, who lives in a state of perpetual excommunication. The boats with their "compromised" rowers, were at readiness.

After coming in contact with any creature thing belonging to the Ottoman Empire it would impossible for us to return to the Austrian territd without undergoing an imprisonment of fourteen da in the odious lazaretto. We felt, therefore, tha before we committed ourselves it was important to take care that none of the arrangements necessary for

[1] A "compromised" person is one who has been in contact with people or things supposed to be capable of conveying infection. As a general rule the whole Ottoman Empire lies constantly under this terrible ban. The "yellow flag" is the ensign of the quarantine establishment.

the journey had been forgotten; and in our anxiety to avoid such a misfortune, we managed the work of departure from Semlin with nearly as much solemnity as if we had been departing this life. Some obliging persons, from whom we had received civilities during our short stay in the place, came down to say their farewell at the river's side; and now, as we stood with them at the distance of three or four yards from the "compromised" officer, they asked if we were perfectly certain that we had wound up all our affairs in Christendom, and whether we had no parting requests to make. We repeated the caution to our servants, and took anxious thought lest by any possibility we might be cut off from some cherished object of affection:—were they quite sure that nothing had been forgotten—that there was no fragrant dressing-case with its gold-compelling letters of credit from which we might be parting for ever? —No; all our treasures lay safely stowed in the boat, and we were ready to follow them to the ends of the earth. Now, therefore, we shook hands with our Semlin friends, who immediately retreated for three or four paces, so as to leave us in the centre of a space between them and the "compromised" officer. The latter then advanced, and asking once more if we had done with the civilised world, held forth his hand. I met it with mine, and there was an end to Christendom for many a day to come.

We soon neared the southern bank of the river, but no sounds came down from the blank walls above, and there was no living thing that we could yet see, except one great hovering bird of the vulture race, flying low, and intent, and wheeling round and round over the pest-accursed city.

But presently there issued from the postern a group

of human beings—beings with immortal souls, and possibly some reasoning faculties; but to me the grand point was this, that they had real, substantial, and incontrovertible turbans. They made for the point towards which we were steering, and when at last I sprang upon the shore, I heard, and saw myself now first surrounded by men of Asiatic blood. I have since ridden through the the land of the Osmanlees, from the Servian border to the Golden Horn—from the Gulf of Satalieh to the tomb of Achilles; but never have I seen such ultra-Turkish looking fellows as those who received me on the banks of the Save. They were men in the humblest order of life, having come to meet our boat in the hope of earning something by carrying our luggage up to the city; but poor though they were, it was plain that they were Turks of the proud old school, and had not yet forgotten the fierce, careless bearing of their once victorious race.

Though the province of Servia generally has obtained a kind of independence, yet Belgrade, as being a place of strength on the frontier, is still garrisoned by Turkish troops under the command of a Pasha. Whether the fellows who now surrounded us were soldiers, or peaceful inhabitants, I did not understand: they wore the old Turkish costume; vests and jackets of many and brilliant colours, divided from the loose petticoat-trousers by heavy volumes of shawl, so thickly folded around their waists as to give the meagre wearers something of the dignity of true corpulence. This cincture enclosed a whole bundle of weapons; no man bore less than one brace of immensely long pistols, and a yataghan (or cutlass), with a dagger or two of various shapes and sizes; most of these arms were

inlaid with silver, and highly burnished, so that they
contrasted shiningly with the decayed grandeur of the
garments to which they were attached (this careful-
ness of his arms is a point of honour with the
Osmanlee, who never allows his bright yataghan to
suffer from his own adversity) ; then the long
drooping mustachios, and the ample folds of the
once white turbans, that lowered over the piercing
eyes, and the haggard features of the men, gave
them an air of gloomy pride, and that appearance of
trying to be disdainful under difficulties, which I
have since seen so often in those of the Ottoman
people who live, and remember old times ; they
seemed as if they were thinking that they would
have been more usefully, more honourably, and more
piously employed in cutting our throats than in
carrying our portmanteaus. The faithful Steel
(Methley's Yorkshire servant) stood aghast for a
moment at the sight of his master's luggage upon the
shoulders of these warlike porters, and when at
last we began to move up he could scarcely avoid
turning round to cast one affectionate look towards
Christendom, but quickly again he marched on with
steps of a man, not frightened exactly, but sternly
prepared for death, or the Koran, or even for
plural wives.

The Moslem quarter of a city is lonely and
desolate. You go up and down, and on over
shelving and hillocky paths through the narrow
lanes walled in by blank, windowless dwellings ; you
come out upon an open space strewed with the
black ruins that some late fire has left; you pass by
a mountain of castaway things, the rubbish of
centuries, and on it you see numbers of big, wolf-
like dogs lying torpid under the sun, with limbs out-

stretched to the full, as if they were dead ; storks, or cranes, sitting fearless upon the low roofs, look gravely down upon you ; the still air that you breathe is loaded with the scent of citron, and pomegranate rinds scorched by the sun, or (as you approach the bazaar) with the dry, dead perfume of strange spices. You long for some signs of life, and tread the ground more heavily, as though you would wake the sleepers with the heel of your boot; but the foot falls noiseless upon the crumbling soil of an Eastern city, and silence follows you still. Again and again you meet turbans, and faces of men, but they have nothing for you—no welcome—no wonder —no wrath—no scorn—they look upon you as we do upon a December's fall of snow—as a " seasonable," unaccountable, uncomfortable work of God, that may have been sent for some good purpose, to be revealed hereafter.

Some people had come down to meet us with an invitation from the Pasha, and we wound our way up to the castle. At the gates there were groups of soldiers, some smoking, and some lying flat like corpses upon the cool stones. We went through courts, ascended steps, passed along a corridor, and walked into an airy, whitewashed room, with an European clock. at one end of it, and Moostapha Pasha at the other ; the fine, old, bearded potentate looked very like Jove—like Jove, too, in the midst of his clouds, for the silvery fumes of the *narghile* [1] hung lightly circling round him.

The Pasha received us with the smooth, kind,

[1] The narghile is a water-pipe upon the plan of the hookah, but more gracefully fashioned ; the smoke is drawn by a very long flexible tube, that winds its snake-like way from the vase to the lips of the beatified smoker.

gentle manner that belongs to well-bred Osmanlees ;
then he lightly clapped his hands, and instantly the
sound filled all the lower end of the room with
slaves ; a syllable dropped from his lips which
bowed all heads, and conjured away the attendants
like ghosts (their coming and their going was thus
swift and quiet, because their feet were bare, and they
passed through no door, but only by the yielding
folds of a purder). Soon the coffee-bearers appeared,
every man carrying separately his tiny cup in a small
metal stand ; and presently to each of us there
came a pipe-bearer, who first rested the bowl of the
tchibouque at a measured distance on the floor, and
then, on this axis, wheeled round the long cheery
stick, and gracefully presented it on half-bended
knee ; already the well-kindled fire was glowing
secure in the bowl, and so, when I pressed the amber
lip [1] to mine, there was no coyness to conquer ; the
willing fume came up, and answered my slightest
sigh, and followed softly every breath inspired, till it
touched me with some faint sense and understanding
of Asiatic contentment.

Asiatic contentment! Yet scarcely, perhaps, one
hour before I had been wanting my bill, and ringing
for waiters, in a shrill and busy hotel.

In the Ottoman dominions there is scarcely any
hereditary influence except that which belongs to the
family of the Sultan ; and wealth, too, is a highly
volatile blessing, not easily transmitted to the
descendant of the owner. From these causes it
results that the people standing in the place of nobles

---

[1] [The wording "amber up to mine," found in many
editions, is evidently a misreading of Kinglake's hand-
writing. He must have made his l's rather small and not
have dotted his i's.]

and gentry are official personages, and though many (indeed the greater number) of these potentates are humbly born and bred, you will seldom, I think, find them wanting in that polished smoothness of manner, and those well-undulating tones which belong to the best Osmanlees. The truth is, that most of the men in authority have risen from their humble station by the arts of the courtier, and they preserve in their high estate those gentle powers of fascination to which they owe their success. Yet unless you can contrive to learn a little of the language, you will be rather bored by your visits of ceremony; the intervention of the interpreter, or dragoman as he is called, is fatal to the spirit of conversation. I think I should mislead you if I were to attempt to give the substance of any particular conversation with Orientals. A traveller may write and say that "the Pasha of So-and-so was particularly interested in the vast progress which has been made in the application of steam, and appeared to understand the structure of our machinery—that he remarked upon the gigantic results of our manufacturing industry—showed that he possessed considerable knowledge of our Indian affairs, and of the constitution of the Company, and expressed a lively admiration of the many sterling qualities for which the people of England are distinguished." But the heap of commonplaces thus quietly attributed to the Pasha will have been founded perhaps on some such talking as this:—

Pasha.—The Englishman is welcome; most blessed among hours is this, the hour of his coming.

Dragoman (to the traveller).—The Pasha pays you his compliments.

Traveller.—Give him my best compliments in

return, and say I'm delighted to have the honour of
seeing him.

Dragoman (to the Pasha).—His lordship, this
Englishman, Lord of London, Scorner of Ireland,
Suppressor of France, has quitted his governments,
and left his enemies to breathe for a moment, and has
crossed the broad waters in strict disguise, with a
small but eternally faithful retinue of fôllowers, in
order that he might look upon the bright countenance
of the Pasha among Pashas—the Pasha of the everlasting Pashalik of Karagholookoldour.

Traveller (to his dragoman).—What on earth
have you been saying about London? The Pasha
will be taking me for a mere cockney. Have not I
told you *always* to say that I am from a branch of
the family of Mudcombe Park, and that I am to be
a magistrate for the county of Bedfordshire, only I've
not qualified, and that I should have been a deputy-
lieutenant if it had not been for the extraordinary
conduct of Lord Mountpromise, and that I was a
candidate for Goldborough at the last election, and
that I should have won easy if my committee had
not been bought. I wish to Heaven that if you *do*
say anything about me, you'd tell the simple truth.

Dragoman [is silent].

Pasha.—What says the friendly Lord of London?
is there aught that I can grant him within the Pashalik
of Karagholookoldour?

Dragoman (growing sulky and literal).—This
friendly Englishman—this branch of Mudcombe—
this head-purveyor of Goldborough — this possible
policeman of Bedfordshire, is recounting his achievements, and the number of his titles.

Pasha.—The end of his honours is more distant
than the ends of the earth, and the catalogue of

his glorious deeds is brighter than the firmament of heaven!

Dragoman (to the traveller).—The Pasha congratulates your Excellency.

Traveller.—About Goldborough? The deuce he does!—but I want to get at his views in relation to the present state of the Ottoman Empire. Tell him the Houses of Parliament have met, and that there has been a speech from the throne, pledging England to preserve the integrity of the Sultan's dominions.

Dragoman (to the Pasha).—This branch of Mudcombe, this possible policeman of Bedfordshire, informs your Highness that in England the talking houses have met, and that the integrity of the Sultan's dominions has been assured for ever and ever by a speech from the velvet chair.

Pasha.—Wonderful chair! Wonderful houses!— whirr! whirr! all by wheels!—whiz! whiz! all by steam!—wonderful chair! wonderful houses! wonderful people!—whirr! whirr! all by wheels! —whiz! whiz! all by steam!

Traveller (to the dragoman).—What does the Pasha mean by that whizzing? he does not mean to say, does he, that our Government will ever abandon their pledges to the Sultan?

Dragoman.—No, your Excellency; but he says the English talk by wheels, and by steam.

Traveller.—That's an exaggeration; but say that the English really have carried machinery to great perfection; tell the Pasha (he'll be struck with that) that whenever we have any disturbances to put down, even at two or three hundred miles from London, we can send troops by the thousand to the scene of action in a few hours.

Dragoman (recovering his temper and freedom of

speech).—His Excellency, this Lord of Mudcombe, observes to your Highness, that whenever the Irish, or the French, or the Indians rebel against the English, whole armies of soldiers, and brigades of artillery, are dropped into a mighty chasm called Euston Square, and in the biting of a cartridge they arise up again in Manchester, or Dublin, or Paris, or Delhi, and utterly exterminate the enemies of England from the face of the earth.

Pasha.—I know it—I know all—the particulars have been faithfully related to me, and my mind comprehends locomotives. The armies of the English ride upon the vapours of boiling caldrons, and their horses are flaming coals!—whirr! whirr! all by wheels!—whiz! whiz! all by steam!

Traveller (to his dragoman).—I wish to have the opinion of an unprejudiced Ottoman gentleman as to the prospects of our English commerce and manufactures; just ask the Pasha to give me his views on the subject.

Pasha (after having received the communication of the dragoman).—The ships of the English swarm like flies; their printed calicoes cover the whole earth; and by the side of their swords the blades of Damascus are blades of grass. All India is but an item in the ledger-books of the merchants, whose lumber-rooms are filled with ancient thrones!— whirr! whirr! all by wheels!—whiz! whiz! all by steam!

Dragoman.—The Pasha compliments the cutlery of England, and also the East India Company.

Traveller.—The Pasha's right about the cutlery (I tried my scimitar with the common officers' swords belonging to our fellows at Malta, and they cut it like the leaf of a novel). Well (to the dragoman), tell the Pasha I am exceedingly gratified to find that he entertains such a high opinion of our manufacturing energy, but I should like him to know, though, that we have got something in England besides that. These foreigners are always fancying that we have nothing but ships, and railways, and East India Companies; do just tell the Pasha that our rural districts deserve his attention, and that even within the last two hundred years there has been an evident improvement in the culture of the turnip, and if he does not take any interest about that, at all events you can explain that we have our virtues in the country—that we are a truth-telling people, and, like the Osmanlees, are faithful in the performance of our promises. Oh! and, by the·bye, whilst you are about it, you may as well just say at the end that the British yeoman is still, thank God! the British yeoman.

Pasha (after hearing the dragoman).—It is true, it is true:—through all Feringhistan the English are foremost and best; for the Russians are drilled swine, and the Germans are sleeping babes, and the Italians are the servants·of songs, and the French are the sons of newspapers, and the Greeks they are weavers of lies, but the English and the Osmanlees are brothers together in righteousness; for the Osmanlees believe in one only God, and cleave to the Koran, and destroy idols; so do the English worship one God, and abominate graven images, and tell the truth, and believe in a book, and though they drink the juice of the grape, yet to say that they worship their prophet as God, or to say that they are eaters of pork, these are lies—lies born of Greeks, and nursed by Jews!

Dragoman.—The Pasha compliments the English.

Traveller (rising).—Well, I've had enough of this. Tell the Pasha I am greatly obliged to him for his hospitality, and still more for his kindness in furnishing me with horses, and say that now I must be off.

Pasha (after hearing the dragoman, and standing up on his divan [1]).—Proud are the sires, and blessed are the dams of the horses that shall carry his Excellency to the end of his prosperous journey. May the saddle beneath him glide down to the gates of the happy city, like a boat swimming on the third river of Paradise. May he sleep the sleep of a child, when his friends are around him; and the while that his enemies are abroad, may his eyes flame red through the darkness—more red than the eyes of ten tigers! Farewell!

Dragoman.—The Pasha wishes your Excellency a pleasant journey.

So ends the visit.

---

[1] That is, if he stands up at all. Oriental etiquette would not warrant his rising, unless his visitor were supposed to be at least his equal in point of rank and station.

CHAPTER II

IN two or three hours our party was ready; the servants, the Tatar, the mounted Suridgees,[1] and the baggage-horses, altogether made up a strong cavalcade. The accomplished Mysseri,[2] of whom you have heard me speak so often, and who served me so faithfully throughout my Oriental journeys, acted as our interpreter, and was, in fact, the brain of our corps. The Tatar, you know, is a Government courier properly employed in carrying despatches, but also sent with travellers to speed them on their way, and answer with his head for their safety. The man whose head was thus pledged for our precious lives was a glorious-looking fellow, with the regular and handsome cast of countenance which is now characteristic of the Ottoman race.[3] His features displayed

[1] [A man in charge of post-horses. At the present day most business connected with horse-transport in European Turkey is managed by Vlachs, a people speaking a language closely akin to Roumanian, and scattered over Macedonia, particularly near the Thessalian frontier.]

[2] [This accomplished gentleman subsequently became the proprietor of an hotel, which was long the principal hostelry of Constantinople. The name still exists, but the building has been burnt down.]

[3] The continual marriages of these people with the chosen beauties of Georgia and Circassia have overpowered the original ugliness of their Tatar ancestors.

14

a good deal of serene pride, self-respect, fortitude, a kind of ingenuous sensuality, and something of instinctive wisdom, without any sharpness of intellect. He had been a Janissary (as I afterwards found), and kept up the odd strut of his old corps, which used to affright the Christians in former times—that rolling gait so comically pompous, that a close imitation of it, even in the broadest farce, would be looked upon as a very rough over-acting of the character. It is occasioned in part by dress and accoutrements. The weighty bundle of weapons carried upon the chest throws back the body so as to give it a wonderful portliness, and, moreover, the immense masses of clothes that swathe his limbs force the wearer in walking to swing himself heavily round from left to right, and from right to left. In truth, this great edifice of woollen, and cotton, and silk, and silver, and brass, and steel is not at all fitted for moving on foot; it cannot even walk without frightfully discomposing its fair proportions; and as to running—our Tatar ran *once* (it was in order to pick up a partridge that Methley had winged with a pistol-shot), and really the attempt was one of the funniest misdirections of human energy that wondering man ever saw. But put him in his stirrups, and then is the Tatar himself again: there he lives at his pleasure, reposing in the tranquillity of that true home (the home of his ancestors) which the saddle seems to afford him, and drawing from his pipe the calm pleasures of his "own fireside," or else dashing sudden over the earth, as though for a moment he felt the mouth of a Turcoman steed, and saw his own Scythian plains lying boundless and open before him.

It was not till his subordinates had nearly completed their preparations for their march that our

Tatar, "commanding the forces," arrived; he came sleek and fresh from the bath (for so is the custom of the Ottomans when they start upon a journey), and was carefully accoutred at every point. From his thigh to his throat he was loaded with arms and other implements of a campaigning life. There is no scarcity of water along the whole road from Belgrade to Stamboul, but the habits of our Tatar were formed by his ancestors and not by himself, so he took good care to see that his leathern water-flask was amply charged and properly strapped to the saddle, along with his blessed *tchibouque*. And now at last he has cursed the Suridgees in all proper figures of speech, and is ready for a ride of a thousand miles; but before he comforts his soul in the marble baths of Stamboul he will be another and a lesser man; his sense of responsibility, his too strict abstemiousness, and his restless energy, disdainful of sleep, will have worn him down to a fraction of the sleek Moostapha that now leads out our party from the gates of Belgrade.

The Suridgees are the men employed to lead the baggage-horses. They are most of them gipsies. Their lot is a sad one: they are the last of the human race, and all the sins of their superiors (including the horses) can safely be visited on them. But the wretched look often more picturesque than their betters; and though all the world despise these poor Suridgees, their tawny skins and their grisly beards will gain them honourable standing in the foreground of a landscape. We had a couple of these fellows with us, each leading a baggage-horse, to the tail of which last another baggage-horse was attached. There was a world of trouble in persuading the stiff angular portmanteaus of Europe to adapt themselves

to their new condition and sit quietly on pack-saddles,
but all was right at last, and it gladdened my eyes to
see our little troop file off through the winding lanes
of the city, and show down brightly in the plain
beneath. The one of our party that seemed to be
most out of keeping with the rest of the scene was
Methley's Yorkshire servant, who always rode
doggedly on in his pantry jacket, looking out for
" gentlemen's seats."

Methley and I had English saddles, but I think
we should have done just as well (I should certainly
have seen more of the country) if we had adopted
saddles like that of our Tatar, who towered so loftily
over the scraggy little beast that carried him.   In
taking thought for the East, whilst in England, I had
made one capital hit which you must not forget—I
had brought with me a pair of common spurs. These
were a great comfort to me throughout my horseback
travels, by keeping up the cheerfulness of the many
unhappy nags that I had to bestride ; the angle of the
Oriental stirrup is a very poor substitute for spurs.

The Ottoman horseman, raised by his saddle to a
great height above the humble level of the back that
he bestrides, and using an awfully sharp bit, is able
to lift the crest of his nag, and force him into a
strangely fast shuffling walk, the orthodox pace for
the journey. My comrade and I, using English
saddles, could not easily keep our beasts up to this
peculiar amble ; besides, we thought it a bore to be
followed by our attendants for a thousand miles, and
we generally, therefore, did duty as the rearguard of
our " grand army " ; we used to walk our horses till
the party in front had got into the distance, and then
retrieve the lost ground by a gallop.

We had ridden on for some two or three hours ;

2

the stir and bustle of our commencing journey had ceased, the liveliness of our little troop had worn off with the declining day, and the night closed in as we entered the great Servian forest. Through this our road was to last for more than a hundred miles. Endless, and endless now on either side, the tall oaks closed in their ranks and stood gloomily lowering over us, as grim as an army of giants with a thousand years' pay in arrear. One strived with listening ear to catch some tidings of that forest world within—some stirring of beasts, some night-bird's scream, but all was quite hushed, except the voice of the cicalas that peopled every bough, and filled the depths of the forest through and through, with one same hum everlasting—more stilling than very silence.

At first our way was in darkness, but after a while the moon got up, and touched the glittering arms and tawny faces of our men with light so pale and mystic, that the watchful Tatar felt bound to look out for demons, and take proper means for keeping them off; forthwith he determined that the duty of frightening away our ghostly enemies (like every other troublesome work) should fall upon the poor Suridgees, who accordingly lifted up their voices, and burst upon the dreadful stillness of the forest with shrieks and dismal howls. These precautions were kept up incessantly, and were followed by the most complete success, for not one demon came near us.

Long before midnight we reached the hamlet in which we were to rest for the night; it was made up of about a dozen clay huts, standing upon a small tract of ground hardly won from the forest. The peasants that lived there spoke a Slavonic dialect, and Mysseri's knowledge of the Russian tongue enabled him to talk with them freely. We took up our quarters in a square room with white walls and an earthen floor, quite bare of furniture, and utterly void of women. They told us, however, that these Servian villagers lived in happy abundance, but that they were careful to conceal their riches, as well as their wives.

The burthens unstrapped from the pack-saddles very quickly furnished our den ; a couple of quilts spread upon the floor, with a carpet-bag at the head of each, became capital sofas — portmanteaus, and hat-boxes, and writing-cases, and books, and maps, and gleaming arms soon lay strewed around us in pleasant confusion. Mysseri's canteen too began to yield up its treasures, but we relied upon finding some provisions in the village. At first the natives declared that their hens were mere old maids and all their cows unmarried ; but our Tatar swore such a grand sonorous oath, and fingered the hilt of his yataghan with such persuasive touch, that the land soon flowed with milk, and mountains of eggs arose.

And soon there was tea before us, with all its unspeakable fragrance, and as we reclined on the floor, we found that a portmanteau was just the right height for a table ; the duty of candlesticks was ably performed by a couple of intelligent natives ; the rest of the villagers stood by the open doorway at the lower end of the room, and watched our banqueting with grave and devout attention.

The first night of your first campaign (though you be but a mere peaceful campaigner) is a glorious time in your life. It is so sweet to find one's self free from the stale civilisation of Europe ! Oh, my dear ally, when first you spread your carpet in the midst of these Eastern scenes, do think for a moment of those your fellow-creatures, that dwell in squares,

and streets, and even (for such is the fate of many!)
in actual country houses; think of the people that are
"presenting their compliments," and "requesting the
honour," and "much regretting,"—of those that are
pinioned at dinner-tables, or stuck up in ballrooms,
or cruelly planted in pews,—ay, think of these, and so
remembering how many poor devils are living in a
state of utter respectability, you will glory the more
in your own delightful escape.

I am bound to confess, however, that with all its
charms a mud floor (like a mercenary match) does
certainly promote early rising. Long before daybreak we were up, and had breakfasted; after this
there was nearly a whole tedious hour to endure
whilst the horses were laden by torchlight; but this
had an end, and at last we went on once more.
Cloaked, and sombre, at first we made our sullen
way through the darkness, with scarcely one barter of
words; but soon the genial morn burst down from
heaven, and stirred the blood so gladly through our
veins, that the very Suridgees, with all their troubles,
could now look up for an instant, and almost seem to
believe in the temporary goodness of God.

The actual movement from one place to another,
in Europeanised countries, is a process so temporary
—it occupies, I mean, so small a proportion of the
traveller's entire time—that his mind remains un-
settled, so long as the wheels are going; he may be
alive enough to external objects of interest, and to
the crowding ideas which are often invited by the
excitement of a changing scene, but he is still conscious of being in a provisional state, and his mind is
constantly recurring to the expected end of his
journey; his ordinary ways of thought have been
interrupted, and before any new mental habits can be

formed he is quietly fixed in his hotel. It will be
otherwise with you when you journey in the East.
Day after day, perhaps week after week and month
after month, your foot is in the stirrup. To taste
the cold breath of the earliest morn, and to lead, or
follow, your bright cavalcade till sunset through
forests and mountain passes, through valleys and
desolate plains, all this becomes your MODE OF LIFE,
and you ride, eat, drink, and curse the mosquitoes as
systematically as your friends in England eat, drink,
and sleep. If you are wise, you will not look upon
the long period of time thus occupied in actual
movement as the mere gulf dividing you from the
end of your journey, but rather as one of those rare
and plastic seasons of your life from which, perhaps,
in after times you may love to date the moulding of
your character—that is, your very identity. Once
feel this, and you will soon grow happy and contented in your saddle-home. As for me and my
comrade, however, in this part of our journey we
often forgot Stamboul, forgot all the Ottoman
Empire, and only remembered old times. We went
back, loitering on the banks of Thames—not grim
old Thames of "after life," that washes the Parliament Houses, and drowns despairing girls — but
Thames, the "old Eton fellow," that wrestled with
us in our boyhood till he taught us to be stronger
than he. We bullied Keate, and scoffed at Larry
Miller, and Okes; we rode along loudly laughing,
and talked to the grave Servian forest as though it
were the "Brocas clump."
    Our pace was commonly very slow, for the
baggage-horses served us for a drag, and kept us to a
rate of little more than five miles in the hour, but now
and then, and chiefly at night, a spirit of movement

would suddenly animate the whole party; the
baggage-horses would be teased into a gallop, and
when once this was done, there would be such a
banging of portmanteaus, and such convulsions of
carpet - bags upon their panting sides, and the
Suridgees would follow them up with such a hurri-
cane of blows, and screams, and curses, that stopping
or relaxing was scarcely possible ; then the rest of us
would put our horses into a gallop, and so, all shouting cheerily, would hunt, and drive the sumpter
beasts like a flock of goats, up hill and down dale,
right on to the end of their journey.

The distances at which we got relays of horses
varied greatly ; some were not more than fifteen or
twenty miles, but twice, I think, we performed a
whole day's journey of more than sixty miles with
the same beasts.

When at last we came out from the forest our
road lay through scenes like those of an English
park. The green sward unfenced, and left to the
free pasture of cattle, was dotted with groups of
stately trees, and here and there darkened over with
larger masses of wood, that seemed gathered together
for bounding the domain, and shutting out some
"infernal" fellow-creature in the shape of a newly
made squire ; in one or two spots the hanging copses
looked down upon a lawn below with such shelter-
ing mien, that seeing the like in England you would
have been tempted almost to ask the name of the
spendthrift, or the madman who had dared to pull
down " the old hall."

There are few countries less infested by "lions"
than the provinces on this part of your route. You
are not called upon to "drop a tear" over the tomb
of "the once brilliant" anybody, or to pay your

"tribute of respect" to anything dead or alive. There are no Servian or Bulgarian litterateurs with whom it would be positively disgraceful not to form an acquaintance ; you have no staring, no praising to get through ; the only public building of any interest that lies on the road is of modern date, but is said to be a good specimen of Oriental architecture; it is of a pyramidical shape, and is made up of thirty thousand skulls, contributed by the rebellions Servians in the early part (I believe) of this century : I am not at all sure of my date, but I fancy it was in the year 1806 that the first skull was laid.[1] I am ashamed to say that in the darkness of the early morning we unknowingly went by the neighbourhood of this triumph of art, and so basely got off from admiring " the simple grandeur of the architect's conception," and " the exquisite beauty of the fretwork."

There being no " lions," we ought at least to have met with a few perils, but the only robbers we saw anything of had been long since dead and gone. The poor fellows had been impaled upon high poles, and so propped up by the transverse spokes beneath them, that their skeletons, clothed with some white, wax-

[1] [The remains of this pyramid, or rather the chapel which is erected over them, can be seen close to the railway immediately after leaving Nish for Pirot and the Bulgarian frontier. Only two or three skulls are now left embedded in masonry. According to the story now told in Servia, Singelich, a Servian leader during the Karageorge insurrection, when hard pressed by the Turks, fired into his powder magazine, and blew up himself and his followers as well as numbers of his enemies. The Turks, in order to intimidate the other Serbs, collected the heads of the victims and built of them a tower or pyramid. In 1878, when Nish became part of the principality of Servia, most of the skulls were removed and buried, but two or three remain.]

like remains of flesh, still sat up lolling in the sunshine, and listlessly stared without eyes.

One day it seemed to me that our path was a little more rugged than usual, and I found that I was deserving for myself the title of Sabalkansky, or "Transcender of the Balcan." The truth is, that, as a military barrier, the Balcan is a fabulous mountain. Such seems to be the view of Major Keppell, who looked on it towards the east with the eye of a soldier, and certainly in the Sophia Pass, which I followed, there is no narrow defile, and no ascent sufficiently difficult to stop, or delay for long time, a train of siege artillery.

Before we reached Adrianople, Methley had been seized with we knew not what ailment, and when we had taken up our quarters in the city he was cast to the very earth by sickness. Andrianople enjoyed an English consul, and I felt sure that, in Eastern phrase, his house would cease to be his house, and would become the house of my sick comrade. I should have judged rightly under ordinary circumstances, but the levelling plague was abroad, and the dread of it had dominion over the consular mind. So now (whether dying or not, one could hardly tell), upon a quilt stretched out along the floor, there lay the best hope of an ancient line, without the material aids to comfort of even the humblest sort, and (sad to say) without the consolation of a friend, or even a comrade worth having. I have a notion that tenderness and pity are affections occasioned in some measure by living within doors; certainly, at the time I speak of, the open-air life which I have been leading, or the wayfaring hardships of the journey, had so strangely blunted me, that I felt intolerant of illness, and looked down upon my companion as if the poor fellow in

falling ill had betrayed a want of spirit. I entertained, too, a most absurd idea—an idea that his
illness was partly affected. You see that I have
made a confession : this I hope—that I may always
hereafter look charitably upon the hard, savage acts
of peasants, and the cruelties of a "brutal" soldiery.
God knows that I strived to melt myself into common
charity, and to put on a gentleness which I could not
feel, but this attempt did not cheat the keenness of
the sufferer ; he could not have felt the less deserted
because that I was with him.

We called to aid a solemn Armenian (I think he
was), half soothsayer, half hakim or doctor, who,
all the while counting his beads, fixed his eyes
steadily upon the patient, and then suddenly dealt
him a violent blow on the chest. Methley bravely
dissembled his pain, for he fancied that the blow was
meant to try whether or not the plague were on
him.

Here was really a sad embarrassment—no bed ;
nothing to offer the invalid in the shape of food save
a piece of thin, tough, flexible, drab-coloured cloth,
made of flour and mill-stones in equal proportions,
and called by the name of "bread" ; then the
patient, of course, had no "confidence in his medical
man," and on the whole, the best chance of saving
my comrade seemed to lie in taking him out of the
reach of his doctor, and bearing him away to the
neighbourhood of some more genial consul. But
how was this to be done ? Methley was much too
ill to be kept in his saddle, and wheel carriages, as
means of travelling, were unknown. There is, however, such a thing as an "araba," a vehicle drawn
by oxen, in which the wives of a rich man are sometimes dragged four or five miles over the grass by

way of recreation. The carriage is rudely framed, but you recognise in the simple grandeur of its design a likeness to things majestic; in short, if your carpenter's son were to make a "Lord Mayor's coach" for little Amy, he would build a carriage very much in the style of a Turkish araba. No one had ever heard of horses being used for drawing a carriage in this part of the world, but necessity is the mother of innovation as well as of invention. I was fully justified, I think, in arguing that there were numerous instances of horses being used for that purpose in our own country—that the laws of nature are uniform in their operation over all the world (except Ireland) — that that which was true in Piccadilly, must be true in Adrianople—that the matter could not fairly be treated as an ecclesiastical question, for that the circumstance of Methley's going on to Stamboul in an araba drawn by horses, when calmly and dispassionately considered, would appear to be perfectly consistent with the maintenance of the Mahometan religion as by law established. Thus poor, dear, patient Reason would have fought her slow battle against Asiatic prejudice, and I am convinced that she would have established the possibility (and perhaps even the propriety) of harnessing horses in a hundred and fifty years; but in the meantime Mysseri, well seconded by our Tatar, put a very quick end to the controversy by having the horses put to.

It was a sore thing for me to see my poor comrade brought to this, for young though he was, he was a veteran in travel. When scarcely yet of age he had invaded India from the frontiers of Russia, and that so swiftly, that measuring by the time of his flight the broad dominions of the king of kings were shrivelled up to a dukedom, and now, poor fellow, he was to be poked into an araba, like a Georgian girl! He suffered greatly, for there were no springs for the carriage, and no road for the wheels ; and so the concern jolted on over the open country with such twists, and jerks, and jumps, as might almost dislocate the supple tongue of Satan.

All day the patient kept himself shut up within the lattice-work of the araba, and I could hardly know how he was faring until the end of the day's journey, when I found that he was not worse, and was buoyed up with the hope of some day reaching Constantinople.

I was always conning over my maps, and fancied that I knew pretty well my line, but after Adrianople I had made more southing than I knew for, and it was with unbelieving wonder, and delight, that I came suddenly upon the shore of the sea. A little while, and its gentle billows were flowing beneath the hoofs of my beast ; but the hearing of the ripple was not enough communion, and the seeing of the blue Propontis was not to know and possess it—I must needs plunge into its depth and quench my longing love in the palpable waves ; and so when old Moostapha (defender against demons) looked round for his charge, he saw with horror and dismay that he for whose life his own life stood pledged was possessed of some devil who had driven him down into the sea—that the rider and the steed had vanished from earth, and that out among the waves was the gasping crest of a post-horse, and the ghostly head of the Englishman moving upon the face of the waters.

We started very early indeed on the last day of our journey, and from the moment of being off until we gained the shelter of the imperial walls we were struggling face to face with an icy storm that swept right down from the steppes of Tartary, keen, fierce, and steady as a northern conqueror. Methley's servant, who was the greatest sufferer, kept his saddle until we reached Stamboul, but was then found to be quite benumbed in limbs, and his brain was so much affected that when he was lifted from his horse he fell away in a state of unconsciousness, the first stage of a dangerous fever.

Our Tatar, worn down by care and toil, and carrying seven heavens full of water in his manifold jackets and shawls, was a mere weak and vapid dilution of the sleek Moostapha, who scarce more than one fortnight before came out like a bridegroom from his chamber to take the command of our party.

Mysseri seemed somewhat over-wearied, but he had lost none of his strangely quiet energy. He wore a grave look, however, for he now had learnt that the plague was prevailing at Constantinople, and he was fearing that our two sick men, and the miserable looks of our whole party, might make us unwelcome at Pera.

We crossed the Golden Horn in a caïque. As soon as we had landed, some woebegone-looking fellows were got together and laden with our baggage. Then on we went, dripping, and sloshing, and looking very like men that had been turned back by the Royal Humane Society as being incurably drowned. Supporting our sick, we climbed up shelving steps and threaded many windings, and at last came up into the main street of Pera, humbly hoping that we might not be judged guilty of plague, and so be cast back with horror from the doors of the shuddering Christians.

Such was the condition of our party, which fifteen days before had filed away so gaily from the gates of Belgrade. A couple of fevers and a north-easterly storm had thoroughly spoiled our looks.

The interest of Mysseri with the house of Giuseppini was too powerful to be denied, and at once, though not without fear and trembling, we were admitted as guests.

CHAPTER III

EVEN if we don't take a part in the chant about
" mosques and minarets," we can still yield
.praises to Stamboul. We can chant about the
harbour; we can say, and sing, that nowhere else
does the sea come so home to a city; there are no
pebbly shores—no sand bars—no slimy river-beds—
no black canals—no locks nor docks to divide the
very heart of the place from the deep waters. If
being in the noisiest mart of Stamboul you would
stroll to the quiet side of the way amidst those
cypresses opposite, you will cross the fathomless
Bosphorus; if you would go from your hotel to the
bazaars, you must go by the bright, blue pathway of
the Golden Horn, that can carry a thousand sail of
the line. You are accustomed to the gondolas that
glide among the palaces of St. Mark, but here at
Stamboul it is a 120-gun ship that meets you in the
street. Venice strains out from the steadfast land,
and in old times would send forth the chief of the
State to woo and wed the reluctant sea; but the
stormy bride of the Doge is the bowing slave of the
Sultan. She comes to his feet with the treasures of
the world—she bears him from palace to palace—by
some unfailing witchcraft she entices the breezes to

follow her [1] and fan the pale cheek of her lord—she
lifts his armed navies to the very gates of his garden
—she watches the walls of his *serai*—she stifles the
intrigues of his ministers—she quiets the scandals of
his courts—she extinguishes his rivals, and hushes
his naughty wives all one by one. So vast are the
wonders of the deep!

All the while that I stayed at Constantinople the
plague was prevailing, but not with any degree of
violence. Its presence, however, lent a mysterious
and exciting, though not very pleasant, interest to my
first knowledge of a great Oriental city; it gave tone
and colour to all I saw, and all I felt—a tone and a
colour sombre enough, but true, and well befitting
the dreary monuments of past power and splendour.
With all that is most truly Oriental in its character
the plague is associated; it dwells with the faithful
in the holiest quarters of their city. The coats and
the hats of Pera are held to be nearly as innocent of
infection as they are ugly in shape and fashion; but
the rich furs and the costly shawls, the broidered
slippers and the gold-laden saddle-cloths, the fragrance
of burning aloes and the rich aroma of patchouli—
these are the signs that mark the familiar home of
plague. You go out from your queenly London—
the centre of the greatest and strongest amongst all
earthly dominions—you go out thence, and travel on
to the capital of an Eastern Prince, you find but a
waning power, and a faded splendour, that inclines
you to laugh and mock; but let the infernal Angel
of Plague be at hand, and he, more mighty than
armies, more terrible than Suleyman in his glory, can

[1] There is almost always a breeze either from the
Marmora or from the Black Sea, that passes along the
course of the Bosphorus.

restore such pomp and majesty to the weakness of the
Imperial city, that if, *when HE is there*, you must
still go prying amongst the shades of this dead empire,
at least you will tread the path with seemly reverence
and awe.

It is the firm faith of almost all the Europeans
living in the East that plague is conveyed by the
touch of infected substances, and that the deadly
atoms especially lurk in all kinds of clothes and furs.
It is held safer to breathe the same air with a man
sick of the plague, and even to come in contact with
his skin, than to be touched by the smallest particle
of woollen or of thread which may have been within
the reach of possible infection. If this be a right
notion, the spread of the malady must be materially
aided by the observance of a custom prevailing
amongst the people of Stamboul. It is this : when
an Osmanlee dies, one of his dresses is cut up, and
a small piece of it is sent to each of his friends as a
memorial of the departed—a fatal present, according
to the opinion of the Franks, for it too often forces
the living not merely to remember the dead man, but
to follow and bear him company.

The Europeans during the prevalence of the
plague, if they are forced to venture into the streets,
will carefully avoid the touch of every human being
whom they pass. Their conduct in this respect
shows them strongly in contrast with the "true
believers"; the Moslem stalks on serenely, as
though he were under the eye of his God, and were
"equal to either fate"; the Franks go crouching
and slinking from death, and some (those chiefly of
French extraction) will fondly strive to fence out
destiny with shining capes of oilskin !

For some time you may manage by great care to

thread your way through the streets of Stamboul without incurring contact, for the Turks, though scornful of the terrors felt by the Franks, are generally very courteous in yielding to that which they hold to be a useless and impious precaution, and will let you pass safe if they can. It is impossible, however, that your immunity can last for any length of time if you move about much through the narrow streets and lanes of a crowded city.

As for me, I soon got "compromised." After one day of rest, the prayers of my hostess began to lose their power of keeping me from the pestilent side of the Golden Horn. Faithfully promising to shun the touch of all imaginable substances, however enticing, I set off very cautiously, and held my way uncompromised till I reached the water's edge ; but before my caïque was quite ready some rueful-looking fellows came rapidly shambling down the steps with a plague-stricken corpse, which they were going to bury amongst the faithful on the other side of the water. I contrived to be so much in the way of this brisk funeral, that I was not only touched by the men bearing the body, but also, I believe, by the foot of the dead man, as it hung lolling out of the bier. This accident gave me such a strong interest in denying the soundness of the contagion theory, that I did in fact deny and repudiate it altogether ; and from that time, acting upon my own convenient view of the matter, I went wherever I chose, without taking any serious pains to avoid a touch. It seems to me now very likely that the Europeans are right, and that the plague may be really conveyed by contagion ; but during the whole time of my remaining in the East, my views on this subject more nearly approached to those of the fatalists ; and so,

when afterwards the plague of Egypt came dealing
his blows around me, I was able to live amongst the
dying without that alarm and anxiety which would
inevitably have pressed upon my mind if I had
allowed myself to believe that every passing touch
was really a probable death-stroke.

And perhaps as you make your difficult way through
a steep and narrow alley, shut in between blank walls,
and little frequented by passers, you meet one of
those coffin-shaped bundles of white linen that implies
an Ottoman lady. Painfully struggling against the
obstacles to progression interposed by the many folds
of her clumsy drapery, by her big mud-boots, and
especially by her two pairs of slippers, she works her
way on full awkwardly enough, but yet there is
something of womanly consciousness in the very
labour and effort with which she tugs and lifts the
burthen of her charms. She is closely followed by
her women slaves. Of her very self you see nothing
except the dark, luminous eyes that stare against your
face, and the tips of the painted fingers depending
like rosebuds from out of the blank bastions of the
fortress. She turns, and turns again, and carefully
glances around her on all sides, to see that she is safe
from the eyes of Mussulmans, and then suddenly
withdrawing the *yashmak*,[1] she shines upon your heart
and soul with all the pomp and might of her beauty.
And this, it is not the light, changeful grace that
leaves you to doubt whether you have fallen in love
with a body, or only a soul ; it is the beauty that
dwells secure in the perfectness of hard, downright

---

[1] The yashmak, you know, is not a mere semi-trans-
parent veil, but rather a good substantial petticoat applied
to the face ; it thoroughly conceals all the features, except
the eyes ; the way of withdrawing it is by pulling it down.

outlines, and in the glow of generous colour. There is fire, though, too—high courage and fire enough in the untamed mind, or spirit, or whatever it is, which drives the breath of pride through those scarcely parted lips.

You smile at pretty women—you turn pale before the beauty that is great enough to have dominion over you. She sees, and exults in your giddiness; she sees and smiles; then presently, with a sudden movement, she lays her blushing fingers upon your arm, and cries out, " Yumourdjak ! " (Plague ! meaning, " there is a present of the plague for you ! ") This is her notion of a witticism. It is a very old piece of fun, no doubt—quite an Oriental Joe Miller ; but the Turks are fondly attached, not only to the institutions, but also to the jokes of their ancestors; so the lady's silvery laugh rings joyously in your ears, and the mirth of her women is boisterous and fresh, as though the bright idea of giving the plague to a Christian had newly lit upon the earth.

Methley began to rally very soon after we had reached Constantinople ; but there seemed at first to be no chance of his regaining strength enough for travelling during the winter, and I determined to stay with my comrade until he had quite recovered ; so I bought me a horse, and a "pipe of tranquillity,"[1] and took a Turkish phrase-master. I troubled myself a great deal with the Turkish tongue, and gained at last some knowledge of its structure. It is enriched, perhaps overladen, with Persian and Arabic words, imported into the language chiefly for

---

[1] The " pipe of tranquillity " is a *tchibouque* too long to be conveniently carried on a journey ; the possession of it therefore implies that its owner is stationary, or, at all events, that he is enjoying a long repose from travel.

the purpose of representing sentiments and religious
dogmas, and terms of art and luxury, entirely
unknown to the Tartar ancestors of the present
Osmanlees; but the body and the spirit of the old
tongue are yet alive, and the smooth words of the
shopkeeper at Constantinople can still carry understanding to the ears of the untamed millions who
rove over the plains of Northern Asia. The
structure of the language, especially in its more
lengthy sentences, is very like to the Latin:[1] the
subject matters are slowly and patiently enumerated,
without disclosing the purpose of the speaker until
he reaches the end of his sentence, and then at last
there comes the clenching word, which gives a
meaning and connection to all that has gone before.
If you listen at all to speaking of this kind, your
attention, rather than be suffered to flag, must grow
more and more lively as the phrase marches on.

The Osmanlees speak well. In countries civilised
according to the European plan the work of trying
to persuade tribunals is almost all performed by a set
of men, the great body of whom very seldom do
anything else; but in Turkey this division of labour

[1] [The structure of Turkish can only be said to resemble
Latin in the general sense that the verb comes at the end
of the sentence, which can be swelled out to enormous, and
indeed preposterous, dimensions. The Turk of the old
school thinks that a letter or document, and even a single
chapter of a book, ought to consist of one sentence; but in
this respect there has been considerable improvement
of late, and modern newspapers and light literature are
written in phrases of relatively reasonable length,—not
longer, say, than German,—and with a much smaller proportion of Arabic and Persian words. The Osmanli gets
few opportunities for public speaking nowadays, but it
is said that the short-lived Turkish Parliament in 1877
furnished a very creditable oratorical display.]

has never taken place, and every man is his own advocate. The importance of the rhetorical art is immense, for a bad speech may endanger the property of the speaker, as well as the soles of his feet and the free enjoyment of his throat. So it results that most of the Turks whom one sees have a lawyer-like habit of speaking connectedly, and at length. Even the treaties continually going on at the bazaar for the buying and selling of the merest trifles are carried on by speechifying rather than by mere colloquies, and the eternal uncertainty as to the market value of things in constant sale gives room enough for discussion. The seller is for ever demanding a price immensely beyond that for which he sells at last, and so occasions unspeakable disgust in many Englishmen, who cannot see why an honest dealer should ask more for his goods than he will really take! The truth is, however, that an ordinary tradesman of Constantinople has no other way of finding out the fair market value of his property. The difficulty under which he labours is easily shown by comparing the mechanism of the commercial system in Turkey with that of our own country. In England, or in any other great mercantile country, the bulk of the things bought and sold goes through the hands of a wholesale dealer, and it is he who higgles and bargains with an entire nation of purchasers by entering into treaty with retail sellers. The labour of making a few large contracts is sufficient to give a clue for finding the fair market value of the goods sold throughout the country; but in Turkey, from the primitive habits of the people, and partly from the absence of great capital and great credit, the importing merchant, the warehouseman, the wholesale dealer, the retail dealer, and the shopman, are all

one person. Old Moostapha, or Abdallah, or Hadgi
Mohamed waddles up from the water's edge with a
small packet of merchandise, which he has bought
out of a Greek brigantine, and when at last he has
reached his nook in the bazaar he puts his goods
before the counter, and himself *upon* it; then laying
fire to his *tchibouque* he "sits in permanence," and
patiently waits to obtain "the best price that can be
got in an open market." This is his fair right as a
seller, but he has no means of finding out what that
best price is except by actual experiment. He
cannot know the intensity of the demand, or the
abundance of the supply, otherwise than by the offers
which may be made for his little bundle of goods;
so he begins by asking a perfectly hopeless price, and
then descends the ladder until he meets a purchaser,
for ever

"Striving to attain
By shadowing out the unattainable."

This is the struggle which creates the continual
occasion for debate. The vendor, perceiving that
the unfolded merchandise has caught the eye of a
possible purchaser, commences his opening speech.
He covers his bristling broadcloths and his meagre
silks with the golden broidery of Oriental praises,
and as he talks, along with the slow and graceful
waving of his arms, he lifts his undulating periods,
upholds and poises them well, till they have gathered
their weight and their strength, and then hurls them
bodily forward with grave, momentous swing. The
possible purchaser listens to the whole speech with
deep and serious attention; but when it is over *his*
turn arrives. He elaborately endeavours to show
why he ought not to buy the things at a price twenty

times larger than their value. Bystanders attracted
to the debate take a part in it as independent members;
the vendor is heard in reply, and coming down with
his price, furnishes the materials for a new debate.
Sometimes, however, the dealer, if he is a very pious
Mussulman, and sufficiently rich to hold back his
ware, will take a more dignified part, maintaining a
kind of judicial gravity, and receiving the applicants
who come to his stall as if they were rather suitors
than customers. He will quietly hear to the end
some long speech that concludes with an offer, and
will answer it all with the one monosyllable "Yok,"
which means distinctly "No."

I caught one glimpse of the old heathen world.
My habits for studying military subjects had been
hardening my heart against poetry; for ever staring
at the flames of battle, I had blinded myself to the
lesser and finer lights that are shed from the imagina-
tions of men. In my reading at this time I delighted
to follow from out of Arabian sands the feet of the
armed believers, and to stand in the broad, manifest
storm-track of Tartar devastation; and thus, though
surrounded at Constantinople by scenes of much
interest to the "classical scholar," I had cast aside
their associations like an old Greek grammar, and
turned my face to the "shining Orient," forgetful of
old Greece and all the pure wealth she left to this
matter-of-fact-ridden world. But it happened to me
one day to mount the high grounds overhanging the
streets of Pera. I sated my eyes with the pomps of
the city and its crowded waters, and then I looked
over where Scutari lay half veiled in her mournful
cypresses. I looked yet farther and higher, and saw
in the heavens a silvery cloud that stood fast and still
against the breeze : it was pure and dazzling white, as

might be the veil of Cytherea, yet touched with such fire, as though from beneath the loving eyes of an immortal were shining through and through. I knew the bearing, but had enormously misjudged its distance and underrated its height, and so it was as a sign and a testimony, almost as a call from the neglected gods, and now I saw and acknowledged the snowy crown of the Mysian Olympus!

CHAPTER IV [1]

THE TROAD

METHLEY recovered almost suddenly, and we determined to go through the Troad together.

My comrade was a capital Grecian. It is true that his singular mind so ordered and disposed his classic lore as to impress it with something of an original and barbarous character — with an almost Gothic quaintness, more properly belonging to a rich native ballad than to the poetry of Hellas. There was a certain impropriety in his knowing so much Greek—an unfitness in the idea of marble fauns, and satyrs, and even Olympian gods, lugged in under the oaken roof and the painted light of an odd, old Norman hall. But Methley, abounding in Homer,

[1] [Since this chapter was written the labours of Schliemann and Dörpfeld have excavated Hissarlik, commonly considered to be the site of Troy, though some prefer to identify the city of the *Iliad* with the ruins of Bunar Bashi, farther inland. Hissarlik is a huge mound, in a singularly desolate plain about an hour's ride from Kum Kale, at the entrance of the Dardanelles, and is said to be composed of the ruins of no less than eight or nine cities placed one on the top of the other. Of the older layers the best preserved are the second and sixth cities. There are no statues, inscriptions, or other indications, so that the structure of this pile of dead towns is excessively difficult

41

really loved him (as I believe) in all truth, without whim or fancy; moreover, he had a good deal of the practical sagacity

" Of a Yorkshireman hippodamoio,"

and this enabled him to apply his knowledge with much more tact than is usually shown by people so learned as he.

to understand, and only becomes intelligible when explained by someone thoroughly acquainted with the course of the excavations; for in order to reach the lower layers it has naturally been necessary to displace the upper ones. The general character of the scene is still excellently described by Byron's lines in *Don Juan*, Cant. iv. :

" Here, on the green and village-cotted hill, is
(Flanked by the Hellespont and by the sea)
Entombed the bravest of the brave, Achilles ;
(They say so—Bryant says the contrary):
And further downward, tall and towering still, is
The tumulus—of whom ? Heaven knows ; 't may be
Patroclus, Ajax, or Protesilaus ;
All heroes, who, if living still, would slay us.

High barrows, without marble or a name,
A vast, untilled, and mountain-skirted plain,
And Ida, in the distance, still the same,
And old Scamander (if 't be he), remain ;
The situation still seems formed for fame—
A hundred thousand men might fight again,
With ease ; but where I looked for Ilion's walls,
The quiet sheep feeds, and the tortoise crawls.

Troops of untended horses; here and there
Some little hamlets, with new names uncouth ;
Some shepherds (not like Paris), led to stare
A moment at the European youth,
Whom to the spot his schoolboy feelings bear ;
A Turk, with beads in hand and pipe in mouth,
Extremely taken with his own religion,
Are what I found there—but the devil a Phrygian."]

I, too, loved Homer, but not with a scholar's love. The most humble and pious among women was yet so proud a mother that she could teach her firstborn son no Watts' hymns, no collects for the day ; she could teach him in earliest childhood no less than this, to find a home in his saddle, and to love old Homer, and all that old Homer sung. True it is, that the Greek was ingeniously rendered into English, the English of Pope even, but not even a mesh like that can screen an earnest child from the fire of Homer's battles.

I poured over the *Odyssey* as over a story-book, hoping and fearing for the hero whom yet I partly scorned. But the *Iliad*—line by line I clasped it to my brain with reverence as well as with love. As an old woman deeply trustful sits reading her Bible because of the world to come, so, as though it would fit me for the coming strife of this temporal world, I read and read the *Iliad*. Even outwardly, it was not like other books ; it was throned in towering folios. There was a preface or dissertation printed in type still more majestic than the rest of the book ; this I read, but not till my enthusiasm for the *Iliad* had already run high. The writer compiling the opinions of many men, and chiefly of the ancients, set forth, I know not how quaintly, that the *Iliad* was all in all to the human race—that it was history, poetry, revelation ; that the works of men's hands were folly and vanity, and would pass away like the dreams of a child, but that the kingdom of Homer would endure for ever and ever.

I assented with all my soul. I read, and still read ; I came to know Homer. A learned commentator knows something of the Greeks, in the same sense as an oil-and-colour man may be said to know

something of painting; but take an untamed child,
and leave him alone for twelve months with any
translation of Homer, and he will be nearer by twenty
centuries to the spirit of old Greece; *he* does not
stop in the ninth year of the siege to admire this or
that group of words; *he* has no books in his tent, but
he shares in vital counsels with the "king of men,"
and knows the inmost souls of the impending gods;
how profanely he exults over the powers divine when
they are taught to dread the prowess of mortals!
and most of all, how he rejoices when the God of
War flies howling from the spear of Diomed, and
mounts into heaven for safety! Then the beautiful
episode of the Sixth Book: the way to feel this is
not to go casting about, and learning from pastors and
masters how best to admire it. The impatient child
is not grubbing for beauties, but pushing the siege;
the women vex him with their delays, and their
talking; the mention of the nurse is personal, and
little sympathy has he for the child that is young
enough to be frightened at the nodding plume of a
helmet; but all the while that he thus chafes at the
pausing of the action, the strong vertical light of
Homer's poetry is blazing so full upon the people
and things of the *Iliad*, that soon to the eyes of the
child they grow familiar as his mother's shawl; yet
of this great gain he is unconscious, and on he goes,
vengefully thirsting for the best blood of Troy, and
never remitting his fierceness till almost suddenly it
is changed for sorrow—the new and generous sorrow
that he learns to feel when the noblest of all his foes
lies sadly dying at the Scæan gate.

Heroic days are these, but the dark ages of schoolboy life come closing over them. I suppose it is all
right in the end, yet, by Jove, at first sight it does

seem a sad intellectual fall from your mother's dressing-room to a buzzing school. You feel so keenly the delights of early knowledge; you form strange mystic friendships with the mere names of mountains, and seas, and continents, and mighty rivers; you learn the ways of the planets, and transcend their narrow limits, and ask for the end of space; you vex the electric cylinder till it yields you, for your toy to play with, that subtle fire in which our earth was forged; you know of the nations that have towered high in the world, and the lives of the men who have saved whole empires from oblivion. What more will you ever learn? Yet the dismal change is ordained, and then, thin meagre Latin (the same for everybody), with small shreds and patches of Greek, is thrown like a pauper's pall over all your early lore. Instead of sweet knowledge, vile, monkish, doggerel grammars and graduses, dictionaries and lexicons, and horrible odds and ends of dead languages, are given you for your portion, and down you fall, from Roman story to a three-inch scrap of "Scriptores Romani,"—from Greek poetry down, down to the cold rations of "Poetæ Græci," cut up by commentators, and served out by schoolmasters!

It was not the recollection of school nor college learning, but the rapturous and earnest reading of my childhood, which made me bend forward so longingly to the plains of Troy.

Away from our people and our horses, Methley and I went loitering along by the willow banks of a stream that crept in quietness through the low, even plain. There was no stir of weather overhead, no sound of rural labour, no sign of life in the land; but all the earth was dead and still, as though it had lain for thrice a thousand years under the leaden gloom of one unbroken Sabbath.

Softly and sadly the poor, dumb, patient stream went winding and winding along through its shifting pathway ; in some places its waters were parted, and then again, lower down, they would meet once more. I could see that the stream from year to year was finding itself new channels, and flowed no longer in its ancient track, but I knew that the springs which fed it were high on Ida—the springs of Simois and Scamander !

It was coldly and thanklessly, and with vacant, unsatisfied eyes that I watched the slow coming and gliding away of the waters. I tell myself now, as a profane fact, that I did stand by that river (Methley gathered some seeds from the bushes that grew there), but since that I am away from his banks, " divine Scamander" has recovered the proper mystery belonging to him as an unseen deity ; a kind of indistinctness, like that which belongs to far antiquity, has spread itself over my memory, of the winding stream that I saw with these very eyes. One's mind regains in absence that dominion over earthly things which has been shaken by their rude contact. You force yourself hardily into the material presence of a mountain, or a river, whose name belongs to poetry and ancient religion, rather than to the external world ; your feelings wound up and kept ready for some sort of half-expected rapture are chilled, and borne down for the time under all this load of real earth and water ; but let these once pass out of sight, and then again the old fanciful notions are restored, and the mere realities which you have just been looking at are thrown back so far into distance, that the very event of your intrusion upon such scenes

begins to look dim and uncertain, as though it belonged to mythology.

It is not over the plain before Troy that the river
now flows ; its waters have edged away far towards
the north, since the day that "divine Scamander"
(whom the gods call Xanthus) went down to do
battle for Ilion, "with Mars, and Phœbus, and Latona,
and Diana glorying in her arrows, and Venus the
lover of smiles."

And now, when I was vexed at the migration of
Scamander, and the total loss or absorption of poor
dear Simois, how happily Methley reminded me
that Homer himself had warned us of some such
changes! The Greeks in beginning their wall had
neglected the hecatombs due to the gods, and so
after the fall of Troy Apollo turned the paths of the
rivers that flow from Ida, and sent them flooding
over the wall, till all the beach was smooth and free
from the unhallowed works of the Greeks. It is
true I see now, on looking to the passage, that
Neptune, when the work of destruction was done,
turned back the rivers to their ancient ways :

" . . . ποταμους δ' ετρεψε νεεσθαι
Καρ' ροον ἡπερ προσθεν ιεν καλλιρροον ὑδωρ,"

but their old channels passing through that light
pervious soil would have been lost in the nine
days' flood, and perhaps the god, when he willed to
bring back the rivers to their ancient beds, may have
done his work but ill : it is easier, they say, to
destroy than it is to restore.

We took to our horses again, and went southward
towards the very plain between Troy and the tents of
the Greeks, but we rode by a line at some distance
from the shore. Whether it was that the lay of the

ground hindered my view towards the sea, or that I
was all intent upon Ida, or whether my mind was in
vacancy, or whether, as is most like, I had strayed
from the Dardan plains all back to gentle England,
there is now no knowing, nor caring, but it was not
quite suddenly indeed, but rather, as it were, in the
swelling and falling of a single wave, that the reality of
that very sea-view, which had bounded the sight of
the Greeks, now visibly acceded to me, and rolled full
in upon my brain. Conceive how deeply that eternal
coastline, that fixed horizon, those island rocks,
must have graven their images upon the minds of the
Grecian warriors by the time that they had reached
the ninth year of the siege! conceive the strength,
and the fanciful beauty, of the speeches with which
a whole army of imagining men must have told their
weariness, and how the sauntering chiefs must have
whelmed that daily, daily scene with their deep
Ionian curses!

And now it was that my eyes were greeted
with a delightful surprise. Whilst we were at
Constantinople, Methley and I had pored over the
map together. We agreed that whatever may have
been the exact site of Troy, the Grecian camp must
have been nearly opposite to the space betwixt the
islands of Imbros and Tenedos,

"Μεσσηγυς Τενεδοιο και Ιμβρου παιπαλοεσσης,"

but Methley reminded me of a passage in the *Iliad* in
which Neptune is represented as looking at the scene
of action before Ilion from above the island of
Samothrace. Now Samothrace, according to the
map, appeared to be not only out of all seeing
distance from the Troad, but to be entirely shut out
from it by the intervening Imbros, which is a larger

island, stretching its length right athwart the line of sight from Samothrace to Troy. Piously allowing that the dread Commoter of our globe might have seen all mortal doings, even from the depth of his own cerulean kingdom, I still felt that if a station were to be chosen from which to see the fight, old Homer, so material in his ways of thought, so averse from all haziness and overreaching, would have *meant* to give the god for his station some spot within reach of men's eyes from the plains of Troy. I think that this testing of the poet's words by map and compass may have shaken a little of my faith in the completeness of his knowledge. Well, now I had come; there to the south was Tenedos, and here at my side was Imbros, all right, and according to the map, but aloft over Imbros, aloft in a far-away heaven, was Samothrace, the watch-tower of Neptune !

So Homer had appointed it, and so it was; the map was correct enough, but could not, like Homer, convey *the whole truth.* Thus vain and false are the mere human surmises and doubts which clash with Homeric writ !

Nobody whose mind had not been reduced to the most deplorable logical condition could look upon this beautiful congruity betwixt the *Iliad* and the material world and yet bear to suppose that the poet may have learned the features of the coast from mere hearsay; now then, I believed; now I knew that Homer had *passed along here,* that this vision of Samothrace over-towering the nearer island was common to him and to me.

After a journey of some few days by the route of Adramiti and Pergamo we reached Smyrna. The letters which Methley here received obliged him to return to England.

4

CHAPTER V

SMYRNA, or Giaour Izmir, "Infidel Smyrna," as the Mussulmans call it, is the main point of commercial contact betwixt Europe and Asia. You are there surrounded by the people, and the confused customs of many and various nations; you see the fussy European adopting the East, and calming his restlessness with the long Turkish "pipe of tranquillity"; you see Jews offering services, and receiving blows;[1] on one side you have a fellow whose dress and beard would give you a good idea of the true Oriental, if it were not for the *gobe-mouche*

---

[1] The Jews of Smyrna are poor, and having little merchandise of their own to dispose of, they are sadly importunate in offering their services as intermediaries their troublesome conduct has led to the custom of beating them in the open streets. It is usual for Europeans to carry long sticks with them, for the express purpose o keeping off the chosen people. I always felt ashamed to strike the poor fellows myself, but I confess to the amuse ment with which I witnessed the observance of this custon by other people. The Jew seldom got hurt much, for h was always expecting the blow, and was ready to reced from it the moment it came: one could not help bein; rather gratified at seeing him bound away so nimbly, with his long robes floating out in the air, and then again whee round, and return with fresh importunities.

expression of countenance with which he is swallowing an article in the *National*; and there, just by, is a genuine Osmanlee, smoking away with all the majesty of a sultan, but before you have time to admire sufficiently his tranquil dignity, and his soft Asiatic repose, the poor old fellow is ruthlessly "run down" by an English midshipman, who had set sail on a Smyrna hack. Such are the incongruities of the "infidel city" at ordinary times; but when I was there, our friend Carrigaholt [1] had imported himself and his oddities as an accession to the other and inferior wonders of Smyrna.

I was sitting alone in my room one day at Constantinople, when I heard Methley approaching my door with shouts of laughter and welcome, and presently I recognised that peculiar cry by which our friend Carrigaholt expresses his emotions; he soon explained to us the final causes by which the fates had worked out their wonderful purpose of bringing him to Constantinople. He was always, you know, very fond of sailing, but he had got into such sad scrapes (including, I think, a lawsuit) on account of his last yacht, that he took it into his head to have a cruise in a merchant vessel, so he went to Liverpool, and looked through the craft lying ready to sail, till he found a smart schooner that perfectly suited his taste. The destination of the vessel was the last thing he thought of; and when he was told that she was bound for Constantinople, he merely assented to that as a part of the arrangement to which he had no objection. As soon as the vessel had sailed, the hapless passenger discovered that his skipper carried on board an enormous wife, with an

[1] [Carrigaholt is said to have been Henry Stuart Burton, of Carrigaholt, County Clare.]

inquiring mind and an irresistible tendency to impart her opinions. She looked upon her guest as upon a piece of waste intellect that ought to be carefully tilled. She tilled him accordingly. If the dons at Oxford could have seen poor Carrigaholt thus absolutely "attending lectures" in the Bay of Biscay, they would surely have thought him sufficiently punished for all the wrongs he did them whilst he was preparing himself under their care for the other and more boisterous University. The voyage did not last more than six or eight weeks, and the philosophy inflicted on Carrigaholt was not entirely fatal to him; certainly he was somewhat emaciated, and, for aught I know, he may have subscribed somewhat too largely to the "Feminine-right-of-reason Society"; but it did not appear that his health had been seriously affected. There was a scheme on foot, it would seem, for taking the passenger back to England in the same schooner—a scheme, in fact, for keeping him perpetually afloat, and perpetually saturated with arguments; but when Carrigaholt found himself ashore, and remembered that the skipperina (who had imprudently remained on board) was not there to enforce her suggestions, he was open to the hints of his servant (a very sharp fellow), who arranged a plan for escaping, and finally brought off his master to Giuseppini's hotel.

Our friend afterwards went by sea to Smyrna, and there he now was in his glory. He had a good, or at all events a gentlemanlike, judgment in matters of taste, and as his great object was to surround himself with all that his fancy could dictate, he lived in a state of perpetual negotiation. He was for ever or the point of purchasing, not only the material productions of the place, but all sorts of such fine ware as "intelligence," "fidelity," and so on. He was most curious, however, as the purchaser of the "affections." Sometimes he would imagine that he had a marital aptitude, and his fancy would sketch a graceful picture, in which he appeared reclining on a divan, with a beautiful Greek woman fondly couched at his feet, and soothing him with the witchery of her guitar. Having satisfied himself with the ideal picture thus created, he would pass into action ; the guitar he would buy instantly, and would give such intimations of his wish to be wedded to a Greek as could not fail to produce great excitement in the families of the beautiful Smyrniotes. Then again (and just in time perhaps to save him from the yoke) his dream would pass away, and another would come in its stead ; he would suddenly feel the yearnings of a father's love, and willing by force of gold to transcend all natural preliminaries, he would issue instructions for the purchase of some dutiful child that could be warranted to love him as a parent. Then at another time he would be convinced that the attachment of menials might satisfy the longings of his affectionate heart, and thereupon he would give orders to his slave-merchant for something in the way of eternal fidelity. You may well imagine that this anxiety of Carrigaholt to purchase not only the scenery, but the many *dramatis personæ* belonging to his dreams, with all their goodness and graces complete, necessarily gave an immense stimulus to the trade and intrigue of Smyrna, and created a demand for human virtues which the moral resources of the place were totally inadequate to supply. Every day after breakfast this lover of the good and the beautiful held a levee, which was often exceedingly amusing. In his ante-room there would be not only the sellers of

pipes and slippers and shawls, and suchlike Oriental
merchandise; not only embroiderers and cunning
workmen patiently striving to realise his visions of
Albanian dresses; not only the servants offering for
places, and the slave-dealer tendering his sable ware;
but there would be the Greek master, waiting to teach
his pupil the grammar of the soft Ionian tongue, in
which he was to delight the wife of his imagination;
and the music-master, who was to teach him some
sweet replies to the anticipated sounds of the fancied
guitar; and then, above all, and proudly eminent with
undisputed preference of *entrée*, and fraught with the
mysterious tidings on which the realisation of the
whole dream might depend, was the mysterious
match-maker,[1] enticing and postponing the suitor, yet
ever keeping alive in his soul the love of that pictured
virtue, whose beauty (unseen by eyes) was half
revealed to the imagination.

You would have thought that this practical dreaming must have soon brought Carrigaholt to a bad end,
but he was in much less danger than you would
suppose; for besides that the new visions of happiness
almost always came in time to counteract the fatal
completion of the preceding scheme, his high breeding
and his delicately sensitive taste almost always came
to his aid at times when he was left without any other
protection; and the efficacy of these qualities in
keeping a man out of harm's way is really immense.
In all baseness and imposture there is a coarse, vulgar
spirit, which, however artfully concealed for a time,
must sooner or later show itself in some little circumstance sufficiently plain to occasion an instant jar upon
the minds of those whose taste is lively and true.

---

[1] Marriages in the East are arranged by professed match-
makers; many of these, I believe, are Jewesses.

To such men a shock of this kind, disclosing the *ugliness* of a cheat, is more effectively convincing than any mere proofs could be.

Thus guarded from isle to isle, and through Greece, and through Albania, this practical Plato with a purse in his hand, carried on his mad chase after the good and the beautiful, and yet returned in safety to his home. But now, poor fellow! the lowly grave, that is the end of men's romantic hopes, has closed over all his rich fancies, and all his high aspirations; he is utterly married! No more hope, no more change for him—no more relays—he must go on Vetturini-wise to the appointed end of his journey!

Smyrna, I think, may be called the chief town and capital of the Grecian race, against which you will be cautioned so carefully as soon as you touch the Levant. You will say that I ought not to confound as one people the Greeks living under a constitutional Government with the unfortunate Rayahs who "groan under the Turkish yoke," but I can't see that political events have hitherto produced any strongly marked difference of character. If I could venture to rely (which I feel that I cannot at all do) upon my own observation, I should tell you that there was more heartiness and strength in the Greeks of the Ottoman Empire than in those of the new kingdom. The truth is, that there is a greater field for commercial enterprise, and even for Greek ambition, under the Ottoman sceptre, than is to be found in the dominions of Otho. Indeed the people, by their frequent migrations from the limits of the constitutional kingdom to the territories of the Porte, seem to show that, on the whole, they prefer "groaning under the Turkish yoke" to the honour

of " being the only true source of legitimate power "
in their own land.

For myself, I love the race ; in spite of all their
vices, and even in spite of all their meannesses, I
remember the blood that is in them, and still love the
Greeks. The Osmanlees are, of course, by nature,
by religion, and by politics, the strong foes of the
Hellenic people ; and as the Greeks, poor fellows!
happen to be a little deficient in some of the virtues
which facilitate the transaction of commercial business
(such as veracity, fidelity, etc.), it naturally follows
that they are highly unpopular with the European
merchants. Now these are the persons through
whom, either directly or indirectly, is derived the
greater part of the information which you gather in
the Levant, and therefore you must make up your
mind to hear an almost universal and unbroken
testimony against the character of the people whose
ancestors invented virtue. And strange to say, the
Greeks themselves do not attempt to disturb this
general unanimity of opinion by any dissent on their
part. Question a Greek on the subject, and he will
tell you at once that the people are *traditori*, and will
then, perhaps, endeavour to shake off his fair share
of the imputation by asserting that his father had been
dragoman to some foreign embassy, and that he (the
son), therefore, by the law of nations, had ceased to
be Greek.

" E dunque no siete traditore ? "

" Possibile, signor, ma almeno Io no sono Greco."

Not even the diplomatic representatives of the
Hellenic kingdom are free from the habit of depreciating their brethren. I recollect that at one of
the ports in Syria a Greek vessel was rather unfairly
kept in quarantine by order of the Board of Health,

which consisted entirely of Europeans. A consular agent from the kingdom of Greece had lately hoisted his flag in the town, and the captain of the vessel drew up a remonstrance, which he requested his consul to present to the Board.

"Now, *is* this reasonable?" said the consul; "is it reasonable that I should place myself in collision with all the principal European gentlemen of the place for the sake of you, a Greek?" The skipper was greatly vexed at the failure of his application, but he scarcely even questioned the justice of the ground which his consul had taken. Well, it happened some time afterwards that I found myself at the same port, having gone thither with the view of embarking for the port of Syra. I was anxious, of course, to elude as carefully as possible the quarantine detentions which threatened me on my arrival, and hearing that the Greek consul had a brother who was a man in authority at Syra, I got myself presented to the former, and took the liberty of asking him to give me such a letter of introduction to his relative at Syra as might possibly have the effect of shortening the term of my quarantine. He acceded to this request with the utmost kindness and courtesy; but when he replied to my thanks by saying that "in serving an Englishman he was doing no more than his strict duty commanded," not even my gratitude could prevent me from calling to mind his treatment of the poor captain who had the misfortune of *not* being an alien in blood to his consul and appointed protector.

I think that the change which has taken place in the character of the Greeks has been occasioned, in great measure, by the doctrines and practice of their religion. The Greek Church has animated the

Muscovite peasant, and inspired him with hopes and
ideas which, however humble, are still better than
none at all; but the faith, and the forms, and the
strange ecclesiastical literature which act so advan-
tageously upon the mere clay of the Russian serf,
seem to hang like lead upon the ethereal spirit of the
Greek. Never in any part of the world have I seen
religious performances so painful to witness as those
of the Greeks. The horror, however, with which
one shudders at their worship is attributable, in some
measure, to the mere effect of costume. In all the
Ottoman dominions, and very frequently too in the
kingdom of Otho, the Greeks wear turbans or other
head-dresses, and shave their heads, leaving only a
rat's-tail at the·crown of the head; they of course
keep themselves covered within doors as well as
abroad, and they never remove their headgear
merely on account of being in a church; but when
the Greek stops to worship at his proper shrine, then,
and then only, he always uncovers; and as you see
him thus with shaven skull and savage tail depending
from his crown, kissing a thing of wood and glass,
and cringing with base prostrations and apparent
terror before a miserable picture, you see superstition
in a shape which, outwardly at least, is sadly abject
and repulsive.

The fasts, too, of the Greek Church produce an
ill effect upon the character of the people, for they
are not a mere farce, but are carried to such an
extent as to bring about a real mortification of the
flesh; the febrile irritation of the frame operating
in conjunction with the depression of the spirits
occasioned by abstinence, will so far answer the
objects of the rite, as to engender some religious
excitement, but this·is of a morbid and gloomy

character, and it seems to be certain, that along with the increase of sanctity, there comes a fiercer desire for the perpetration of dark crimes. The number of murders committed during Lent is greater, I am told, than at any other time of the year. A man under the influence of a bean dietary (for this is the principal food of the Greeks during their fasts) will be in an apt humour for enriching the shrine of his saint, and passing a knife through his next-door neighbour. The moneys deposited upon the shrines are appropriated by priests; the priests are married men, and have families to provide for; they "take the good with the bad," and continue to recommend fasts.

Then, too, the Greek Church enjoins her followers to keep holy such a vast number of saints' days as practically to shorten the lives of the people very materially. I believe that one-third out of the number of days in the year are "kept holy," or rather, *kept stupid*, in honour of the saints; no great portion of the time thus set apart is spent in religious exercises, and the people don't betake themselves to any such animating pastimes as might serve to strengthen the frame, or invigorate the mind, or exalt the taste. On the contrary, the saints' days of the Greeks in Smyrna are passed in the same manner as the Sabbaths of well-behaved Protestant housemaids in London—that is to say, in a steady and serious contemplation of street scenery. The men perform this duty *at the doors* of their houses, the women *at the windows*, which the custom of Greek towns has so decidedly appropriated to them as the proper station of their sex, that a man would be looked upon as utterly effeminate if he ventured to choose that situation for the keeping of the saints' days. I was present one day at a treaty for the hire of some apartments at Smyrna, which was carried on between Carrigaholt and the Greek woman to whom the rooms belonged. Carrigaholt objected that the windows commanded no view of the street. Immediately the brow of the majestic matron clouded, and with all the scorn of a Spartan mother she coolly asked Carrigaholt, and said, "Art thou a tender damsel that thou wouldst sit and gaze from windows?" The man whom she addressed, however, had not gone to Greece with any intention of placing himself under the laws of Lycurgus, and was not to be diverted from his views by a Spartan rebuke, so he took care to find himself windows after his own heart, and there, I believe, for many a month, he kept the saints' days, and all the days intervening, after the fashion of Grecian women.

Oh! let me be charitable to all who write, and to all who lecture, and to all who preach, since even I, a layman not forced to write at all, can hardly avoid chiming in with some tuneful cant! I have had the heart to talk about the pernicious effects of the Greek holidays, to which I owe some of my most beautiful visions! I will let the words stand, as a humbling proof that I am subject to that immutable law which compels a man with a pen in his hand to be uttering every now and then some sentiment not his own. It seems as though the power of expressing regrets and desires by written symbols were coupled with a condition that the writer should from time to time express the regrets and desires of other people; as though, like a French peasant under the old régime, one were bound to perform a certain amount of work *upon the public highways.* I rebel as stoutly as I can against this horrible *corvée.* I try not to deceive

you—I try to set down the thoughts which are fresh
within me, and not to pretend any wishes, or griefs,
which I do not really feel ; but no sooner do I cease
from watchfulness in this regard, than my right hand
is, as it were, seized by some false angel, and even
now, you see, I have been forced to put down such
words and sentences as I ought to have written if
really and truly I had wished to disturb the saints'
days of the beautiful Smyrniotes !

Which, Heaven forbid ! for as you move through
the narrow streets of the city at these times of festival,
the transom-shaped windows suspended over your
head on either side are filled with the beautiful
descendants of the old Ionian race ; all (even yonder
empress that sits throned at the window of that
humblest mud cottage) are attired with seeming
magnificence ; their classic heads are crowned with
scarlet, and loaded with jewels or coins of gold, the
whole wealth of the wearer ; [1] their features are
touched with a savage pencil, which hardens the
outline of eyes and eyebrows, and lends an unnatural
fire to the stern, grave looks with which they pierce
your brain. Endure their fiery eyes as best you
may, and ride on slowly and reverently, for facing
you from the side of the transom, that looks longwise
through the street, you see the one glorious shape
transcendant in its beauty ; you see the massive braid
of hair as it catches a touch of light on its jetty
surface, and the broad, calm, angry brow ; the large
black eyes, deep set, and self-relying like the eyes of

[1] A Greek woman wears her whole fortune upon her
person in the shape of jewels or gold coins ; I believe that
this mode of investment is adopted in great measure for
safety's sake. It has the advantage of enabling a suitor
to *reckon* as well as to admire the objects of his affection.

a conqueror, with their rich shadows of thought lying darkly around them ; you see the thin fiery nostril, and the bold line of the chin and throat disclosing all the fierceness, and all the pride, passion, and power that can live along with the rare womanly beauty of those sweetly turned lips. But then there is a terrible stillness in this breathing image ; it seems like the stillness of a savage that sits intent and brooding, day by day, upon some one fearful scheme of vengeance, but yet more like it seems to the stillness of an Immortal, whose will must be known, and obeyed without sign or speech. Bow down !—Bow down and adore the young Persephonie, transcendent Queen of Shades !

CHAPTER VI

GREEK MARINERS

I SAILED from Smyrna in the *Amphitrite*, a Greek brigantine, which was confidently said to be bound for the coast of Syria ; but I knew that this announcement was not to be relied upon with positive certainty, for the Greek mariners are practically free from the stringency of ship's papers, and where they will, there they go. However, I had the whole of the cabin for myself and my attendant, Mysseri, subject only to the society of the captain at the hour of dinner. Being at ease in this respect, being furnished too with plenty of books, and finding an unfailing source of interest in the thorough Greekness of my captain and my crew, I felt less anxious than most people would have been about the probable length of the cruise. I knew enough of Greek navigation to be sure that our vessel would cling to earth like a child to its mother's knee, and that I should touch at many an isle before I set foot upon the Syrian coast ; but I had no invidious preference for Europe, Asia, or Africa, and I felt that I could defy the winds to blow me upon a coast that was blank and void of interest. My patience was extremely useful to me, for the cruise altogether endured some forty days, and that in the midst of winter.

According to me, the most interesting of all the Greeks (male Greeks) are the mariners, because their pursuits and their social condition are so nearly the same as those of their famous ancestors. You will say, that the occupation of commerce must have smoothed down the salience of their minds; and this would be so perhaps, if their mercantile affairs were conducted according to the fixed business-like routine of Europeans; but the ventures of the Greeks are surrounded by such a multitude of imagined dangers (and from the absence of regular marts, in which the true value of merchandise can be ascertained), are so entirely speculative, and besides, are conducted in a manner so wholly determined upon by the wayward fancies and wishes of the crew, that they belong to enterprise rather than to industry, and are very far indeed from tending to deaden any freshness of character.

The vessels in which war and piracy were carried on during the years of the Greek Revolution became merchantmen at the end of the war; but the tactics of the Greeks, as naval warriors, were so exceedingly cautious, and their habits as commercial mariners are so wild, that the change has been more slight than you might imagine. The first care of Greeks (Greek Rayahs) when they undertake a shipping enterprise is to procure for their vessel the protection of some European power. This is easily managed by a little intriguing with the dragoman of one of the embassies at Constantinople, and the craft soon glories in the ensign of Russia, or the dazzling Tricolor, or the Union Jack. Thus, to the great delight of her crew, she enters upon the ocean world with a flaring lie at her peak, but the appearance of the vessel does no discredit to the borrowed flag;

she is frail indeed, but is gracefully built, and smartly rigged; she always carries guns, and, in short, gives good promise of mischief and speed.

The privileges attached to the vessel and her crew ' by virtue of the borrowed flag are so great, as to imply a liberty wider even than that which is often enjoyed in our more strictly civilised countries, so that there is no pretence for saying that the development of the true character belonging to Greek mariners is prevented by the dominion of the Ottoman. These men are free, too, from the power of the great capitalist, whose sway is more withering than despotism itself to the enterprises of humble venturers. The capital employed is supplied by those whose labour is to render it productive. The crew receive no wages, but have all a share in the venture, and in general, I believe, they are the owners of the whole freight. They choose a captain, to whom they entrust just power enough to keep the vessel on her course in fine weather, but not quite enough for a gale of wind; they also elect a cook and a mate. The cook whom we had on board was particularly careful about the ship's reckoning, and when under the influence of the keen sea-breezes we grew fondly expectant of an instant dinner, the great author of *pilafs* would be standing on deck with an ancient quadrant in his hands, calmly affecting to take an observation. But then to make up for this the captain would be exercising a controlling influence over the soup, so that all in the end went well. Our mate was a Hydriot, a native of that island rock which grows nothing but mariners and mariners' wives. His character seemed to be exactly that which is generally attributed to the Hydriot race; he was fierce, and gloomy, and lonely in his ways.

5

One of his principal duties seemed to be that of acting as counter-captain, or leader of the opposition, denouncing the first symptoms of tyranny, and protecting even the cabin-boy from oppression. Besides this, when things went smoothly he would begin to prognosticate evil, in order that his more lighthearted comrades might not be puffed up with the seeming good fortune of the moment.

It seemed to me that the personal freedom of these sailors, who own no superiors except those of their own choice, is as like as may be to that of their seafaring ancestors. And even in their mode of navigation they have admitted no such an entire change as you would suppose probable. It is true that they have so far availed themselves of modern discoveries as to look to the compass instead of the stars, and that they have superseded the immortal gods of their forefathers by St. Nicholas in his glass case,[1] but they are not yet so confident either in their needle, or their saint, as to love an open sea, and they still hug their shores as fondly as the Argonauts of old. Indeed, they have a most unsailor-like love for the land, and I really believe that in a gale of wind they would rather have a rock-bound coast on their lee than no coast at all. According to the notions of an English seaman, this kind of navigation would soon bring the vessel on which it might be practised to an evil end. The Greek, however, is unaccountably successful in escaping the consequences of being " jammed in," as it is called, upon a leeshore.

These seamen, like their forefathers, rely upon no

---

[1] St. Nicholas is the great patron of Greek sailors. A small picture of him enclosed in a glass case is hung up like a barometer at one end of the cabin.

winds unless they are right astern or on the quarter ;
they rarely go *on* a wind if it blows at all fresh, and
if the adverse breeze approaches to a gale, they at
once fumigate St. Nicholas, and put up the helm.
The consequence, of course, is that under the ever-
varying winds of the Ægean they are blown about
in the most whimsical manner. I used to think that
Ulysses, with his ten years' voyage, had taken his
time in making Ithaca, but my experience in Greek
navigation soon made me understand that he had had,
in point of fact, a pretty good "average passage."

Such are now the mariners of the Ægean : free,
equal amongst themselves, navigating the seas of their
forefathers with the same heroic, and yet childlike,
spirit of venture, the same half-trustful reliance upon
heavenly aid, they are the liveliest images of true old
Greeks that time and the new religions have spared
to us.

With one exception, our crew were "a solemn
company," [1] and yet, sometimes, when all things
went well, they would relax their austerity, and
show a disposition to fun, or rather to quiet humour.
When this happened, they invariably had recourse
to one of their number, who went by the name of
"Admiral Nicolou." He was an amusing fellow,
the poorest, I believe, and the least thoughtful of
the crew, but full of rich humour. His oft-told
story of the events by which he had gained the
sobriquet of "Admiral" never failed to delight his
hearers, and when he was desired to repeat it for my
benefit, the rest of the crew crowded round with as
much interest as if they were listening to the tale
for the first time. A number of Greek brigs and
brigantines were at anchor in the bay of Beyrout.

[1] Hanmer.

A festival of some kind, particularly attractive to the sailors, was going on in the town, and whether with or without leave I know not, but the crews of all the craft, except that of Nicolou, had gone ashore. On board his vessel, however, which carried dollars, there was, it would seem, a more careful, or more influential captain, who was able to enforce his determination that one man, at least, should be left on board. Nicolou's good nature was with him so powerful an impulse, that he could not resist the delight of volunteering to stay with the vessel whilst his comrades went ashore. His proposal was accepted, and the crew and captain soon left him alone on the deck of his vessel. The sailors, gathering together from their several ships, were amusing themselves in the town, when suddenly there came down from betwixt the mountains one of those sudden hurricanes which sometimes occur in southern climes. Nicolou's vessel, together with four of the craft which had been left unmanned, broke from her moorings, and all five of the vessels were carried out seaward. The town is on a salient point at the southern side of the bay, so that "that Admiral" was close under the eyes of the inhabitants and the shore-gone sailors when he gallantly drifted out at the head of his little fleet. If Nicolou could not entirely control the manœuvres of the squadron, there was at least no human power to divide his authority, and thus it was that he took rank as "Admiral." Nicolou cut his cable, and thus for the time saved his vessel; for the rest of the fleet under his command were quickly wrecked, whilst "the Admiral" go away clear to the open sea. The violence of the squall soon passed off, but Nicolou felt that his chance of one day resigning his high duties as an

admiral for the enjoyments of private life on the
steadfast shore mainly depended upon his success in
working the brig with his own hands, so after calling
on his namesake, the saint (not for the first time, I
take it), he got up some canvas, and took the helm:
he became equal, he told us, to a score of Nicolous,
and the vessel, as he said, was "manned with his
terrors." For two days, it seems, he cruised at
large, but at last, either by his seamanship, or by the
natural instinct of the Greek mariners for finding
land, he brought his craft close to an unknown shore,
that promised well for his purpose of running in the
vessel; and he was preparing to give her a good
berth on the beach, when he saw a gang of ferocious-
looking fellows coming down to the point for which
he was making. Poor Nicolou was a perfectly un-
lettered and untutored genius, and for that reason,
perhaps, a keen listener to tales of terror. His mind
had been impressed with some horrible legend of
cannibalism, and he now did not doubt for a moment
that the men awaiting him on the beach were the
monsters at whom he had shuddered in the days of
his childhood. The coast on which Nicolou was
running his vessel was somewhere, I fancy, at the
foot of the Anzairie Mountains, and the fellows who
were preparing to give him a reception were probably
very rough specimens of humanity. It is likely
enough that they might have given themselves the
trouble of putting "the Admiral" to death, for the
purpose of simplifying their claim to the vessel and
preventing litigation, but the notion of their cannibalism was of course utterly unfounded. Nicolou's
terror had, however, so graven the idea on his mind,
that he could never afterwards dismiss it. Having
once determined the character of his expectant hosts,

the Admiral naturally thought that it would be better to keep their dinner waiting any length of time than to attend their feast in the character of a roasted Greek, so he put about his vessel, and tempted the deep once more. After a further cruise the lonely commander ran his vessel upon some rocks at another part of the coast, where she was lost with all her treasures, and Nicolou was but too glad to scramble ashore, though without one dollar in his girdle. These adventures seem flat enough as I repeat them, but the hero expressed his terrors by such odd terms of speech, and such strangely humorous gestures, that the story came from his lips with an unfailing zest, so that the crew, who had heard the tale so often, could still enjoy to their hearts' content the rich fright of the Admiral, and still shuddered with unabated horror when he came to the loss of the dollars.

The power of listening to long stories (for which, by the bye, I am giving you large credit) is common, I fancy, to most sailors, and the Greeks have it to a high degree, for they can be perfectly patient under a narrative of two or three hours' duration. These long stories are mostly founded upon Oriental topics, and in one of them I recognised with some alteration an old friend of the *Arabian Nights*. I inquired as to the source from which the story had been derived, and the crew all agreed that it had been handed down unwritten from Greek to Greek. Their account of the matter does not, perhaps, go very far towards showing the real origin of the tale; but when I afterwards took up the *Arabian Nights*, I became strongly impressed with a notion that they must have sprung from the brain of a Greek. It seems to me that these stories, whilst they disclose a complete and habitual *knowledge* of things Asiatic, have about them so much of freshness and life, so much of the stirring and volatile European character, that they cannot have owed their conception to a mere Oriental, who for creative purposes is a thing dead and dry—a mental mummy, that may have been a live king just after the Flood, but has since lain balmed in spice. At the time of the Caliphat the Greek race was familiar enough to Baghdad : they were the merchants, the pedlars, the barbers, and intriguers-general of south-western Asia, and therefore the Oriental materials with which the Arabian tales were wrought must have been completely at the command of the inventive people to whom I would attribute their origin.

We were nearing the isle of Cyprus when there arose half a gale of wind, with a heavy chopping sea. My Greek seamen considered that the weather amounted not to a half, but to an integral gale of wind at the very least, so they put up the helm, and scudded for twenty hours. When we neared the mainland of Anadoli the gale ceased, and a favourable breeze sprung up, which brought us off Cyprus once more. Afterwards the wind changed again, but we were still able to lay our course by sailing close-hauled.

We were at length in such a position, that by holding on our course for about half an hour we should get under the lee of the island and find ourselves in smooth water, but the wind had been gradually freshening; it now blew hard, and there was a heavy sea running.

As the grounds for alarm arose, the crew gathered together in one close group; they stood pale and grim under their hooded capotes like monks awaiting a massacre, anxiously looking by turns along the pathway of the storm and then upon each other, and then upon the eye of the captain who stood by the helmsman. Presently the Hydriot came aft, more moody than ever, the bearer of fierce remonstrance against the continuing of the struggle ; he received a resolute answer, and still we held our course. Soon there came a heavy sea, that caught the bow of the brigantine as she lay jammed in betwixt the waves; she bowed her head low under the waters, and shuddered through all her timbers, then gallantly stood up again over the striving sea, with bowsprit entire. But where were the crew ? It was a crew no longer, but rather a gathering of Greek citizens ; the shout of the seamen was changed for the murmuring of the people—the spirit of the old Demos was alive. The men came aft in a body, and loudly asked that the vessel should be put about, and that the storm be no longer tempted. Now then, for speeches. The captain, his eyes flashing fire, his frame all quivering with emotion—wielding his every limb, like another and a louder voice, pours forth the eloquent torrent of his threats and his reasons, his commands and his prayers ; he promises, he vows, he swears that there is safety in holding on —safety, *if Greeks will be brave !* The men hear and are moved; but the gale rouses itself once more, and again the raging sea comes trampling over the timbers that are the life of all. The fierce Hydriot advances one step nearer to the captain, and the angry growl of the people goes floating down the wind, but they listen ; they waver once more, and once more resolve, then waver again, thus doubtfully hanging between the terrors of the storm and the persuasion of glorious speech, as though it were the

Athenian that talked, and Philip of Macedon that thundered on the weather-bow.

Brave thoughts winged on Grecian words gained their natural mastery over terror ; the brigantine held on her course, and reached smooth water at last. I landed at Limasol, the westernmost port of Cyprus, leaving the vessel to sail for Larnaca, where she was to remain for some days.

CHAPTER VII

CYPRUS

THERE was a Greek at Limasol who hoisted his flag as an English vice-consul, and he insisted upon my accepting his hospitality. With some difficulty, and chiefly by assuring him that I could not delay my departure beyond an early hour in the afternoon, I induced him to allow my dining with his family instead of banqueting all alone with the representative of my Sovereign in consular state and dignity. The lady of the house, it seemed, had never sat at table with a European. She was very shy about the matter, and tried hard to get out of the scrape, but the husband, I fancy, reminded her that she was theoretically an Englishwoman, by virtue of the flag that waved over her roof, and that she was bound to show her nationality by sitting at meat with me. Finding herself inexorably condemned to bear with the dreaded gaze of European eyes, she tried to save her innocent children from the hard fate awaiting herself, but I obtained that all of them (and I think there were four or five) should sit at the table. You will meet with abundance of stately receptions and of generous hospitality, too, in the East, but rarely, very rarely in those regions (or even, so far as I know, in any part of southern Europe) does one gain an opportunity of seeing the familiar and indoor life of the people.

This family party of the good consul's (or rather of mine, for I originated the idea, though he furnished the materials) went off very well. The mamma was shy at first, but she veiled the awkwardness which she felt by affecting to scold her children, who had all of them, I think, immortal names — names too which they owed to tradition, and certainly not to any classical enthusiasm of their parents. Every instant I was delighted by some such phrases as these, " Themistocles, my love, don't fight."—" Alcibiades, can't you sit still? "—" Socrates, put down the cup." — " Oh, fie! Aspasia don't. Oh! don't be naughty! " It is true that the names were pronounced Socrāhtie, Aspāhsie—that is, according to accent, and not according to quantity—but I suppose it is scarcely now to be doubted that they were so sounded in ancient times.

To me it seems, that of all the lands I know (you will see in a minute how I connect this piece of prose with the Isle of Cyprus), there is none in which mere wealth, mere unaided wealth, is held half so cheaply; none in which a poor devil of a millionaire, without birth, or ability, occupies so humble a place as in England. My Greek host and I were sitting together, I think, upon the roof of the house (for that is the lounging-place in Eastern climes), when the former assumed a serious air, and intimated a wish to converse upon the subject of the British Constitution, with which he assured me that he was thoroughly acquainted. He presently, however, informed me that there was one anomalous circumstance attended upon the practical working of our political system which he had never been able to hear explained in a manner satisfactory to himself. From the fact of his having found a difficulty in his subject, I began to think that my host might really know rather more of it than his announcement of a thorough knowledge had led me to expect. I felt interested at being about to hear from the lips of an intelligent Greek, quite remote from the influence of European opinions, what might seem to him the most astonishing and incomprehensible of all those results which have followed from the action of our political institutions. The anomaly, the only anomaly which had been detected by the vice-consular wisdom, consisted in the fact that Rothschild (the late money-monger) had never been the Prime Minister of England! I gravely tried to throw some light upon the mysterious causes that had kept the worthy Israelite out of the Cabinet, but I think I could see that my explanation was not satisfactory. Go and argue with the flies of summer that there is a power divine, yet greater than the sun in the heavens, but never dare hope to convince the people of the south that there is any other God than Gold.

My intended journey was to the site of the Paphian temple. I take no antiquarian interest in ruins, and care little about them, unless they are either striking in themselves, or else serve to mark some spot on which my fancy loves to dwell. I knew that the ruins of Paphos were scarcely, if at all, discernible, but there was a will and a longing more imperious than mere curiosity that drove me thither.

For this just then was my pagan soul's desire— that (not forfeiting my inheritance for the life to come) it had yet been given me to live through this world — to live a favoured mortal under the old Olympian dispensation—to speak out my resolves to the listening Jove, and hear him answer with approving thunder—to be blessed with divine councils from the lips of Pallas Athēnie—to believe—ay, only to believe—to believe for one rapturous moment that in the gloomy depths of the grove, by the mountain's side, there were some leafy pathway that crisped beneath the glowing sandal of Aphrodētie — Aphrodētie, not coldly. disdainful of even a mortal's love! And this vain, heathenish longing of mine was father to the thought of visiting the scene of the ancient worship.

The isle is beautiful. From the edge of the rich, flowery fields on which I trod to the midway sides of the snowy Olympus, the ground could only here and there show an abrupt crag, or a high straggling ridge that up - shouldered itself from out of the wilderness of myrtles, and of the thousand bright-leaved shrubs that twined their arms together in lovesome tangles. The air that came to my lips was warm and fragrant as the ambrosial breath of the goddess, infecting me, not (of course) with a faith in the old religion of the isle, but with a sense and apprehension of its mystic power—a power that was still to be obeyed—obeyed by *me*, for why otherwise did I toil on with sorry horses to " where, for HER, the hundred altars glowed with Arabian incense, and breathed with the fragrance of garlands ever fresh " ? [1]

I passed a sadly disenchanting night in the cabin of a Greek priest—not a priest of the goddess, but of the Greek Church ; there was but one humble room, or rather shed, for man, and priest, and beast. The next morning I reached Baffa (Paphos), a

[1] ". . . ubi templum illi, centumque Sabæo
Thure calent aræ, sertisque recentibus halant."
—*Æneid,* i. 415.

village not far distant from the site of the temple.
There was a Greek husbandman there who (not for
emolument, but for the sake of the protection and
dignity which it afforded) had got leave from the
man at Limasol to hoist his flag as a sort of deputy-
provisionary-sub-vice-pro-acting-consul of the British
sovereign: the poor fellow instantly changed his
Greek headgear for the cap of consular dignity, and
insisted upon accompanying me to the ruins. I
would not have stood this if I could have felt the
faintest gleam of my yesterday's pagan piety, but I
had ceased to dream, and had nothing to dread from
any new disenchanters.

The ruins (the fragments of one or two prostrate
pillars) lie upon a promontory, bare and unmystified
by the gloom of surrounding groves. My Greek
friend in his consular cap stood by, respectfully
waiting to see what turn my madness would take,
now that I had come at last into the presence of the
old stones. If you have no taste for research, and
can't affect to look for inscriptions, there is some
awkwardness in coming to the end of a merely
sentimental pilgrimage; when the feeling which
impelled you has gone, you have nothing to do but
to laugh the thing off as well as you can, and, by
the bye, it is not a bad plan to turn the conversation
(or rather, allow the natives to turn it) towards the
subject of hidden treasures. This is a topic on
which they will always speak with eagerness, and if
they can fancy that you, too, take an interest in such
matters, they will not only think you perfectly sane,
but will begin to give you credit for some more than
human powers of forcing the obscure earth to show
you its hoards of gold.

When we returned to Baffa, the vice-consul seized

a club with the quietly determined air of a brave
man resolved to do some deed of note. He went
into the yard adjoining his cottage, where there were
some thin, thoughtful, canting cocks, and serious,
low-church-looking hens, respectfully listening, and
chickens of tender years so well brought up, as
scarcely to betray in their conduct the careless levity
of youth. The vice-consul stood for a moment
quite calm, collecting his strength; then suddenly he
rushed into the midst of the congregation, and began
to deal death and destruction on all sides. He
spared neither sex nor age; the dead and dying
were immediately removed from the field of slaughter,
and in less than an hour, I think, they were brought
on the table, deeply buried in mounds of snowy rice.

My host was in all respects a fine, generous fellow.
I could not bear the idea of impoverishing him by
my visit, and I consulted my faithful Mysseri, who
not only assured me that I might safely offer money
to the vice-consul, but recommended that I should
give no more to him than to " the other," meaning
any other peasant. I felt, however, that there was
something about the man, besides the flag and the
cap, which made me shrink from offering coin, and
as I mounted my horse on departing I gave him the
only thing fit for a present that I happened to have
with me, a rather handsome clasp-dagger, brought
from Vienna. The poor fellow was ineffably
grateful, and I had some difficulty in tearing myself
from out of the reach of his thanks. At last I gave
him what I supposed to be the last farewell, and rode
on, but I had not gained more than about a hundred
yards when my host came bounding and shouting
after me, with a goat's-milk cheese in his hand,
which he implored me to accept. In old times the

shepherd of Theocritus, or (to speak less dishonestly) the shepherd of the "Poetæ Græci," sung his best song; I in this latter age presented my best dagger, and both of us received the same rustic reward.

It had been known that I should return to Limasol, and when I arrived there I found that a noble old Greek had been hospitably plotting to have me for his guest. I willingly accepted his offer. The day of my arrival happened to be the birthday of my host, and in consequence of this there was a constant influx of visitors, who came to offer their congratulations. A few of these were men, but most of them were young, graceful girls. Almost all of them went through the ceremony with the utmost precision and formality; each in succession spoke her blessing, in the tone of a person repeating a set formula, then deferentially accepted the invitation to sit, partook of the proffered sweetmeats and the cold, glittering water, remained for a few minutes either in silence or engaged in very thin conversation, then arose, delivered a second benediction, followed by an elaborate farewell, and departed.

The bewitching power attributed at this day to the women of Cyprus is curious in connection with the worship of the sweet goddess, who called their isle her own. The Cypriote is not, I think, nearly so beautiful in face as the Ionian queens of Izmir, but she is tall, and slightly formed; there is a high-souled meaning and expression, a seeming consciousness of gentle empire, that speaks in the wavy line of the shoulder, and winds itself like Cytherea's own cestus around the slender waist; then the richly-abounding hair (not enviously gathered together under the head-dress) descends the neck, and passes the waist in sumptuous braids. Of all other women with Grecian blood in their veins the costume is graciously beautiful, but these, the maidens of Limasol —their robes are more gently, more sweetly imagined, and fall like Julia's cashmere in soft, luxurious folds. The common voice of the Levant allows that in face the women of Cyprus are less beautiful than their brilliant sisters of Smyrna ; and yet, says the Greek, he may trust himself to one and all the bright cities of the Ægean, and may yet weigh anchor with a heart entire, but that so surely as he ventures upon the enchanted isle of Cyprus, so surely will he know the rapture or the bitterness of love. The charm, they say, owes its power to that which the people call the astonishing "politics" (πολιτικη) of the women, meaning, I fancy, their tact and their witching ways : the word, however, plainly fails to express one half of that which the speakers would say. I have smiled to hear the Greek, with all his plenteousness of fancy, and all the wealth of his generous language, yet vainly struggling to describe the ineffable spell which the Parisians dispose of in their own smart way by a summary " Je ne sçai quoi."

I went to Larnaca, the chief city of the isle, and over the water at last to Beyrout.

6

CHAPTER VIII

LADY HESTER STANHOPE [1]

BEYROUT on its land side is hemmed in by the Druses, who occupy all the neighbouring highlands.

Often enough I saw the ghostly images of the women with their exalted horns stalking through the streets, and I saw too in travelling the affrighted groups of the mountaineers as they fled before me, under the fear that my party might be a company of income-tax commissioners, or a pressgang enforcing the conscription for Mehemet Ali; but nearly all my knowledge of the people, except in regard of their mere costume and outward appearance, is drawn from books and despatches, to which I have the honour to refer you.

I received hospitable welcome at Beyrout from the Europeans as well as from the Syrian Christians, and I soon discovered that their standing topic of interest was the Lady Hester Stanhope, who lived in an old

---

[1] The writer advises that none should attempt to read the following account of the late Lady Hester Stanhope except those who may already chance to feel an interest in the personage to whom it relates. The chapter (which has been written and printed for the reasons mentioned in the preface) is chiefly filled with the detailed conversation, or rather discourse, of a highly eccentric gentlewoman.

convent on the Lebanon range, at the distance of about a day's journey from the town. The lady's habit of refusing to see Europeans added the charm of mystery to a character which, even without that aid, was sufficiently distinguished to command attention.

Many years of Lady Hester's early womanhood had been passed with Lady Chatham at Burton Pynsent, and during that inglorious period of the heroine's life her commanding character, and (as they would have called it in the language of those days) her "condescending kindness" towards my mother's family, had increased in them those strong feelings of respect and attachment which her rank and station alone would have easily won from people of the middle class. You may suppose how deeply the quiet women in Somersetshire must have been interested, when they slowly learned by vague and uncertain tidings that the intrepid girl who had been used to break their vicious horses for them was reigning in sovereignty over the wandering tribes of Western Asia! I know that her name was made almost as familiar to me in my childhood as the name of Robinson Crusoe—both were associated with the spirit of adventure; but whilst the imagined life of the castaway mariner never failed to seem glaringly real, the true story of the Englishwoman ruling over Arabs always sounded to me like fable. I never had heard, nor indeed, I believe, had the rest of the world ever heard, anything like a certain account of the heroine's adventures; all I knew was, that in one of the drawers which were the delight of my childhood, along with attar of roses and fragrant wonders from Hindustan, there were letters carefully treasured, and trifling presents which I was taught to think valuable

because they had come from the queen of the desert,
who dwelt in tents, and reigned over wandering
Arabs.

This subject, however, died away, and from the
ending of my childhood up to the period of my
arrival in the Levant, I had seldom even heard a
mentioning of the Lady Hester Stanhope, but now,
wherever I went, I was met by the name so familiar
in sound, and yet so full of mystery from the vague,
fairy-tale sort of idea which it brought to my mind;
I heard it, too, connected with fresh wonders, for it
was said that the woman was now acknowledged as
an inspired being by the people of the mountains, and
it was even hinted with horror that she claimed to be
more than a prophet.

I felt at once that my mother would be sadly sorry
to hear that I had been within a day's ride of her
early friend without offering to see her, and I therefore despatched a letter to the recluse, mentioning the
maiden name of my mother (whose marriage was
subsequent to Lady Hester's departure), and saying
that if there existed on the part of her ladyship any
wish to hear of her old Somersetshire acquaintance,
I should make a point of visiting her. My letter
was sent by a foot-messenger, who was to take an
unlimited time for his journey, so that it was not, I
think, until either the third or the fourth day that the
answer arrived. A couple of horsemen covered with
mud suddenly dashed into the little court of the
"locanda" in which I was staying, bearing themselves as ostentatiously as though they were carrying
a cartel from the Devil to the Angel Michael: one
of these (the other being his attendant) was an Italian
by birth (though now completely orientalised), who
lived in my lady's establishment as doctor nominally,

but practically as an upper servant; he presented me a very kind and appropriate letter of invitation.

It happened that I was rather unwell at this time, so that I named a more distant day for my visit than I should otherwise have done, and after all, I did not start at the time fixed. Whilst still remaining at Beyrout I received this letter, which certainly betrays no symptom of the pretensions to divine power which were popularly attributed to the writer :—

"Sir,—I hope I shall be disappointed in seeing you on Wednesday, for the late rains have rendered the river Damoor if not dangerous, at least very unpleasant to pass for a person who has been lately indisposed, for if the animal swims, you would be immerged in the waters. The weather will probably change after the 21st of the moon, and after a couple of days the roads and the river will be passable, therefore I shall expect you either Saturday or Monday.

"It will be a great satisfaction to me to have an opportunity of inquiring after your mother, who was a sweet, lovely girl when I knew her.—Believe me, sir, yours sincerely,   Hester Lucy Stanhope."

Early one morning I started from Beyrout. There are no regularly established relays of horses in Syria, at least not in the line which I took, and you therefore hire your cattle for the whole journey, or at all events for your journey to some large town. Under these circumstances you have no occasion for a Tatar (whose principal utility consists in his power to compel the supply of horses). In other respects, the mode of travelling through Syria differs very little from that which I have described as prevailing in Turkey. I hired my horses and mules (for I had some of both) for the whole of the journey from Beyrout to Jerusalem. The owner of the beasts (who had a couple of fellows under him) was the most dignified member of my party ; he was, indeed, a magnificent old man, and was called Shereef, or " holy "—a title of honour which, with the privilege of wearing the green turban, he well deserved, not only from the blood of the Prophet that flowed in his veins, but from the well-known sanctity of his life and the length of his blessed beard.

Mysseri, of course, still travelled with me, but the Arabic was not one of the seven languages which he spoke so perfectly, and I was therefore obliged to hire another interpreter. I had no difficulty in finding a proper man for the purpose—one Demetrius, or, as he was always called, Dthemetri, a native of Zante, who had been tossed about by fortune in all directions. He spoke the Arabic very well, and communicated with me in Italian. The man was a very zealous member of the Greek Church. He had been a tailor. He was as ugly as the devil, having a thoroughly Tatar countenance, which expressed the agony of his body or mind, as the case might be, in the most ludicrous manner imaginable. He embellished the natural caricature of his person by suspending about his neck and shoulders and waist quantities of little bundles and parcels, which he thought too valuable to be entrusted to the jerking of pack-saddles. The mule that fell to his lot on this journey every now and then, forgetting that his rider was a saint, and remembering that he was a tailor, took a quiet roll upon the ground, and stretched his limbs calmly and lazily, like a good man awaiting a sermon. Dthemetri never got seriously hurt, but the subversion and dislocation of his bundles made him for the moment a sad spectacle of ruin, and when he regained his legs, his wrath with the mule became very amusing. He always addressed the beast in language which implied that he, as a Christian and saint, had been personally insulted and oppressed by a Mahometan mule. Dthemetri, however, on the whole proved to be a most able and capital servant. I suspected him of now and then leading me out of my way in order that he might have the opportunity of visiting the shrine of a saint; and on one occasion, as you will see by and by, he was induced by religious motives to commit a gross breach of duty; but putting these pious faults out of the question (and they were faults of the right side), he was always faithful and true to me.

I left Saïde (the Sidon of ancient times) on my right, and about an hour, I think, before sunset began to ascend one of the many low hills of Lebanon. On the summit before me was a broad, grey mass of irregular building, which from its position, as well as from the gloomy blankness of its walls, gave the idea of a neglected fortress. It had, in fact, been a convent of great size, and like most of the religious houses in this part of the world, had been made strong enough for opposing an inert resistance to any mere casual band of assailants who might be un-provided with regular means of attack : this was the dwelling-place of the Chatham's fiery granddaughter.

The aspect of the first court which I entered was such as to keep one in the idea of having to do with a fortress rather than a mere peaceable dwelling-place. A number of fierce-looking and ill-clad Albanian soldiers were hanging about the place, and striving to bear the curse of tranquillity as well as they could : two or three of them, I think, were smoking their *tchibouques*, but the rest of them were lying torpidly upon the flat stones, like the bodies of departed brigands. I rode on to an inner part of the building, and at last, quitting my horses, was conducted through a doorway that led me at once from an open court into an apartment on the ground floor. As I entered, an Oriental figure in male costume approached me from the farther end of the room with many and profound bows, but the growing shades of evening prevented me from distinguishing the features of the personage who was receiving me with this solemn welcome. I had always, however, understood that Lady Hester Stanhope wore the male attire, and I began to utter in English the common civilities that seemed to be proper on the commencement of a visit by an uninspired mortal to a renowned prophetess; but the figure which I addressed only bowed so much the more, prostrating itself almost to the ground, but speaking to me never a word. I feebly strived not to be outdone in gestures of respect; but presently my bowing opponent saw the error under which I was acting, and suddenly convinced me that, at all events, I was not *yet* in the presence of a superhuman being, by declaring that he was not " miladi," but was, in fact, nothing more or less god-like than the poor doctor, who had brought his mistress's letter to Beyrout.

Her ladyship, in the right spirit of hospitality, now sent and commanded me to repose for a while after the fatigues of my journey, and to dine.

The cuisine was of the Oriental kind, which is highly artificial, and I thought it very good. I rejoiced too in the wine of the Lebanon.

Soon after the ending of the dinner the doctor arrived with miladi's compliments, and an intimation that she would be happy to receive me if I were so disposed. It had now grown dark, and the rain was falling heavily, so that I got rather wet in following my guide through the open courts that I had to pass in order to reach the presence chamber. At last I was ushered into a small apartment, which was protected from the draughts of air passing through the doorway by a folding screen; passing this, I came alongside of a common European sofa, where sat the lady prophetess. She rose from her seat very formally, spoke to me a few words of welcome, pointed to a chair which was placed exactly opposite to her sofa at a couple of yards' distance, and remained standing up to the full of her majestic height, perfectly still and motionless, until I had taken my appointed place; she then resumed her seat, not packing herself up according to the mode of the Orientals, but allowing her feet to rest on the floor or the footstool; at the moment of seating herself she covered her lap with a mass of loose white drapery which she held in her hand. It occurred to me at the time that she did this in order to avoid the awkwardness of sitting in manifest trousers under the eye of a European, but I can hardly fancy now that with her wilful nature she would have brooked such a compromise as this.

The woman before me had exactly the person of a prophetess—not, indeed, of the divine sibyl imagined by Domenichino, so sweetly distracted betwixt love and mystery, but of a good business-like, practical prophetess, long used to the exercise of her sacred calling. I have been told by those who knew Lady Hester Stanhope in her youth, that any notion of a resemblance betwixt her and the great Chatham must have been fanciful; but at the time of my seeing her, the large commanding features of the gaunt woman, then sixty years old or more, certainly reminded me of the statesman that lay dying [1] in the House of Lords, according to Copley's picture. Her face was of the most astonishing whiteness; [2] she wore a very large turban, which seemed to be of pale cashmere shawls, so disposed as to conceal the hair; her dress, from the chin down to the point at which it was concealed by the drapery which she held over her lap, was a mass of white linen loosely folding—an ecclesiastical sort of affair, more like a surplice than any of those blessed creations which our souls love under the names of "dress" and "frock" and "bodice" and "collar" and "habit-shirt" and sweet "chemisette."

Such was the outward seeming of the personage that sat before me, and indeed she was almost bound by the fame of her actual achievements, as well as by her sublime pretensions, to look a little differently from the rest of womankind. There had been something of grandeur in her career. After the death of Lady Chatham, which happened in 1803, she lived under the roof of her uncle, the second Pitt, and when he resumed the Government in 1804, she became the dispenser of much patronage, and sole secretary of state for the department of Treasury banquets. Not having seen the lady until late in her life, when she was fired with spiritual ambition, I can hardly fancy that she could have performed her political duties in the saloons of the Minister with much of feminine sweetness and patience. I am told, however, that she managed matters very well indeed: perhaps it was better for the lofty-minded

[1] Historically "*fainting*"; the death did not occur until long afterwards.
[2] I am told that in youth she was exceedingly sallow.

leader of the House to have his reception-rooms
guarded by this stately creature, than by a merely
clever and managing woman; it was fitting that the
wholesome awe·with which he filled the minds of
the country gentlemen should be aggravated by the
presence of his majestic niece. But the end was
approaching. The sun of Austerlitz showed the
Czar madly sliding his splendid army like a weaver's
shuttle from his right hand to his left, under the very
eyes—the deep, grey, watchful eyes of Napoleon;
before night came, the coalition was a vain thing—
meet for history, and the heart of its great author
was crushed with grief when the terrible tidings came
to his ears. In the bitterness of his despair he cried
out to his niece, and bid her " ROLL UP THE MAP OF
EUROPE "; there was a little more of suffering, and
at last, with his swollen tongue (so they say) still
muttering something for England, he died by the
noblest of all sorrows.

Lady Hester, meeting the calamity in her own
fierce way, seems to have scorned the poor island
that had not enough of God's grace to keep the
" heaven-sent " Minister alive. I can hardly tell
why it should be, but there is a longing for the East
very commonly felt by proud-hearted people when
goaded by sorrow. Lady Hester Stanhope obeyed
this impulse. For some time, I believe, she was at
Constantinople, where her magnificence and near
alliance to the late Minister gained her great influence.
Afterwards she passed into Syria. The people of
that country, excited by the achievements of Sir
Sidney Smith, had begun to imagine the possibility
of their land being occupied by the English, and
many of them looked upon Lady Hester as a princess
who came to prepare the way for the expected

conquest. I don't know it from her own lips, or
indeed from any certain authority, but I have been
told that she began her connection with the Bedouins
by making a large present of money (£500 it was
said—immense in piastres) to the Sheik whose
authority was recognised in that part of the desert
which lies between Damascus and Palmyra. The
prestige created by the rumours of her high and
undefined rank, as well as of her wealth and
corresponding magnificence, was well sustained by
her imperious character and her dauntless bravery.
Her influence increased. I never heard anything
satisfactory as to the real extent or duration of her
sway, but it seemed that for a time at least she
certainly exercised something like sovereignty amongst
the wandering tribes.[1] And now that her earthly
kingdom had passed away she strove for spiritual
power, and impiously dared, as it was said, to boast
some mystic union with the very God of very God!

A couple of black slave girls came at a signal, and
supplied their mistress as well as myself with lighted
tchibouques and coffee.

The custom of the East sanctions, and almost
commands, some moments of silence whilst you are
inhaling the first few breaths of the fragrant pipe.
The pause was broken, I think, by my lady, who
addressed to me some inquiries respecting my mother,
and particularly as to her marriage; but before I

[1] This was my impression at the time of writing the
above passage, an impression created by the popular and
uncontradicted accounts of the matter, as well as by the
tenor of Lady Hester's conversation. I have now some
reason to think that I was deceived, and that her sway in
the desert was much more limited than I had supposed.
She seems to have had from the Bedouins a fair five
hundred pounds' worth of respect, and not much more.

had communicated any great amount of family facts, the spirit of the prophetess kindled within her, and presently (though with all the skill of a woman of the world) she shuffled away the subject of poor, dear Somersetshire, and bounded onward into loftier spheres of thought.

My old acquaintance with some of "the twelve" enabled me to bear my part (of course a very humble one) in a conversation relative to occult science. Milnes once spread a report, that every gang of gipsies was found upon inquiry to have come last from a place to the westward, and to be about to make the next move in an eastern direction; either therefore they were to be all gathered together towards the rising of the sun by the mysterious finger of Providence, or else they were to revolve round the globe for ever and ever: both of these suppositions were highly gratifying, because they were both marvellous; and though the story on which they were founded plainly sprang from the inventive brain of a poet, no one had ever been so odiously statistical as to attempt a contradiction of it. I now mentioned the story as a report to Lady Hester Stanhope, and asked her if it were true. I could not have touched upon any imaginable subject more deeply interesting to my hearer, more closely akin to her habitual train of thinking. She immediately threw off all the restraint belonging to an interview with a stranger; and when she had received a few more similar proofs of my aptness for the marvellous, she went so far as to say that she would adopt me as her *élève* in occult science.

For hours and hours this wondrous white woman poured forth her speech, for the most part concerning sacred and profane mysteries; but every now and then she would stay her lofty flight and swoop down upon the world again. Whenever this happened I was interested in her conversation.

She adverted more than once to the period of her lost sway amongst the Arabs, and mentioned some of the circumstances that aided her in obtaining influence with the wandering tribes. The Bedouin, so often engaged in irregular warfare, strains his eyes to the horizon in search of a coming enemy just as habitually as the sailor keeps his " bright look-out " for a strange sail. In the absence of telescopes a far-reaching sight is highly valued, and Lady Hester possessed this quality to an extraordinary degree. She told me that on one occasion, when there was good reason to expect a hostile attack, great excitement was felt in the camp by the report of a far-seeing Arab, who declared that he could just distinguish some moving objects upon the very farthest point within the reach of his eyes. Lady Hester was consulted, and she instantly assured her comrades in arms that there were indeed a number of horses within sight, but that they were without riders. The assertion proved to be correct, and from that time forth her superiority over all others in respect of far sight remained un- disputed.

Lady Hester related to me this other anecdote of her Arab life. It was when the heroic qualities of the Englishwoman were just beginning to be felt amongst the people of the desert, that she was march- ing one day, along with the forces of the tribe to which she had allied herself. She perceived that preparations for an engagement were going on, and upon her making inquiry as to the cause, the Sheik at first affected mystery and concealment, but at last confessed that war had been declared against his tribe on account of its alliance with the English princess, and that they were now unfortunately about to be attacked by a very superior force. He made it appear that Lady Hester was the sole cause of hostility betwixt his tribe and the impending enemy, and that his sacred duty of protecting the English-woman whom he had admitted as his guest was the only obstacle which prevented an amicable arrange-ment of the dispute. The Sheik hinted that his tribe was likely to sustain an almost overwhelming blow, but at the same time declared, that no fear of the consequences, however terrible to him and his whole people, should induce him to dream of abandon-ing his illustrious guest. The heroine instantly took her part: it was not for her to be a source of danger to her friends, but rather to her enemies, so she resolved to turn away from the people, and trust for help to none save only her haughty self. The Sheiks affected to dissuade her from so rash a course, and fairly told her that although they (having been freed from her presence) would be able to make good terms for themselves, yet that there were no means of allaying the hostility felt towards her, and that the whole face of the desert would be swept by the horse-men of her enemies so carefully as to make her escape into other districts almost impossible. The brave woman was not to be moved by terrors of this kind, and bidding farewell to the tribe which had honoured and protected her, she turned her horse's head and rode straight away from them, without friend or follower. Hours had elapsed, and for some time she had been alone in the centre of the round horizon, when her quick eye perceived some horsemen in the distance. The party came nearer and nearer; soon it was plain that they were making towards her, and presently some hundreds of Bedouins, fully armed, galloped up to her, ferociously shouting, and apparently intending to take her life at the instant with their pointed spears. Her face at the time was covered with the *yashmak*, according to Eastern usage, but at the moment when the foremost of the horsemen had all but reached her with their spears, she stood up in her stirrups, withdrew the *yashmak* that veiled the terrors of her countenance, waved her arm slowly and disdainfully, and cried out with a loud voice "Avaunt!"[1] The horsemen recoiled from her glance, but not in terror. The threatening yells of the assailants were suddenly changed for loud shouts of joy and admiration at the bravery of the stately Englishwoman, and festive gunshots were fired on all sides around her honoured head. The truth was, that the party belonged to the tribe with which she had allied herself, and that the threatened attack as well as the pretended apprehension of an engagement had been contrived for the mere purpose of testing her courage. The day ended in a great feast prepared to do honour to the heroine, and from that time her power over the minds of the people grew rapidly. Lady Hester related this story with great spirit, and I recollect that she put up her *yashmak* for a moment in order to give me a better idea of the effect which she produced by suddenly revealing the awfulness of her countenance.

With respect to her then present mode of life, Lady Hester informed me, that for her sin she had subjected herself during many years to severe penance,

---

[1] She spoke it, I daresay, in English; the words would not be the less effective for being spoken in an unknown tongue. Lady Hester, I believe, never learnt to speak the Arabic with a perfect accent.

and that her self-denial had not been without its reward. "Vain and false," said she, "is all the pretended knowledge of the Europeans—their doctors will tell you that the drinking of milk gives yellowness to the complexion; milk is my only food, and you see if my face be not white." Her abstinence from food intellectual was carried as far as her physical fasting. She never, she said, looked upon a book or a newspaper, but trusted alone to the stars for her sublime knowledge ; she usually passed the nights in communing with these heavenly teachers, and lay at rest during the daytime. She spoke with great contempt of the frivolity and benighted ignorance of the modern Europeans, and mentioned in proof of this, that they were not only untaught in astrology, but were unacquainted with the common and every-day phenomena produced by magic art. She spoke as if she would make me understand that all sorcerous spells were completely at her command, but that the exercise of such powers would be derogatory to her high rank in the heavenly kingdom. She said that the spell by which the face of an absent person is thrown upon a mirror was within the reach of the humblest and most contemptible magicians, but that the practice of such-like arts was unholy as well as vulgar.

We spoke of the bending twig by which, it is said, precious metals may be discovered. In relation to this, the prophetess told me a story rather against herself, and inconsistent with the notion of her being perfect in her science ; but I think that she mentioned the facts as having happened before the time at which she attained to the great spiritual authority which she now arrogated. She told me that vast treasures were known to exist in a

situation which she mentioned, if I rightly remember, as being near Suez; that Napoleon,
profanely brave, thrust his arm into the cave
containing the coveted gold, and that instantly his
flesh became palsied, but the youthful hero (for she
said he was great in his generation) was not to
be thus daunted ; he fell back characteristically upon
his brazen resources, and ordered up his artillery;
but man could not strive with demons, and Napoleon
was foiled. In after years came Ibrahim Pasha,
with heavy guns, and wicked spells to boot, but the
infernal guardians of the treasure were too strong for
him. It was after this that Lady Hester passed by
the spot, and she described with animated gesture the
force and energy with which the divining twig had
suddenly leaped in her hands. She ordered excavations, and no demons opposed her enterprise;
the vast chest in which the treasure had been
deposited was at length discovered, but, lo and
behold, it was full of pebbles ! She said, however,
that the times were approaching in which the hidden
treasures of the earth would become available to those
who had true knowledge.

Speaking of Ibrahim Pasha, Lady Hester said
that he was a bold, bad man, and was possessed of
some of those common and wicked magical arts upon
which she looked down with so much contempt.
She said, for instance, that Ibrahim's life was charmed
against balls and steel, and that after a battle he
loosened the folds of his shawl and shook out the
bullets like dust.

It seems that the St. Simonians once made overtures
to Lady Hester. She told me that the Père
Enfantin (the chief of the sect) had sent her a
service of plate, but that she had declined to receive

it. She delivered a prediction as to the probability of the St. Simonians finding the "mystic mother," and this she did in a way which would amuse you. Unfortunately I am not at liberty to mention this part of the woman's prophecies ; why, I cannot tell, but so it is, that she bound me to eternal secrecy. Lady Hester told me that since her residence at Djoun she had been attacked by a terrible illness, which rendered her for a long time perfectly helpless ; all her attendants fled, and left her to perish. Whilst she lay thus alone, and quite unable to rise, robbers came and carried away her property.[1] She told me that they actually unroofed a great part of the building, and employed engines with pulleys, for the purpose of hoisting out such of her valuables as were too bulky to pass through doors. It would seem that before this catastrophe Lady Hester had been rich in the possession of Eastern luxuries ; for she told me that when the chiefs of the Ottoman force took refuge with her after the fall of Acre, they brought their wives also in great

---

[1] The proceedings thus described to me by Lady Hester as having taken place during her illness, were afterwards re-enacted at the time of her death. Since I wrote the words to which this note is appended, I received from Warburton an interesting account of the heroine's death, or rather the circumstances attending the discovery of the event ; and I caused it to be printed in the former editions of this work. I must now give up the borrowed ornament, and omit my extract from my friend's letter, for the rightful owner has reprinted it in *The Crescent and the Cross.* I know what a sacrifice I am making, for in noticing the first edition of this book reviewers turned aside from the text to the note, and remarked upon the interesting information which Warburton's letter contained. [This narrative is reproduced in an Appendix to the present edition.]

numbers. To all of these Lady Hester, as she said, presented magnificent dresses; but her generosity occasioned strife only instead of gratitude, for every woman who fancied her present less splendid than that of another with equal or less pretension, became absolutely furious: all these audacious guests had now been got rid of, but the Albanian soldiers, who had taken refuge with Lady Hester at the same time, still remained under her protection.

In truth, this half-ruined convent, guarded by the proud heart of an English gentlewoman, was the only spot throughout all Syria and Palestine in which the will of Mehemet Ali and his fierce lieutenant was not the law. More than once had the Pasha of Egypt commanded that Ibrahim should have the Albanians delivered up to him, but this white woman of the mountain (grown classical not by books, but by very pride) answered only with a disdainful invitation to "come and take them." Whether it was that Ibrahim was acted upon by any superstitious dread of interfering with the prophetess (a notion not at all incompatible with his character as an able Oriental commander), or that he feared the ridicule of putting himself in collision with a gentlewoman, he certainly never ventured to attack the sanctuary, and so long as the Chatham's granddaughter breathed a breath of life there was always this one hillock, and that too in the midst of a most populous district, which stood out, and kept its freedom. Mehemet Ali used to say, I am told, that the Englishwoman had given him more trouble than all the insurgent people of Syria and Palestine.

The prophetess announced to me that we were upon the eve of a stupendous convulsion, which would destroy the then recognised value of all property upon earth ; and declaring that those only who should be in the East at the time of the great change could hope for greatness in the new life that was now close at hand, she advised me, whilst there was yet time, to dispose of my property in poor frail England, and gain a station in Asia. She told me that, after leaving her, I should go into Egypt, but that in a little while I should return into Syria. I secretly smiled at this last prophecy as a " bad shot," for I had fully determined after visiting the Pyramids to take ship from Alexandria for Greece. But men struggle vainly in the meshes of their destiny. The unbelieved Cassandra was right after all ; the plague came, and the necessity of avoiding the quarantine, to which I should have been subjected if I had sailed from Alexandria, forced me to alter my route. I went down into Egypt, and stayed there for a time, and then crossed the desert once more, and came back to the mountains of the Lebanon, exactly as the prophetess had foretold.

Lady Hester talked to me long and earnestly on the subject of religion, announcing that the Messiah was yet to come. She strived to impress me with the vanity and the falseness of all European creeds, as well as with a sense of her own spiritual greatness : throughout her conversation upon these high topics she carefully insinuated, without actually asserting, her heavenly rank.

Amongst other much more marvellous powers, the lady claimed to have one which most women, I fancy, possess, namely, that of reading men's characters in their faces. She examined the line of my features very attentively, and told me the result, which, however, I mean to keep hidden.

One favoured subject of discourse was that of
" race," upon which she was very diffuse, and yet
rather mysterious. She set great value upon the
ancient French [1] (not Norman blood, for that she
vilified), but did not at all appreciate that which we
call in this country "an old family." She had a
vast idea of the Cornish miners on account of their
race, and said, if she chose, she could give me
the means of rousing them to the most tremendous
enthusiasm.

Such are the topics on which the lady mainly
conversed, but very often she would descend to more
worldly chat, and then she was no longer the
prophetess, but the sort of woman that you sometimes
see, I am told, in London drawing-rooms—cool,
decisive in manner, unsparing of enemies, full of
audacious fun, and saying the downright things that
the sheepish society around her is afraid to utter. I
am told that Lady Hester was in her youth a capital
mimic, and she showed me that not all the queenly
dulness to which she had condemned herself, not all
her fasting and solitude, had destroyed this terrible
power. The first whom she crucified in my presence
was poor Lord Byron. She had seen him, it
appeared, I know not where, soon after his arrival in
the East, and was vastly amused at his little affecta-

---

[1] In a letter which I afterwards received from Lady
Hester, she mentioned incidentally Lord Hardwicke, and
said that he was "the kindest-hearted man existing—a
most manly, firm character. He comes from a good breed
—all the Yorkes excellent, with *ancient* French blood in
their veins." The underscoring of the word "ancient"
is by the writer of the letter, who had certainly no great
love or veneration for the French of the present day : she
did not consider them as descended from her favourite
stock.

tions. He had picked up a few sentences of the Romanic, with which he affected to give orders to his Greek servant. I can't tell whether Lady Hester's mimicry of the bard was at all close, but it was amusing; she attributed to him a curiously coxcombical lisp.

Another person whose style of speaking the lady took off very amusingly was one who would scarcely object to suffer by the side of Lord Byron—I mean Lamartine, who had visited her in the course of his travels. The peculiarity which attracted her ridicule was an over-refinement of manner: according to my lady's imitation of Lamartine (I have never seen him myself), he had none of the violent grimace of his countrymen, and not even their usual way of talking, but rather bore himself mincingly, like the humbler sort of English dandy.[1]

Lady Hester seems to have heartily despised everything approaching to exquisiteness. She told me, by the bye (and her opinion upon that subject is worth having), that a downright manner, amounting even to brusqueness, is more effective than any other with the Oriental; and that amongst the English of all ranks and all classes there is no man so attractive to the Orientals, no man who can negotiate with

---

[1] It is said that deaf people can hear what is said concerning themselves, and it would seem that those who live without books or newspapers know all that is written about them. Lady Hester Stanhope, though not admitting a book or newspaper into her fortress, seems to have known the way in which M. Lamartine mentioned her in his book, for in a letter which she wrote to me after my return to England she says, "Although neglected, as Monsieur le M." (referring, as I believe, to M. Lamartine) "describes, and without books, yet my head is organised to supply the want of them as well as acquired knowledge."

them half so effectively, as a good, honest, open-hearted, and positive naval officer of the old school.

I have told you, I think, that Lady Hester could deal fiercely with those she hated. One man above all others (he is now uprooted from society, and cast away for ever) she blasted with her wrath. You would have thought that in the scornfulness of her nature she must have sprung upon her foe with more of fierceness than of skill; but this was not so, for with all the force and vehemence of her invective she displayed a sober, patient, and minute attention to the details of vituperation, which contributed to its success a thousand times more than mere violence.

During the hours that this sort of conversation, or rather discourse, was going on our *tchibouques* were from time to time replenished, and the lady as well as I continued to smoke with little or no intermission till the interview ended. I think that the fragrant fumes of the latakiah must have helped to keep me on my good behaviour as a patient disciple of the prophetess.

It was not till after midnight that my visit for the evening came to an end. When I quitted my seat the lady rose and stood up in the same formal attitude (almost that of a soldier in a state of " attention ") which she had assumed at my entrance ; at the same time she let go the drapery which she had held over her lap whilst sitting and allowed it to fall to the ground.

The next morning after breakfast I was visited by my lady's secretary—the only European, except the doctor, whom she retained in her household. This secretary, like the doctor, was Italian, but he pre-served more signs of European dress and European pretensions than his medical fellow-slave. He spoke little or no English, though he wrote it pretty well, having been formerly employed in a mercantile house connected with England. The poor fellow was in an unhappy state of mind. In order to make you understand the extent of his spiritual anxieties, I ought to have told you that the doctor [1] (who had sunk into the complete Asiatic, and had condescended accordingly to the performance of even menial services) had adopted the common faith of all the neighbouring people, and had become a firm and happy believer in the divine power of his mistress. Not so the secretary. When I had strolled with him to a distance from the building, which rendered him safe from being overheard by human ears, he told me in a hollow voice, trembling with emotion, that there were times at which he doubted the divinity of "milèdi." I said nothing to encourage the poor fellow in that frightful state of scepticism which, if indulged, might end in positive infidelity. I found that her ladyship had rather arbitrarily abridged the amusements of her secretary, forbidding him from shooting small birds on the mountain-side. This oppression had aroused in him a spirit of inquiry that might end fatally, perhaps for himself, perhaps for the "religion of the-place."

The secretary told me that his mistress was greatly disliked by the surrounding people, whom she oppressed by her exactions, and the truth of this

[1] I have been recently told that this Italian's pretensions to the healing art were thorougly unfounded. My informant is a gentleman who enjoyed during many years the esteem and confidence of Lady Hester Stanhope; his adventures in the Levant were most curious and interesting.

statement was borne out by the way in which my lady spoke to me of her neighbours. But in Eastern countries hate and veneration are very commonly felt for the same object, and the general belief in the superhuman power of this wonderful white lady, her resolute and imperious character, and above all, perhaps, her fierce Albanians (not backward to obey an order for the sacking of a village), inspired sincere respect amongst the surrounding inhabitants. Now the being "respected" amongst Orientals is not an empty or merely honorary distinction, but carries with it a clear right to take your neighbour's corn, his cattle, his eggs, and his honey, and almost anything that is his, except his wives. This law was acted upon by the princess of Djoun, and her establishment was supplied by contributions apportioned amongst the nearest of the villages.

I understood that the Albanians (restrained, I suppose, by the dread of being delivered up to Ibrahim) had not given any very troublesome proofs of their unruly natures. The secretary told me that their rations, including a small allowance of coffee and tobacco, were served out to them with tolerable regularity.

I asked the secretary how Lady Hester was off for horses, and said that I would take a look at the stable. The man did not raise any opposition to my proposal, and affected no mystery about the matter, but said that the only two steeds which then belonged to her ladyship were of a very humble sort. This answer, and a storm of rain then beginning to descend, prevented me at the time from undertaking my journey to the stable, which was at some distance from the part of the building in which I was quartered, and I don't know that I ever thought of the matter afterwards until my return to England, when I saw Lamartine's eye-witnessing account of the horse saddled by the hands of his Maker!

When I returned to my apartment (which, as my hostess told me, was the only one in the whole building that kept out the rain) her ladyship sent to say that she would be glad to receive me again. I was rather surprised at this, for I had understood that she reposed during the day, and it was now little later than noon. "Really," said she, when I had taken my seat and my pipe, "we were together for hours last night, and still I have heard nothing at all of my old friends; now *do* tell me something of your dear mother and her sister; I never knew your father —it was after I left Burton Pynsent that your mother married." I began to make slow answer, but my questioner soon went off again to topics more sublime, so that this second interview, which lasted two or three hours, was occupied by the same sort of varied discourse as that which I have been describing.

In the course of the afternoon the captain of an English man-of-war arrived at Djoun, and her ladyship determined to receive him for the same reason as that which had induced her to allow my visit, namely, an early intimacy with his family. I and the new visitor, who was a pleasant, amusing person, dined together, and we were afterwards invited to the presence of my lady, with whom we sat smoking and talking till midnight. The conversation turned chiefly, I think, upon magical science. I had determined to be off at an early hour the next morning, and so at the end of this interview I bade my lady farewell. With her parting words she once more advised me to abandon Europe and seek my reward in the East, and she urged me too to give the like counsels to my father, and tell him that " *She had said it.*"

Lady Hester's unholy claim to supremacy in the spiritual kingdom was, no doubt, the suggestion of fierce and inordinate pride most perilously akin to madness, but I am quite sure that the mind of the woman was too strong to be thoroughly overcome by even this potent feeling. I plainly saw that she was not an unhesitating follower of her own system, and I even fancied that I could distinguish the brief moments during which she contrived to believe in herself, from those long and less happy intervals in which her own reason was too strong for her.

As for the lady's faith in astrology and magic science, you are not for a moment to suppose that this implied any aberration of intellect. She believed these things in common with those around her, for she seldom spoke to anybody except crazy old dervishes, who received her alms, and fostered her extravagancies, and even when (as on the occasion of my visit) she was brought into contact with a person entertaining different notions, she still remained un-contradicted. This *entourage* and the habit of fasting from books and newspapers were quite enough to make her a facile recipient of any marvellous story.

I think that in England we are scarcely sufficiently conscious of the great debt we owe to the wise and watchful press which presides over the formation of our opinions, and which brings about this splendid result, namely, that in matters of belief the humblest of us are lifted up to the level of the most sagacious, so that really a simple cornet in the Blues is no more likely to entertain a foolish belief about ghosts ; or witchcraft, or any other supernatural topic, than the Lord High Chancellor or the Leader of the House

of Commons. How different is the intellectual
régime of Eastern countries! In Syria and Palestine
and Egypt you might as well dispute the efficacy of
grass or grain as of magic. There is no controversy
about the matter. The effect of this, the unanimous
belief of an ignorant people upon the mind of a
stranger, is extremely curious, and well worth noticing.
A man coming freshly from Europe is at first proof
against the nonsense with which he is assailed, but
often it happens that after a little while the social
atmosphere in which he lives will begin to infect him,
and if he has been unaccustomed to the cunning of
fence by which Reason prepares the means of guard-
ing herself against fallacy, he will yield himself at
last to the faith of those around him, and this he will
do by sympathy, it would seem, rather than from
conviction. I have been much interested in observing
that the mere "practical man," however skilful and
shrewd in his own way, has not the kind of power
that will enable him to resist the gradual impression
made upon his mind by the common opinion of those
whom he sees and hears from day to day. Even
amongst the English (whose good sense and sound
religious knowledge would be likely to guard them
from error) I have known the calculating merchant,
the inquisitive traveller, and the post-captain, with
his bright, wakeful eye of command—I have known
all these surrender themselves to the *really* magic-like
influence of other people's minds. Their language
at first is that they are "staggered," leading you by
that expression to suppose that they had been witnesses
to some phenomenon, which it was very difficult to
account for otherwise than by supernatural causes;
but when I have questioned further, I have always
found that these "staggering" wonders were not

even specious enough to be looked upon as good
"tricks." A man in England who gained his whole
livelihood as a conjurer would soon be starved to
death if he could perform no better miracles than
those which are wrought with so much effect in
Syria and Egypt; *sometimes*, no doubt, a magician
will make a good hit (Sir John once said a "good
thing"), but all such successes range, of course,
under the head of mere "tentative miracles," as
distinguished by the strong-brained Paley.

CHAPTER IX

I CROSSED the plain of Esdraelon and entered amongst the hills of beautiful Galilee. It was at sunset that my path brought me sharply round into the gorge of a little valley, and close upon a grey mass of dwellings that lay happily nestled in the lap of the mountain. There was one only shining point still touched with the light of the sun, who had set for all besides; a brave sign this to " holy " Shereef and the rest of my Moslem men, for the one glittering summit was the head of a minaret, and the rest of the seeming village that had veiled itself so meekly under the shades of evening was Christian Nazareth!

Within the precincts of the Latin convent in which I was quartered there stands the great Catholic church which encloses the sanctuary, the dwelling of the blessed Virgin.[1] This is a grotto of about ten

---

[1] The Greek Church does not recognise this as the true sanctuary, and many Protestants look upon all the traditions by which it is attempted to ascertain the holy places of Palestine as utterly fabulous. For myself, I do not mean either to affirm or deny the correctness of the opinion which has fixed upon this as the true site, but merely to mention it as a belief entertained without question by my brethren of the Latin Church, whose guest I was at the time. It would be a great aggravation of the trouble of

111

feet either way, forming a little chapel or recess, to which you descend by steps. It is decorated with splendour. On the left hand a column of granite hangs from the top of the grotto to within a few feet of the ground; immediately beneath it is another column of the same size, which rises from the ground as if to meet the one above; but between this and the suspended pillar there is an interval of more than a foot; these fragments once formed a single column, against which the angel leant when he spoke and told to Mary the mystery of her awful blessedness. Hard by, near the altar, the holy Virgin was kneeling.

I had been journeying (cheerily indeed, for the voices of my followers were ever within my hearing, but yet), as it were, in solitude, for I had no comrade to whet the edge of my reason, or wake me from my noonday dreams. I was left all alone to be taught and swayed by the beautiful circumstances of Palestine travelling—by the clime, and the land, and the name of the land, with all its mighty import; by the glittering freshness of the sward, and the abound-

writing about these matters if I were to stop in the midst of every sentence for the purpose of saying "so called" or "so it is said," and would besides sound very ungraciously: yet I am anxious to be literally true in all I write. Now, thus it is that I mean to get over my difficulty. Whenever in this great bundle of papers or book (if book it is to be) you see any words about matters of religion which would seem to involve the assertion of my own opinion, you are to understand me just as if one or other of the qualifying phrases above mentioned had been actually inserted in every sentence. My general direction for you to construe me thus will render all that I write as strictly and actually true as if I had every time lugged in a formal declaration of the fact that I was merely expressing the notions of other people.

ing masses of flowers that furnished my sumptuous
pathway; by the bracing and fragrant air that seemed
to poise me in my saddle, and to lift me along as a
planet appointed to glide through space.

And the end of my journey was Nazareth, the
home of the blessed Virgin! In the first dawn of
my manhood the old painters of Italy had taught me
their dangerous worship of the beauty that is more
than mortal, but those images all seemed shadowy
now, and floated before me so dimly, the one overcasting the other, that they left me no one sweet idol
on which I could look and look again and say,
"Maria mia!" Yet they left me more than an
idol; they left me (for to them I am wont to trace
it) a faint apprehension of beauty not compassed with
lines and shadows; they touched me (forgive, proud
Marie of Anjou!)—they touched me with a faith in
loveliness transcending mortal shapes.

I came to Nazareth, and was led from the convent
to the sanctuary. Long fasting will sometimes heat
my brain and draw me away out of the world—will
disturb my judgment, confuse my notions of right and
wrong, and weaken my power of choosing the right:
I had fasted perhaps too long, for I was fevered with
the zeal of an insane devotion to the heavenly queen
of Christendom. But I knew the feebleness of this
gentle malady, and knew how easily my watchful
reason, if ever so slightly provoked, would drag me
back to life. Let there but come one chilling breath
of the outer world, and all this loving piety would
cower and fly before the sound of my own bitter
laugh. And so as I went I trod tenderly, not
looking to the right nor to the left, but bending my
eyes to the ground.

The attending friar served me well; he led me

8

down quietly and all but silently to the Virgin's home. The mystic air was so burnt with the consuming flames of the altar, and so laden with incense, that my chest laboured strongly, and heaved with luscious pain. There—there with beating heart the Virgin knelt and listened. I strived to grasp and hold with my riveted eyes some one of the feigned Madonnas, but of all the heaven-lit faces imagined by men there was none that would abide with me in this the very sanctuary. Impatient of vacancy, I grew madly strong against Nature, and if by some awful spell, some impious rite, I could—Oh most sweet Religion, that bid me fear God, and be pious, and yet not cease from loving! Religion and gracious custom commanded me that I fall down loyally and kiss the rock that blessed Mary pressed. With a half consciousness, with the semblance of a thrilling hope that I was plunging deep, deep into my first knowledge of some most holy mystery, or of some new rapturous and daring sin, I knelt, and bowed down my face till I met the smooth rock with my lips. One moment—one moment my heart, or some old pagan demon within me, woke up, and fiercely bounded; my bosom was lifted, and swung, as though I had touched her warm robe. One moment, one more, and then the fever had left me. I rose from my knees. I felt hopelessly sane. The mere world reappeared. My good old monk was there, dangling his key with listless patience, and as he guided me from the church, and talked of the refectory and the coming repast, I listened to his words with some attention and pleasure.

CHAPTER X

THE MONKS OF PALESTINE

WHENEVER you come back to me from Palestine we will find some " golden wine " [1] of Lebanon, that we may celebrate with apt libations the monks of the Holy Land, and though the poor fellows be theoretically "dead to the world," we will drink to every man of them a good long life, and a merry one! Graceless is the traveller who forgets his obligations to these saints upon earth; little love has he for merry Christendom if he has not rejoiced with great joy to find in the very midst of water-drinking infidels those lowly monasteries, in which the blessed juice of the grape is quaffed in peace. Ay! ay! we will fill our glasses till they look like cups of amber, and drink profoundly to our gracious hosts in Palestine.

Christianity permits, and sanctions, the drinking of wine, and of all the holy brethren in Palestine there are none who hold fast to this gladsome rite so strenuously as the monks of Damascus; not that they are more zealous Christians than the rest of their fellows in the Holy Land, but that they have better wine. Whilst I was at Damascus I had my quarters at the Franciscan convent there, and very soon after

[1] " Vino d'oro."

my arrival I asked one of the monks to let me know
something of the spots that deserved to be seen.   I
made my inquiry in reference to the associations with
which the city had been hallowed by the sojourn and
adventures of St. Paul.   "There is nothing in all
Damascus," said the good man, "half so well worth
seeing as our cellars;" and forthwith he invited me
to go, see, and admire the long range of liquid
treasure that he and his brethren had laid up for
themselves on earth.   And these I soon found were not
as the treasures of the miser, that lie in unprofitable
disuse; for day by day, and hour by hour, the golden
juice ascended from the dark recesses of the cellar to ·
the uppermost brains of the friars.   Dear old fellows!
in the midst of that solemn land their Christian
laughter rang loudly and merrily, their eyes kept
flashing with joyous bonfires, and their heavy woollen
petticoats could no more weigh down the springiness
of their paces, than the filmy gauze of a *danseuse* can
clog her bounding step.

   You would be likely enough to fancy that these
monastics are men who have retired to the sacred
sites of Palestine from an enthusiastic longing to
devote themselves to the exercise of religion in the
midst of the very land on which its first seeds were
cast; and this is partially, at least, the case with the
monks of the Greek Church, but it is not with
enthusiasts that the Catholic establishments are filled.
The monks of the Latin convents are chiefly persons
of the peasant class from Italy and Spain, who have
been handed over to these remote asylums by order
of their ecclesiastical superiors, and can no more
account for their being in the Holy Land, than men
of marching regiments can explain why they are in
"stupid quarters."   I believe that these monks are

for the most part well conducted men, punctual in
their ceremonial duties, and altogether humble-minded
Christians. Their humility is not at all misplaced,
for you see at a glance (poor fellows!) that they
belong to the *lag remove* of the human race. If the
taking of the cowl does not imply a complete
renouncement of the world, it is at least (in these
days) a thorough farewell to every kind of useful and
entertaining knowledge, and accordingly the low
bestial brow and the animal caste of those almost
Bourbon features show plainly enough that all the
intellectual vanities of life have been really and truly
abandoned. But it is hard to quench altogether the
spirit of inquiry that stirs in the human breast, and
accordingly these monks inquire — they are *always*
inquiring—inquiring for " news " ! Poor fellows !
they could scarcely have yielded themselves to the
sway of any passion more difficult of gratification,
for they have no means of communicating with the
busy world except through European travellers ; and
these, in consequence I suppose of that restlessness
and irritability that generally haunt their wanderings,
seem to have always avoided the bore of giving any
information to their hosts. As for me, I am more
patient and good-natured, and when I found that the
kind monks who gathered round me at Nazareth
were longing to know the real truth about the
General Bonaparte who had recoiled from the siege
of Acre, I softened my heart down to the good
humour of Herodotus, and calmly began to " sing
history," telling my eager hearers of the French
Empire and the greatness of its glory, and of
Waterloo and the fall of Napoleon ! Now my story
of this marvellous ignorance on the part of the poor
monks is one upon which (though depending on my

own testimony) I look " with considerable suspicion."
It is quite true (how silly it would be to *invent*
anything so witless !), and yet I think I could satisfy
the mind of a " reasonable man " that it is false.
Many of the older monks must have been in Europe
at the time when the Italy and the Spain from which
they came were in act of taking their French lessons,
or had parted so lately with their teachers, that not
to know of "the Emperor" was impossible, and
these men could scarcely, therefore, have failed to
bring with them some tidings of Napoleon's career.
Yet I say that that which I have written is true—the
one who believes because I have said it will be right
(she always is), whilst poor Mr. "reasonable man,"
who is convinced by the weight of my argument,
will be completely deceived.

.In Spanish politics, however, the monks are better
instructed. The revenues of the monasteries, which
had been principally supplied by the bounty of their
most Catholic majesties, have been withheld since
Ferdinand's death, and the interests of these establishments being thus closely involved in the destinies of
Spain, it is not wonderful that the brethren should
be a little more knowing in Spanish affairs than in
other branches of history. Besides, a large proportion
of the monks were natives of the Peninsula. To these,
I remember, Mysseri's familiarity with the Spanish
language and character was a source of immense
delight ; they were always gathering around him,
and it seemed to me that they treasured like gold
the few Castilian words which he deigned to spare
them.

The monks do a world of good in their way ; and
there can be no doubting that previously to the
arrival of Bishop Alexander, with his numerous

young family and his pretty English nursemaids, they were the chief propagandists of Christianity in Palestine. My old friends of the Franciscan convent at Jerusalem some time since gave proof of their goodness by delivering themselves up to the peril of death for the sake of duty. When I was their guest they were forty I believe in number, and I don't recollect that there was one of them whom I should have looked upon as a desirable life-holder of any property to which I might be entitled in expectancy. Yet these forty were reduced in a few days to nineteen. The plague was the messenger that summoned them to a taste of real death; but the circumstances under which they perished are rather curious; and though I have no authority for the story except an Italian newspaper, I harbour no doubt of its truth, for the facts were detailed with minuteness, and strictly corresponded with all that I knew of the poor fellows to whom they related.

It was about three months after the time of my leaving Jerusalem that the plague set his spotted foot on the Holy City. The monks felt great alarm; they did not shrink from their duty, but for its performance they chose a plan most sadly well fitted for bringing down upon them the very death which they were striving to ward off. They imagined themselves almost safe so long as they remained within their walls; but then it was quite needful that the Catholic Christians of the place, who had always looked to the convent for the supply of their spiritual wants, should receive the aids of religion in the hour of death. A single monk therefore was chosen, either by lot or by some other fair appeal to destiny. Being thus singled out, he was to go forth into the plague-stricken city, and to perform with exactness

his priestly duties; then he was to return, not to
the interior of the convent, for fear of infecting
his brethren, but to a detached building (which I
remember) belonging to the establishment, but at
some little distance from the inhabited rooms. He
was provided with a bell, and at a certain hour in
the morning he was ordered to ring it, *if he could*;
but if no sound was heard at the appointed time,
then knew his brethren that he was either delirious
or dead, and another martyr was sent forth to take
his place. In this way twenty-one of the monks
were carried off. One cannot well fail to admire
the steadiness with which the dismal scheme was
carried through; but if there be any truth in the
notion that disease may be invited by a frightening
imagination, it is difficult to conceive a more dangerous plan than that which was chosen by these poor
fellows. The anxiety with which they must have
expected each day the sound of the bell, the silence
that reigned instead of it, and then the drawing of
the lots (the odds against death being one point
lower than yesterday), and the going forth of the
newly-doomed man — all this must have widened
the gulf that opens to the shades below. When
his victim had already suffered so much of mental
torture, it was but easy work for big bullying pestilence to follow a forlorn monk from the beds of the
dying, and wrench away his life from him as he lay
all alone in an outhouse.

In most, I believe in all, of the Holy Land convents there are two personages so strangely raised
above their brethren in all that dignifies humanity,
that their bearing the same habit, their dwelling
under the same roof, their worshipping the same
God (consistent as all this is with the spirit of their

religion), yet strikes the mind with a sense of wondrous incongruity; the men I speak of are the "Padre Superiore," and the "Padre Missionario." The former is the supreme and absolute governor of the establishment over which he is appointed to rule, the latter is entrusted with the more active of the spiritual duties attaching to the Pilgrim Church. He is the shepherd of the good Catholic flock, whose pasture is prepared in the midst of Mussulmans and schismatics; he keeps the light of the true faith ever vividly before their eyes, reproves their vices, supports them in their good resolves, consoles them in their afflictions, and teaches them to hate the Greek Church. Such are his labours, and you may conceive that great tact must be needed for conducting with success the spiritual interests of the Church under circumstances, so odd as those which surround it in Palestine.

But the position of the Padre Superiore is still more delicate; he is almost unceasingly in treaty with the powers that be, and the worldly prosperity of the establishment over which he presides is in great measure dependent upon the extent of diplomatic skill which he can employ in its favour. I know not from what class of churchmen these personages are chosen, for there is a mystery attending their origin and the circumstance of their being stationed in these convents, which Rome does not suffer to be penetrated. I have heard it said that they are men of great note, and, perhaps, of too high ambition in the Catholic Hierarchy, who, having fallen under the grave censure of the Church, are banished for fixed periods to these distant monasteries. I believe that the term during which they are condemned to remain in the Holy Land is from eight to twelve years. By the natives of the country, as well as by the rest of the brethren, they are looked upon as superior beings; and rightly too, for Nature seems to have crowned them in her own true way.

The chief of the Jerusalem convent was a noble creature; his worldly and spiritual authority seemed to have surrounded him, as it were, with a kind of "court," and the manly gracefulness of his bearing did honour to the throne which he filled. There were no lords of the bedchamber, and no gold sticks and stones in waiting, yet everybody who approached him looked as though he were being "presented"; every interview which he granted wore the air of an "audience"; the brethren as often as they came near bowed low and kissed his hand; and if he went out, the Catholics of the place that hovered about the convent would crowd around him with devout affection, and almost scramble for the blessing which his touch could give. He bore his honours all serenely, as though calmly conscious of his power to "bind and to loose."

CHAPTER XI

GALILEE

NEITHER old "sacred"[1] himself, nor any of
his helpers, knew the road which I meant to
take from Nazareth to the Sea of Galilee and from
thence to Jerusalem, so I was forced to add another
to my party by hiring a guide. The associations of
Nazareth, as well as my kind feeling towards the
hospitable monks, whose guest I had been, inclined
me to set at naught the advice which I had received
against employing Christians. I accordingly engaged
a lithe, active young Nazarene, who was recommended to me by the monks, and who affected to
be familiar with the line of country through which I
intended to pass. My disregard of the popular prejudices against Christians was not justified in this
particular instance by the result of my choice. This
you will see by and by.

I passed by Cana and the house in which the
water had been turned into wine; I came to the
field in which our Saviour had rebuked the Scotch
Sabbath-keepers of that period, by suffering His
disciples to pluck corn on the Lord's Day; I rode
over the ground on which the fainting multitude
had been fed, and they showed me some massive

[1] Shereef.

fragments—the relics, they said, of that wondrous banquet, now turned into stone. The petrifaction was most complete.

I ascended the height on which our Lord was standing when He wrought the miracle. The hill was lofty enough to show me the fairness of the land on all sides, but I have an ancient love for the mere features of a lake, and so forgetting all else when I reached the summit, I looked away eagerly to the eastward. There she lay, the Sea of Galilee. Less stern than Wast Water, less fair than gentle Windermere, she had still the winning ways of an English lake ; she caught from the smiling heavens unceasing light and changeful phases of beauty, and with all this brightness on her face, she yet clung so fondly to the dull he-looking mountain at her side, as though she would

> "Soothe him with her finer fancies,
> Touch him with her lighter thought." [1]

If one might judge of men's real thoughts by their writings, it would seem that there are people who can visit an interesting locality and follow up continuously the exact train of thought that ought to be suggested by the historical associations of the place. A person of this sort can go to Athens and think of nothing later than the age of Pericles ; can live with the Scipios as long as he stays in Rome ; can go up in a balloon, and think how resplendently in former times the now vacant and desolate air was peopled with angels, how prettily it was crossed at intervals by the rounds of Jacob's ladder ! I don't possess this power at all ; it is only by snatches, and for few

[1] Tennyson.

moments together, that I can really associate a place with its proper history.

"There at Tiberias, and along this western shore towards the north, and upon the bosom too of the lake, our Saviour and His disciples"— away flew those recollections, and my mind strained eastward, because that that farthest shore was the end of the world that belongs to man the dweller, the beginning of the other and veiled world that is held by the strange race, whose life (like the pastime of Satan) is a "going to and fro upon the face of the earth." From those grey hills right away to the gates of Bagdad stretched forth the mysterious "desert"— not a pale, void, sandy tract, but a land abounding in rich pastures, a land without cities or towns, without any "respectable" people or any "respectable" things, yet yielding its eighty thousand cavalry to the beck of a few old men. But once more—"Tiberias —the plain of Gennesareth—the very earth on which I stood—that the deep low tones of the Saviour's voice should have gone forth into eternity from out of the midst of these hills and these valleys!"— Ay, ay, but yet again the calm face of the lake was uplifted, and smiled upon my eyes with such familiar gaze, that the "deep low tones" were hushed, the listening multitudes all passed away, and instead there came to me a dear old memory from over the seas in England, a memory sweeter than Gospel to that poor wilful mortal, me.

I went to Tiberias, and soon got afloat upon the water. In the evening I took up my quarters in the Catholic church, and the building being large enough, the whole of my party were admitted to the benefit of the same shelter. With portmanteaus and carpet bags, and books and maps, and fragrant tea, Mysseri soon made me a home on the southern side of the church. One of old Shereef's helpers was an enthusiastic Catholic, and was greatly delighted at having so sacred a lodging. He lit up the altar with a number of tapers, and when his preparations were complete, he began to perform his orisons in the strangest manner imaginable. His lips muttered the prayers of the Latin Church, but he bowed himself down and laid his forehead to the stones beneath him after the manner of a Mussulman. The universal aptness of a religious system for all stages of civilisation, and for all sorts and conditions of men, well befits its claim of divine origin. She is of all nations, and of all times, that wonderful Church of Rome!

Tiberias is one of the four holy cities,[1] according to the Talmud, and it is from this place, or the immediate neighbourhood of it, that the Messiah is to arise.

Except at Jerusalem, never think of attempting to sleep in a "holy city." Old Jews from all parts of the world go to lay their bones upon the sacred soil, and as these people never return to their homes, it follows that any domestic vermin which they may bring with them are likely to become permanently resident, so that the population is continually increasing. No recent census had been taken when I was at Tiberias, but I know that the congregation of fleas which attended at my church alone must have been something enormous. It was a carnal, self-seeking congregation, wholly inattentive to the service which was going on, and devoted to the one object of having my blood. The fleas of all nations were there. The smug, steady, importunate flea from

---

[1] The other three cities held holy by Jews are Jerusalem, Hebron, and Safet.

Holywell Street; the pert, jumping *puce* from hungry France, the wary, watchful *pulce* with his poisoned stiletto; the vengeful *pulga* of Castile with his ugly knife; the German *floh* with his knife and fork, insatiate, not rising from table; whole swarms from all the Russias, and Asiatic hordes unnumbered —all these were there, and all rejoiced in one great international feast. I could no more defend myself against my enemies than if I had been *pain à discretion* in the hands of a French patriot, or English gold in the claws of a Pennsylvanian Quaker. After passing a night like this you are glad to pick up the wretched remains of your body long, long before morning dawns. Your skin is scorched, your temples throb, your lips feel withered and dried, your burning eyeballs are screwed inwards against the brain. You have no hope but only in the saddle and the freshness of the morning air.

CHAPTER XII

MY FIRST BIVOUAC

THE course of the Jordan is from the north to
the south, and in that direction, with very little
of devious winding, it carries the shining waters of
Galilee straight down into the solitudes of the Dead
Sea. Speaking roughly, the river in that meridian is
a boundary between the people living under roofs and
the tented tribes that wander on the farther side.
And so, as I went down in my way from Tiberias
towards Jerusalem, along the western bank of the
stream, my thinking all propended to the ancient
world of herdsmen and warriors that lay so close over
my bridle arm.

If a man, and an Englishman, be not born of his
mother with a natural Chiffney-bit in his mouth,
there comes to him a time for loathing the wearisome
ways of society; a time for not liking tamed people;
a time for not dancing quadrilles, not sitting in pews;
a time for pretending that Milton and Shelley, and
all sorts of mere dead people, were greater in death
than the first living Lord of the Treasury; a time,
in short, for scoffing and railing, for speaking lightly
of the very opera, and all our most cherished institutions. It is from nineteen to two or three and
twenty perhaps that this war of the man against men

s like to be waged most sullenly. You are yet in his smiling England, but you find yourself wending way to the dark sides of her mountains, climbing the dizzy crags, exulting in the fellowship of mists and clouds, and watching the storms how they gather, or roving the mettle of your mare upon the broad and dreary downs, because that you feel congenially with he yet unparcelled earth. A little while you are free and unlabelled, like the ground that you compass; out civilisation is coming and coming; you and your much-loved waste lands will be surely enclosed, and sooner or later brought down to a state of mere usefulness; the ground will be curiously sliced into acres and roods and perches, and you, for all you sit so smartly in your saddle, you will be caught, you will be taken up from travel as a colt from grass, to be rained and tried, and matched and run. All this in time, but first come Continental tours and the moody longing for Eastern travel. The downs and the moors of England can hold you no longer; with large strides you burst away from these slips and patches of free land; you thread your path through the crowds of Europe, and at last, on the banks of Jordan, you joyfully know that you are upon the very frontier of all accustomed respectabilities. There, on the other side of the river (you can swim it with one arm), there reigns the people that will be like to put you to death for *not* being a vagrant, for *not* being a robber, for *not* being armed and houseless. There is comfort in that—health, comfort, and strength to one who is dying from very weariness of that poor, dear, middle-aged, deserving, accomplished, pedantic, and painstaking governess, Europe.

I had ridden for some hours along the right bank of Jordan when I came to the Djesr el Medjamé (an

9

old Roman bridge, I believe), which crossed the river. My Nazarene guide was riding ahead of the party, and now, to my surprise and delight, he turned leftwards, and led on over the bridge. I knew that the true road to Jerusalem must be mainly by the right bank of Jordan, but I supposed that my guide was crossing the bridge at this spot in order to avoid some bend in the river, and that he knew of a ford lower down by which we should regain the western bank. I made no question about the road, for I was but too glad to set my horse's hoofs upon the land of the wandering tribes. None of my party except the Nazarene knew the country. On we went through rich pastures upon the eastern side of the water. I looked for the expected bend of the river, but far as I could see it kept a straight southerly course; I still left my guide unquestioned.

The Jordan is not a perfectly accurate boundary betwixt roofs and tents, for soon after passing the bridge I came upon a cluster of huts. Some time afterwards the guide, upon being closely questioned by my servants, confessed that the village which we had left behind was the last that we should see, but he declared that he knew a spot at which we should find an encampment of friendly Bedouins, who would receive me with all hospitality. I had long determined not to leave the East without seeing something of the wandering tribes, but I had looked forward to this as a pleasure to be found in the desert between El Arish and Egypt; I had no idea that the Bedouins on the east of Jordan were accessible. My delight was so great at the near prospect of bread and salt in the tent of an Arab warrior, that I wilfully allowed my guide to go on and mislead me. I saw that he was taking me out of the straight route towards Jerusalem, and was drawing me into the midst of the Bedouins; but the idea of his betraying me seemed (I know not why) so utterly absurd, that I could not entertain it for a moment. I fancied it possible that the fellow had taken me out of my route in order to attempt some little mercantile enterprise with the tribe for which he was seeking, and I was glad of the opportunity which I might thus gain of coming in contact with the wanderers.

Not long after passing the village a horseman met us. It appeared that some of the cavalry of Ibrahim Pasha had crossed the river for the sake of the rich pastures on the eastern bank, and that this man was one of the troopers. He stopped and saluted; he was obviously surprised at meeting an unarmed, or half-armed, cavalcade, and at last fairly told us that we were on the wrong side of the river, and that if we proceeded we must lay our account with falling amongst robbers. All this while, and throughout the day, my Nazarene kept well ahead of the party, and was constantly up in his stirrups, straining forward and searching the distance for some objects which still remained unseen.

For the rest of the day we saw no human being; we pushed on eagerly in the hope of coming up with the Bedouins before nightfall. Night came, and we still went on in our way till about ten o'clock. Then the thorough darkness of the night, and the weariness of our beasts (which had already done two good days' journey in one), forced us to determine upon coming to a standstill. Upon the heights to the eastward we saw lights; these shone from caves on the mountain-side, inhabited, as the Nazarene told us, by rascals of a low sort — not real Bedouins, men whom we might frighten into harmlessness, but

from whom there was no willing hospitality to be
expected.

We heard at a little distance the brawling of a
rivulet, and on the banks of this it was determined to
establish our bivouac. We soon found the stream,
and following its course for a few yards, came to a
spot which was thought to be fit for our purpose. It
was a sharply cold night in February, and when I
dismounted I found myself standing upon some wet
rank herbage that promised ill for the comfort of our
resting-place. I had bad hopes of a fire, for the
pitchy darkness of the night was a great obstacle to
any successful search for fuel, and, besides, the boughs
of trees or bushes would be so full of sap in this early
spring, that they would not be easily persuaded to
burn. However, we were not likely to submit to a
dark and cold bivouac without an effort, and my
fellows groped forward through the darkness, till
after advancing a few paces they were happily stopped
by a complete barrier of dead prickly bushes. Before
our swords could be drawn to reap this welcome
harvest it was found to our surprise that the fuel was
already hewn and strewed along the ground in a thick
mass. A spot for the fire was found with some
difficulty, for the earth was moist and the grass high
and rank. At last there was a clicking of flint and
steel, and presently there stood out from darkness one
of the tawny faces of my muleteers, bent down to
near the ground, and suddenly lit up by the glowing
of the spark which he courted with careful breath.
Before long there was a particle of dry fibre or leaf
that kindled to a tiny flame; then another was lit
from that, and then another. Then small crisp twigs,
little bigger than bodkins, were laid athwart the
glowing fire. The swelling cheeks of the muleteer,

laid level with the earth, blew tenderly at first and
then more boldly upon the young flame, which was
daintily nursed and fed, and fed more plentifully
when it gained good strength. At last a whole
armful of dry bushes was piled up over the fire, and
presently, with a loud cheery crackling and crackling,
a royal tall blaze shot up from the earth and showed
me once more the shapes and faces of my men, and
the dim outlines of the horses and mules that stood
grazing hard by.

My servants busied themselves in unpacking the
baggage as though we had arrived at an hotel—
Shereef and his helpers unsaddled their cattle. We
had left Tiberias without the slightest idea that we
were to make our way to Jerusalem along the
desolate side of the Jordan, and my servants
(generally provident in those matters) had brought
with them only, I think, some unleavened bread
and a rocky fragment of goat's-milk cheese. These
treasures were produced. Tea and the contrivances
for making it were always a standing part of my
baggage. My men gathered in circle round the fire.
The Nazarene was in a false position from having
misled us so strangely, and he would have shrunk
back, poor devil, into the cold and outer darkness,
but I made him draw near and share the luxuries of
the night. My quilt and my pelisse were spread,
and the rest of my party had all their capotes or
pelisses, or robes of some sort, which furnished their
couches. The men gathered in circle, some kneeling, some sitting, some lying reclined around our
common hearth. Sometimes on one, sometimes on
another, the flickering light would glare more fiercely.
Sometimes it was the good Shereef that seemed
the foremost, as he sat with venerable beard the

image of manly piety—unknowing of all geography, unknowing where he was or whither he might go, but trusting in the goodness of God and the clinching power of fate and the good star of the Englishman. Sometimes, like marble, the classic face of the Greek Mysseri would catch the sudden light, and then again by turns the ever - perturbed Dthemetri, with his old Chinaman's eye and bristling, terrier-like moustache, shone forth illustrious.

I always liked the men who attended me on these Eastern travels, for they were all of them brave, cheery-hearted fellows ; and although their following my career brought upon them a pretty large share of those toils and hardships which are so much more amusing to gentlemen than to servants, yet not one of them ever uttered or hinted a syllable of complaint, or even affected to put on an air of resignation. I always liked them, but never perhaps so much as when they were thus grouped together under the light of the bivouac fire. I felt towards them as my comrades rather than as my servants, and took delight in breaking bread with them, and merrily passing the cup.

The love of tea is a glad source of fellow-feeling between the Englishman and the Asiatic. In Persia it is drunk by all, and although it is a luxury that is rarely within the reach of the Osmanlees, there are few of them who do not know and love the blessed *tchäi*. Our camp-kettle, filled from the brook, hummed doubtfully for a while, then busily bubbled under the sidelong glare of the flames ; cups clinked and rattled ; the fragrant steam ascended, and soon this little circlet in the wilderness grew warm and genial as my lady's drawing-room.

And after this there came the *tchibouque*—great comforter of those that are hungry and wayworn.

And it has this virtue—it helps to destroy the *gêne*
and awkwardness which one sometimes feels at being
in company with one's dependants; for whilst the
amber is at your lips, there is nothing ungracious in
your remaining silent, or speaking pithily in short
inter-whiff sentences. And for us that night there
was pleasant and plentiful matter of talk; for the
where we should be on the morrow, and the where-
withal we should be fed, whether by some ford we
should regain the western bank of Jordan, or find
bread and salt under the tents of a wandering tribe,
or whether we should fall into the hands of the
Philistines, and so come to see death—the last and
greatest of all "the fine sights" that there be—these
were questionings not dull nor wearisome to us, for
we were all concerned in the answers. And it was
not an all-imagined morrow that we probed with our
sharp guesses, for the lights of those low Philistines,
the men of the caves, still hung over our heads, and
we knew by their yells that the fire of our bivouac
had shown us.

At length we thought it well to seek for sleep.
Our plans were laid for keeping up a good watch
through the night. My quilt and my pelisse and my
cloak were spread out so that I might lie spokewise,
with my feet towards the central fire. I wrapped
my limbs daintily round, and gave myself positive
orders to sleep like a veteran soldier. But I found
that my attempt to sleep upon the earth that God
gave me was more new and strange than I had fancied
it. I had grown used to the scene which was before
me whilst I was sitting or reclining by the side of
the fire, but now that I laid myself down at length it
was the deep black mystery of the heavens that hung
over my eyes—not an earthly thing in the way from

my own very forehead right up to the end of all space. I grew proud of my boundless bedchamber. I might have "found sermons" in all this greatness (if I had I should surely have slept), but such was not then my way. If this cherished self of mine had built the universe, I should have dwelt with delight on "the wonders of creation." As it was, I felt rather the vain-glory of my promotion from out of mere rooms and houses into the midst of that grand, dark, infinite palace.

And then, too, my head, far from the fire, was in cold latitudes, and it seemed to me strange that I should be lying so still and passive, whilst the sharp night breeze walked free over my cheek, and the cold damp clung to my hair, as though my face grew in the earth and must bear with the footsteps of the wind and the falling of the dew as meekly as the grass of the field. Besides, I got puzzled and distracted by having to endure heat and cold at the same time, for I was always considering whether my feet were not over-devilled and whether my face was not too well iced. And so when from time to time the watch quietly and gently kept up the languishing fire, he seldom, I think, was unseen to my restless eyes. Yet, at last, when they called me and said that the morn would soon be dawning, I rose from a state of half-oblivion not much unlike to sleep, though sharply qualified by a sort of vegetable's consciousness of having been growing still colder and colder for many and many an hour.

CHAPTER XIII

THE DEAD SEA

THE grey light of the morning showed us for the first time the ground which we had chosen for our resting - place. We found that we had bivouacked upon a little patch of barley plainly belonging to the men of the caves. The dead bushes which we found so happily placed in readiness for our fire had been strewn as a fence for the protection of the little crop. This was the only cultivated spot of ground which we had seen for many a league, and I was rather sorry to find that our night fire and our cattle had spread so much ruin upon this poor solitary slip of corn-land.

The saddling and loading of our beasts was a work which generally took nearly an hour, and before this was half over daylight came. We could now see the men of the caves. They collected in a body, amounting, I should think, to nearly fifty, and rushed down towards our quarters with fierce shouts and yells. But the nearer they got the slower they went; their shouts grew less resolute in tone, and soon ceased altogether. The fellows, however, advanced to a thicket within thirty yards of us, and behind this "took up their position." My men without premeditation did exactly that which was best; they kept steadily to their work of loading the beasts without fuss or hurry; and whether it was that they instinctively felt the wisdom of keeping quiet, or that they merely obeyed the natural inclination to silence which one feels in the early morning, I cannot tell, but I know that, except when they exchanged a syllable or two relative to the work they were about, not a word was said. I now believe that this quietness of our party created an undefined terror in the minds of the cave-holders and scared them from coming on; it gave them a notion that we were relying on some resources which they knew not of. Several times the fellows tried to lash themselves into a state of excitement which might do instead of pluck. They would raise a great shout and sway forward in a dense body from behind the thicket; but when they saw that their bravery thus gathered to a head did not even suspend the strapping of a portmanteau or the tying of a hatbox, their shout lost its spirit, and the whole mass was irresistibly drawn back like a wave receding from the shore.

These attempts at an onset were repeated several times, but always with the same result. I remained under the apprehension of an attack for more than half an hour, and it seemed to me that the work of packing and loading had never been done so slowly. I felt inclined to tell my fellows to make their best speed, but just as I was going to speak I observed that every one was doing his duty already; I therefore held my peace and said not a word, till at last Mysseri led up my horse and asked me if I were ready to mount.

We all marched off without hindrance.

After some time we came across a party of Ibrahim's cavalry, which had bivouacked at no great distance from us. The knowledge that such a force was in the neighbourhood may have conduced to the forbearance of the cave-holders.

We saw a scraggy-looking fellow nearly black, and wearing nothing but a cloth round the loins; he was tending flocks. Afterwards I came up with another of these goatherds, whose helpmate was with him. They gave us some goat's milk, a welcome present. I pitied the poor devil of a goatherd for having such a very plain wife. I spend an enormous quantity of pity upon that particular form of human misery.

About midday I began to examine my map and to question my guide, who at last fell on his knees and confessed thaat he knew nothing of the country in which we were. I was thus thrown upon my own resources, and calculating that on the preceding day we had nearly performed a two days' journey, I concluded that the Dead Sea must be near. In this I was right, for at about three or four o'clock in the afternoon I caught a first sight of its dismal face.

I went on and came near to those waters of death. They stretched deeply into the southern desert, and before me, and all around, as far away as the eye could follow, blank hills piled high over hills, pale, yellow, and naked, walled up in her tomb for ever the dead and damned Gomorrah. There was no fly that hummed in the forbidden air, but instead a deep stillness; no grass grew from the earth, no weed peered through the void sand; but in mockery of all life there were trees borne down by Jordan in some ancient flood, and these, grotesquely planted upon the forlorn shore, spread out their grim skeleton arms, all scorched and charred to blackness by the heats of the long silent years.

I now struck off towards the débouchure of the river ; but I found that the country, though seemingly quite flat, was intersected by deep ravines, which did not show themselves until nearly approached. For some time my progress was much obstructed ; but at last I came across a track which led towards the river, and which might, as I hoped, bring me to a ford. I found, in fact, when I came to the river's side that the track reappeared upon the opposite bank, plainly showing that the stream had been fordable at this place. Now, however, in consequence of the late rains the river was quite impracticable for baggage-horses. A body of waters about equal to the Thames at Eton, but confined to a narrower channel, poured down in a current so swift and heavy, that the idea of passing with laden baggage-horses was utterly forbidden. I could have swum across myself, and I might, perhaps, have succeeded in swimming a horse over ; but this would have been useless, because in such case I must have abandoned not only my baggage, but all my attendants, for none of them were able to swim, and without that resource it would have been madness for them to rely upon the swimming of their beasts across such a powerful stream. I still hoped, however, that there might be a chance of passing the river at the point of its actual junction with the Dead Sea, and I therefore went on in that direction.

Night came upon us whilst labouring across gullies and sandy mounds, and we were obliged to come to a standstill quite suddenly upon the very edge of a precipitous descent. Every step towards the Dead Sea had brought us into a country more and more dreary ; and this sandhill, which we were forced to choose for our resting-place, was dismal enough. A few slender blades of grass, which here and there singly pierced the sand, mocked bitterly the hunger of our jaded beasts, and with our small remaining fragment of goat's-milk rock by way of supper, we were not much better off than our horses. We wanted, too, the great requisite of a cheery bivouac—fire. Moreover, the spot on which we had been so suddenly brought to a standstill was relatively high and unsheltered, and the night wind blew swiftly and cold.

The next morning I reached the débouchure of the Jordan, where I had hoped to find a bar of sand that might render its passage possible. The river, however, rolled its eddying waters fast down to the " sea " in a strong, deep stream that shut out all hope of crossing.

It now seemed necessary either to construct a raft of some kind, or else to retrace my steps and remount the banks of the Jordan. I had once happened to give some attention to the subject of military bridges—a branch of military science which includes the construction of rafts and contrivances of the like sort—and I should have been very proud indeed if I could have carried my party and my baggage across by dint of any idea gathered from Sir Howard Douglas or Robinson Crusoe. But we were all faint and languid from want of food, and besides there were no materials. Higher up the river there were bushes and river plants, but nothing like timber; and the cord with which my baggage was tied to the pack-saddles amounted altogether to a very small quantity, not nearly enough to haul any sort of craft across the stream.

And now it was, if I remember rightly, that Dthemetri submitted to me a plan for putting to death the Nazarene, whose misguidance had been the cause of our difficulties. There was something fascinating in this suggestion, for the slaying of the guide was of course easy enough, and would look like an act of what politicians call " vigour." If it were only to become known to my friends in England that I had calmly killed a fellow-creature for taking me out of my way, I might remain perfectly quiet and tranquil for all the rest of my days, quite free from the danger of being considered "slow "; I might ever after live on upon my reputation, like " single-speech Hamilton " in the last century, or " single sin—" in this, without being obliged to take the trouble of doing any more harm in the world. This was a great temptation to an indolent person, but the motive was not strengthened by any sincere feeling of anger with the Nazarene. Whilst the question of his life and death was debated he was riding in front of our party, and there was something in the anxious writhing of his supple limbs that seemed to express a sense of his false position, and struck me as highly comic. I had no crotchet at that time against the punishment of death, but I was unused to blood, and the proposed victim looked so thoroughly capable of enjoying life (if he could only get to the other side of the river), that I thought it would be hard for him to die merely in order to give me a character for energy. Acting on the result of these considerations, and reserving to myself a free and unfettered discretion to have the poor villain shot at any future moment, I magnanimously decided that for the present he should live, and not die.

I bathed in the Dead Sea. The ground covered by the water sloped so gradually, that I was not only forced to " sneak in," but to walk through the water nearly a quarter of a mile before I could get out of my depth. When at last I was able to attempt to dive, the salts held in solution made my eyes smart so sharply, that the pain which I thus suffered, together with the weakness occasioned by want of food, made me giddy and faint for some moments, but I soon grew better. I knew beforehand the impossibility of sinking in this buoyant water, but I was surprised to find that I could not swim at my accustomed pace; my legs and feet were lifted so high and dry out of the the lake, that my stroke was baffled, and I found myself kicking against the thin air instead of the dense fluid upon which I was swimming. The water is perfectly bright and clear; its taste detestable. After finishing my attempts at swimming and diving, I took some time in regaining the shore, and before I began to dress I found that the sun had already evaporated the water which clung to me, and that my skin was thickly encrusted with salts.

CHAPTER XIV

THE BLACK TENTS

MY steps were reluctantly turned towards the north. I had ridden some way, and still it seemed that all life was fenced and barred out from the desolate ground over which I was journeying. On the west there flowed the inpassable Jordan, on the east stood an endless range of barren mountains, and on the south lay that desert sea that knew not the plashing of an oar; greatly therefore was I surprised when suddenly there broke upon my ear the long, ludicrous, persevering bray of a donkey. I was riding at this time some few hundred yards ahead of all my party except the Nazarene (who by a wise instinct kept closer to me than to Dthemetri), and I instantly went forward in the direction of the sound, for I fancied that where there were donkeys, there too most surely would be men. The ground on all sides of me seemed thoroughly void and lifeless, but at last I got down into a hollow, and presently a sudden turn brought me within thirty yards of an Arab encampment. The low black tents which I had so long lusted to see were right before me, and and they were all teeming with live Arabs—men, women, and children.

I wished to have let my party behind know

where I was, but I recollected that they would be able to trace me by the prints of my horse's hoofs in the sand ; and having to do with Asiatics, I felt the danger of the slightest movement which might be looked upon as a sign of irresolution. Therefore, without looking behind me, without looking to the right or to the left, I rode straight up towards the foremost tent. Before this was strewed a semi-circular fence of dead boughs, through which there was an opening opposite to the front of the tent. As I advanced, some twenty or thirty of the most uncouth-looking fellows imaginable came forward to meet me. In their appearance they showed nothing of the Bedouin blood ; they were of many colours, from dingy brown to jet black, and some of these last had much of the negro look about them. They were tall, powerful fellows, but awfully ugly. They wore nothing but the Arab shirts, confined at the waist by leathern belts.

I advanced to the gap left in the fence, and at once alighted from my horse. The chief greeted me after his fashion by alternately touching first my hand and then his own forehead, as if he were conveying the virtue of the touch like a spark of electricity. Presently I found myself seated upon a sheepskin, which was spread for me under the sacred shade of Arabian canvas. The tent was of a long, narrow, oblong form, and contained a quantity of men, women, and children so closely huddled together, that there was scarcely one of them who was not in actual contact with his neighbour. The moment I had taken my seat the chief repeated his salutations in the most enthusiastic manner, and then the people having gathered densely about me, got hold of my unresisting hand and passed it round like a claret jug

for the benefit of everybody. The women soon
brought me a wooden bowl full of buttermilk, and
welcome indeed came the gift to my hungry and
thirsty soul.

After some time my party, as I had expected,
came up, and when poor Dthemetri saw me on my
sheepskin, "the life and soul" of this ragamuffin
party, he was so astounded, that he even failed to
check his cry of horror; he plainly thought that
now, at last, the Lord had delivered me (interpreter
and all) into the hands of the lowest Philistines.

Mysseri carried a tobacco-pouch slung at his belt,
and as soon as its contents were known the whole
population of the tent began begging like spaniels for
bits of the beloved weed. I concluded from the
abject manner of these people that they could not
possibly be thoroughbred Bedouins, and I saw, too,
that they must be in the very last stage of misery,
for poor indeed is the man in these climes who
cannot command a pipeful of tobacco. I began to
think that I had fallen amongst thorough savages,
and it seemed likely enough that they would gain
their very first knowledge of civilisation by ravishing
and studying the contents of my dearest portmanteaus,
but still my impression was that they would hardly
venture upon such an attempt. I observed, indeed,
that they did not offer me the bread and salt which
I had understood to be the pledges of peace amongst
wandering tribes, but I fancied that they refrained
from this act of hospitality, not in consequence of
any hostile determination, but in order that the notion
of robbing me might remain for the present an "open
question." I afterwards found that the poor fellows
had no bread to offer. They were literally "out at
grass." It is true that they had a scanty supply of

milk from goats, but they were living almost entirely upon certain grass stems, which were just in season at that time of the year. These, if not highly nourishing, are pleasant enough to the taste, and their acid juices come gratefully to thirsty lips.

CHAPTER XV

A ND now Dthemetri began to enter into a negotiation with my hosts for a passage over the river. I never interfered with my worthy dragoman upon these occasions, because from my entire ignorance of the Arabic I should have been quite unable to exercise any real control over his words, and it would have been silly to break the stream of his eloquence to no purpose. I have reason to fear, however, that he lied transcendently, and especially in representing me as the bosom friend of Ibrahim Pasha. The mention of that name produced immense agitation and excitement, and the Sheik explained to Dthemetri the grounds of the infinite respect which he and his tribe entertained for the Pasha. A few weeks before Ibrahim had craftily sent a body of troops across the Jordan. The force went warily round to the foot of the mountains on the east, so as to cut off the retreat of this tribe, and then surrounded them as they lay encamped in the vale; their camels, and indeed all their possessions worth taking, were carried off by the soldiery, and moreover the then Sheik, together with every tenth man of the tribe, was brought out and shot. You would think that this conduct on

148

the part of the Pasha might not procure for his "friend" a very gracious reception amongst the people whom he had thus despoiled and decimated ; but the Asiatic seems to be animated with a feeling of profound respect, almost bordering upon affection, for all who have done him any bold and violent wrong; and there is always, too, so much of vague and undefined apprehension mixed up with his really well-founded alarms, that I can see no limit to the yielding and bending of his mind when it is wrought upon by the idea of power.

After some discussion the Arabs agreed, as I thought, to conduct me to a ford, and we moved on towards the river, followed by seventeen of the most able-bodied of the tribe, under the guidance of several grey-bearded elders, and Sheik Ali Djoubran at the head of the whole detachment. Upon leaving the encampment a sort of ceremony was performed, for the purpose, it seemed, of ensuring, if possible, a happy result for the undertaking. There was an uplifting of arms, and a repeating of words that sounded like formulæ, but there were no prostrations, and I did not understand that the ceremony was of a religious character. The tented Arabs are looked upon as very bad Mahometans.[1]

We arrived upon the banks of the river—not at a ford, but at a deep and rapid part of the stream, and I now understood that it was the plan of these men,

---

[1] [The tented Arabs are no doubt very bad Mohammedans, but the assumption which Kinglake seems to make that prostrations are essential to a Moslem religious ceremony is not correct. The form of prayer called in Turkey Namaz, which ought to be performed by every devout Moslem five times a day, does necessarily involve prostrations in which the forehead touches the ground, but it is by no means the only, though doubtless the most important,

if they helped me at all, to transport me across the river by some species of raft. But a reaction had taken place in the opinions of many, and a violent dispute arose upon a motion which seemed to have been made by some honourable member with a view to robbery. The fellows all gathered together in circle, at a little distance from my party, and there disputed with great vehemence and fury for nearly two hours. I can't give a correct report of the debate, for it was held in a barbarous dialect of the Arabic unknown to my dragoman. I recollect I sincerely felt at the time that the arguments in favour of robbing me must have been almost unanswerable, and I gave great credit to the speakers on my side for the ingenuity and sophistry which they must have shown in maintaining the fight so well.

During the discussion I remained lying in front of my baggage, which had all been taken from the pack-saddles and placed upon the ground. I was so languid from want of food, that I had scarcely animation enough to feel as deeply interested as you would suppose in the result of the discussion. I thought, however, that the pleasantest toys to play with during this interval were my pistols, and now and then, when I listlessly visited my loaded barrels with the swivel ramrods, or drew a sweet, musical click from my English firelocks, it seemed to me that I exercised a slight and gentle influence on the debate. Thanks to Ibrahim Pasha's terrible visitation the men of the tribe were wholly unarmed, and my

act of worship sanctioned by Islam. In the present case the ceremony was probably a blessing, which is generally given by closing the eyes and uplifting the arms with the hands bent back and the palms open. I have often seen such benedictions given when a party sets out for a pilgrimage or any other purpose.]

advantage in this respect might have counterbalanced in some measure the superiority of numbers.

Mysseri (not interpreting in Arabic) had no duty to perform, and he seemed to be faint and listless as myself. Shereef looked perfectly resigned to any fate. But Dthemetri (faithful terrier!) was bristling with zeal and watchfulness. He could not understand the debate, which indeed was carried on at a distance too great to be easily heard, even if the language had been familiar; but he was always on the alert, and now and then conferring with men who had straggled out of the assembly. At last he found an opportunity of making a proposal, which at once produced immense sensation; he offered, on my behalf, that if the tribe should bear themselves loyally towards me, and take my party and my baggage in safety to the other bank of the river, I should give them a *teskeri*, or written certificate of their good conduct, which might avail them hereafter in the hour of their direst need. This proposal was received and instantly accepted by all the men of the tribe there present with the utmost enthusiasm. I was to give the men, too, a *baksheish*, that is, a present of money, which is usually made upon the conclusion of any sort of treaty; but although the people of the tribe were so miserably poor, they seemed to look upon the pecuniary part of the arrangement as a matter quite trivial in comparison with the *teskeri*. Indeed the sum which Dthemetri promised them was extremely small, and not the slightest attempt was made to extort any further reward.

The council now broke up, and most of the men rushed madly towards me, and overwhelmed me with vehement gratulations; they caressed my boots with much affection, and my hands were severely kissed.

The Arabs now went to work in right earnest to effect the passage of the river. They had brought with them a great number of the skins which they use for carrying water in the desert; these they filled with air, and fastened several of them to small boughs which they cut from the banks of the river. In this way they constructed a raft not more than about four or five feet square, but rendered buoyant by the inflated skins which supported it. On this a portion of my baggage was placed, and was firmly tied to it by the cords used on my pack-saddles. The little raft with its weighty cargo was then gently lifted into the water, and I had the satisfaction to see that it floated well.

Twelve of the Arabs now stripped, and tied inflated skins to their loins; six of the men went down into the river, got in front of the little raft, and pulled it off a few feet from the bank. The other six then dashed into the stream with loud shouts, and swam along after the raft, pushing it from behind. Off went the craft in capital style at first, for the stream was easy on the eastern side; but I saw that the tug was to come, for the main torrent swept round in a bend near the western bank of the river.

The old men, with their long grey grisly beards, stood shouting and cheering, praying and commanding. At length the raft entered upon the difficult part of its course; the whirling stream seized and twisted it about, and then bore it rapidly downwards; the swimmers flagged, and seemed to be beaten in the struggle. But now the old men on the bank, with their rigid arms uplifted straight, sent forth a cry and a shout that tore the wide air into tatters, and then to make their urging yet more strong they shrieked out the dreadful syllables, "'Brahim Pasha!" The swimmers, one moment before so blown and so weary, found lungs to answer the cry, and shouting back the name of their great destroyer, they dashed on through the torrent, and bore the raft in safety to the western bank.

Afterwards the swimmers returned with the raft, and attached to it the rest of my baggage. I took my seat upon the top of the cargo, and the raft thus laden passed the river in the same way, and with the same struggle as before. The skins, however, not being perfectly air-tight, had lost a great part of their buoyancy, so that I, as well as the luggage that passed on this last voyage, got wet in the waters of Jordan. The raft could not be trusted for another trip, and the rest of my party passed the river in a different and (for them) much safer way. Inflated skins were fastened to their loins, and thus supported, they were tugged across by Arabs swimming on either side of them. The horses and mules were thrown into the water and forced to swim over. The poor beasts had a hard struggle for their lives in that swift stream; and I thought that one of the horses would have been drowned, for he was too weak to gain a footing on the western bank, and the stream bore him down. At last, however, he swam back to the side from which he had come. Before dark all had passed the river except this one horse and old Shereef. He, poor fellow, was shivering on the eastern bank, for his dread of the passage was so great, that he delayed it as long as he could, and at last it became so dark that he was obliged to wait till the morning.

I lay that night on the banks of the river, and at a little distance from me the Arabs kindled a fire, round which they sat in a circle. They were made most savagely happy by the tobacco with which I supplied them, and they soon determined that the whole night should be one smoking festival. The poor fellows had only a cracked bowl, without any tube at all, but this morsel of a pipe they handed round from one to the other, allowing to each a fixed number of whiffs. In that way they passed the whole night.

The next morning old Shereef was brought across. It was a strange sight to see this solemn old Mussulman, with his shaven head and his sacred beard, sprawling and puffing upon the surface of the water. When at last he reached the bank the people told him that by his baptism in Jordan he had surely become a mere Christian. Poor Shereef!—the holy man! the descendant of the Prophet!—he was sadly hurt by the taunt, and the more so as he seemed to feel that there was some foundation for it, and that he really might have absorbed some Christian errors.

When all was ready for departure I wrote the *teskeri* in French and delivered it to Sheik Ali Djoubran, together with the promised *haksheish*; he was exceedingly grateful, and I parted in a very friendly way from this ragged tribe.

In two or three hours I gained Rihah, a village said to occupy the site of ancient Jericho. There was one building there which I observed with some emotion, for although it may not have been actually standing in the days of Jericho, it contained at this day a most interesting collection of—modern loaves.

Some hours after sunset I reached the convent of Santo Saba, and there remained for the night.

CHAPTER XVI

THE enthusiasm that had glowed, or seemed to glow, within me for one blessed moment when I knelt by the shrine of the Virgin at Nazareth, was not rekindled at Jerusalem. In the stead of the solemn gloom and the deep stillness that of right belonged to the Holy City, there was the hum and the bustle of active life. It was the "height of the season." The Easter ceremonies drew near. The pilgrims were flocking, in from all quarters; and although their objects were partly at least of a religious character, yet their "arrivals" brought as much stir and liveliness to the city as if they had come up to marry their daughters.

The votaries who every year crowd to the Holy Sepulchre are chiefly of the Greek and Armenian Churches. They are not drawn into Palestine by a mere sentimental longing to stand upon the ground trodden by our Saviour, but rather they perform the pilgrimage as a plain duty strongly inculcated by their religion. A very great proportion of those who belong to the Greek Church contrive at some time or other in the course of their lives to achieve the enterprise. Many in their infancy and childhood are brought to the holy sites by their parents, but those who have not had this advantage will often make it the main object of their lives to save money enough for this holy undertaking.

The pilgrims begin to arrive in Palestine some weeks before the Easter festival of the Greek Church. They come from Egypt, from all parts of Syria, from Armenia and Asia Minor, from Stamboul, from Roumelia, from the provinces of the Danube, and from all the Russias. Most of these people bring with them some articles of merchandise, but I myself believe (notwithstanding the common taunt against pilgrims) that they do this rather as a mode of paying the expenses of their journey, than from a spirit of mercenary speculation. They generally travel in families, for the women are of course more ardent than their husbands in undertaking these pious enterprises, and they take care to bring with them all their children, however young; for the efficacy of the rites does not depend upon the age of the votary, so that people whose careful mothers have obtained for them the benefit of the pilgrimage in early life, are saved from the expense and trouble of undertaking the journey at a later age. The superior veneration so often excited by objects that are distant and unknown shows not perhaps the wrongheadedness of a man, but rather the transcendent power of his imagination. However this may be, and whether it is by mere obstinacy that they poke their way through intervening distance, or whether they come by the winged strength of fancy, quite certainly the pilgrims who flock to Palestine from the most remote homes are the people most eager in the enterprise, and in number too they bear a very high proportion to the whole mass.

The great bulk of the pilgrims make their way by

sea to the port of Jaffa. A number of families will charter a vessel amongst them, all bringing their own provisions, which are of the simplest and cheapest kind. On board every vessel thus freighted there is, I believe, a priest, who helps the people in their religious exercises, and tries (and fails) to maintain something like order and harmony. The vessels employed in this service are usually Greek brigs or brigantines and schooners, and the number of passengers stowed in them is almost always horribly excessive. The voyages are sadly protracted, not only by the land-seeking, storm-flying habits of the Greek seamen, but also by their endless schemes and speculations, which are for ever tempting them to touch at the nearest port. The voyage, too, must be made in winter, in order that Jerusalem may be reached some weeks before the Greek Easter, and thus by the time they attain to the holy shrines the pilgrims have really and truly undergone a very respectable quantity of suffering. I once saw one of these pious cargoes put ashore on the coast of Cyprus, where they had touched for the purpose of visiting (not Paphos, but) some Christian sanctuary. I never saw (no, never even in the most horridly stuffy ballroom) such a discomfortable collection of human beings. Long huddled together in a pitching and rolling prison, fed on beans, exposed to some real danger and to terrors without end, they had been tumbled about for many wintry weeks in the chopping seas of the Mediterranean. As soon as they landed they stood upon the beach and chanted a hymn of thanks; the chant was morne and doleful, but really the poor people were looking so miserable, that one could not fairly expect from them any lively outpouring of gratitude.

When the pilgrims have landed at Jaffa they hire camels, horses, mules, or donkeys, and make their way as well as they can to the Holy City. The space fronting the Church of the Holy Sepulchre soon becomes a kind of bazaar, or rather, perhaps, reminds you of an English fair. On this spot the pilgrims display their merchandise, and there too the trading residents of the place offer their goods for sale. I have never, I think, seen elsewhere in Asia so much commercial animation as upon this square of ground by the church door; the "money-changers" seemed to be almost as brisk and lively as if they had been *within* the temple.

When I entered the church I found a babel of worshippers. Greek, Roman, and Armenian priests were performing their different rites in various nooks and corners, and crowds of disciples were rushing about in all directions, some laughing and talking, some begging, but most of them going round in a regular and methodical way to kiss the sanctified spots, and speak the appointed syllables, and lay down the accustomed coin. If this kissing of the shrines had seemed as though it were done at the bidding of enthusiasm, or of any poor sentiment even feebly approaching to it, the sight would have been less odd to English eyes; but as it was, I stared to see grown men thus steadily and carefully embracing the sticks and the stones, not from love or from zeal (else God forbid that I should have stared!), but from a calm sense of duty; they seemed to be not "working out," but *transacting* the great business of salvation.

Dthemetri, however, who generally came with me when I went out, in order to do duty as interpreter, really had in him some enthusiasm. He was a

zealous and almost fanatical member of the Greek
Church, and had long since performed the pilgrimage,
so now great indeed was the pride and delight with
which he guided me from one holy spot to another.
Every now and then, when he came to an unoccupied
shrine, he fell down on his knees and performed
devotion; he was almost distracted by the tempta-
tions that surrounded him; there were so many
stones absolutely requiring to be kissed, that he
rushed about happily puzzled and sweetly teased, like
" Jack among the maidens."

A Protestant, familiar with the Holy Scriptures,
but ignorant of tradition and the geography of modern
Jerusalem, finds himself a good deal " mazed " when
he first looks for the sacred sites. The Holy
Sepulchre is not in a field without the walls, but in
the midst, and in the best part of the town, under the
roof of the great church which I have been talking
about. It is a handsome tomb of oblong form,
partly subterranean and partly above ground, and
closed in on all sides except the one by which it is
entered. You descend into the interior by a few
steps, and there find an altar with burning tapers.
This is the spot which is held in greater sanctity than
any other at Jerusalem. When you have seen
enough of it you feel perhaps weary of the busy
crowd, and inclined for a gallop; you ask your
dragoman whether there will be time before sunset to
procure horses and take a ride to Mount Calvary.
Mount Calvary, signor?—eccolo! it is *upstairs—on
the first floor*. In effect you ascend, if I remember
rightly, just thirteen steps, and then you are shown
the now golden sockets in which the crosses of our
Lord and the two thieves were fixed. All this is
startling, but the truth is, that the city having

gathered round the Sepulchre, which is the main point of interest, has crept northward, and thus in great measure are occasioned the many geographical surprises that puzzle the " Bible Christian."

The Church of the Holy Sepulchre comprises very compendiously almost all the spots associated with the closing career of our Lord. Just there, on your right, He stood and wept; by the pillar, on your left, He was scourged ; on the spot, just before you, He was crowned with the crown of thorns ; up there He was crucified, and down here He was buried. A locality is assigned to every, the minutest, event connected with the recorded history of our Saviour ; even the spot where the cock crew when Peter denied his Master is ascertained, and surrounded by the walls of an Armenian convent. Many Protestants are wont to treat these traditions contemptuously, and those who distinguish themselves from their brethren by the appellation of " Bible Christians " are almost fierce in their denunciation of these supposed errors.

It is admitted, I believe, by everybody that the formal sanctification of these spots was the act of the Empress Helena, the mother of Constantine, but I think it is fair to suppose that she was guided by a careful regard to the then prevailing traditions. Now the nature of the ground upon which Jerusalem stands is such, that the localities belonging to the events there enacted might have been more easily, and permanently, ascertained by tradition than those of any city that I know of. Jerusalem, whether ancient or modern, was built upon and surrounded by sharp, salient rocks intersected by deep ravines. Up to the time of the siege Mount Calvary of course must have been well enough known to the people of

Jerusalem; the destruction of the mere buildings could not have obliterated from any man's memory the names of those steep rocks and narrow ravines in the midst of which the city had stood. It seems to me, therefore, highly probable that in fixing the site of Calvary the Empress was rightly guided. Recollect, too, that the voice of tradition at Jerusalem is quite unanimous, and that Romans, Greeks, Armenians, and Jews, all hating each other sincerely, concur in assigning the same localities to the events told in the Gospel. I concede, however, that the attempt of the Empress to ascertain the sites of the minor events cannot be safely relied upon. With respect, for instance, to the certainty of the spot where the cock crew, I am far from being convinced.

Supposing that the Empress acted arbitrarily in fixing the holy sites, it would seem that she followed the Gospel of St. John, and that the geography sanctioned by her can be more easily reconciled with that history than with the accounts of the other Evangelists.

The authority exercised by the Mussulman Government in relation to the holy sites is in one view somewhat humbling to the Christians, for it is almost as an arbitrator between the contending sects (this always, of course, for the sake of pecuniary advantage) that the Mussulman lends his contemptuous aid; he not only grants, but enforces toleration. All persons, of whatever religion, are allowed to go as they will into every part of the Church of the Holy Sepulchre, but in order to prevent indecent contests, and also from motives arising out of money payments, the Turkish Government assigns the peculiar care of each sacred spot to one of the

11

ecclesiastic bodies. Since this guardianship carries
with it the receipt of the coins which the pilgrims
leave upon the shrines, it is strenuously fought for by
all the rival Churches, and the artifices of intrigue
are busily exerted at Stamboul in order to procure
the issue or revocation of the firmans by which the
coveted privilege is granted. In this strife the Greek
Church has of late years signally triumphed, and the
most famous of the shrines are committed to the care
of their priesthood. They possess the golden socket
in which stood the cross of our Lord, whilst the
Latins are obliged to content themselves with the
apertures in which were inserted the crosses of the
two thieves. They are naturally discontented with
that poor privilege, and sorrowfully look back to the
days of their former glory—the days when Napoleon
was Emperor, and Sebastiani ambassador at the Porte.
It seems that the "citizen" sultan, old Louis
Philippe, has done very little indeed for Holy
Church in Palestine.

Although the pilgrims perform their devotions at
the several shrines with so little apparent enthusiasm,
they are driven to the verge of madness by the miracle
displayed before them on Easter Saturday. Then it
is that the Heaven-sent fire issues from the Holy
Sepulchre. The pilgrims all assemble in the great
church, and already, long before the wonder is
worked, they are wrought by anticipation of God's
sign, as well as by their struggles for room and
breathing space, to a most frightful state of excitement. At length the chief priest of the Greeks,
accompanied (of all people in the world) by the
Turkish Governor, enters the tomb. After this,
there is a long pause, and then suddenly from out of
the small apertures on either side of the sepulchre

there issue long, shining flames. The pilgrims now rush forward, madly struggling to light their tapers at the holy fire. This is the dangerous moment, and many lives are often lost.

The year before that of my going to Jerusalem, Ibrahim Pasha, from some whim, or motive of policy, chose to witness the miracle. The vast church was of course thronged, as it always is on that awful day. It seems that the appearance of the fire was delayed for a very long time, and that the growing frenzy of the people was heightened by suspense. Many, too, had already sunk under the effect of the heat and the stifling atmosphere, when at last the fire flashed from the sepulchre. Then a terrible struggle ensued; many sunk and were crushed. Ibrahim had taken his station in one of the galleries, but now, feeling perhaps his brave blood warmed by the sight and sound of such strife, he took upon himself to quiet the people by his personal presence, and descended into the body of the church with only a few guards. He had forced his way into the midst of the dense crowd, when unhappily he fainted away; his guards shrieked out, and the event instantly became known. A body of soldiers recklessly forced their way through the crowd, trampling over every obstacle that they might save the life of their general. Nearly two hundred people were killed in the struggle.

The following year, however, the Government took better measures for the prevention of these calamities. I was not present at the ceremony, having gone away from Jerusalem some time before, but I afterwards returned into Palestine, and I then learned that the day had passed off without any disturbance of a fatal kind. It is, however, almost too

much to expect that so many ministers of peace can
assemble without finding some occasion for strife,
and in that year a tribe of wild Bedouins became the
subject of discord. These men, it seems, led an
Arab life in some of the desert tracts bordering on
the neighbourhood of Jerusalem, but were not connected with any of the great ruling tribes. Some
whim or notion of policy had induced them to
embrace Christianity ; but they were grossly ignorant
of the rudiments of their adopted faith, and having
no priest with them in their desert, they had as little
knowledge of religious ceremonies as of religion
itself. They were not even capable of conducting
themselves in a place of worship with ordinary
decorum, but would interrupt the service with
scandalous cries and warlike shouts. Such is the
account the Latins give of them, but I have never
heard the other side of the question. These wild
fellows, notwithstanding their entire ignorance of
all religion, are yet claimed by the Greeks, not only
as proselytes who have embraced Christianity generally, but as converts to the particular doctrines and
practice of their Church. The people thus alleged
to have concurred in the great schism of the Eastern
Empire are never, I believe, within the walls of a
church, or even of any building at all, except upon
this occasion of Easter ; and as they then never fail
to find a row of some kind going on by the side of
the sepulchre, they fancy, it seems, that the ceremonies there enacted are funeral games of a martial
character, held in honour of a deceased chieftain,
and that a Christian festival is a peculiar kind of
battle, fought between walls, and without cavalry.
It does not appear, however, that these men are
guilty of any ferocious acts, or that they attempt to

commit depredations. The charge against them is merely that by their way of applauding the performance, by their horrible cries and frightful gestures, they destroy the solemnity of divine service, and upon this ground the Franciscans obtained a firman for the exclusion of such tumultuous worshippers. The Greeks, however, did not choose to lose the aid of their wild converts merely because they were a little backward in their religious education, and they therefore persuaded them to defy the firman by entering the city *en masse* and overawing their enemies. The Franciscans, as well as the Government authorities, were obliged to give way, and the Arabs triumphantly marched into the church. The festival, however, must have seemed to them rather flat, for although there may have been some "casualties" in the way of eyes black and noses bloody, and women "missing," there was no return of "killed."

Formerly the Latin Catholics concurred in acknowledging (but not, I hope, in working) the annual miracle of the heavenly fire, but they have for many years withdrawn their countenance from this exhibition, and they now repudiate it as a trick of the Greek Church. Thus of course the violence of feeling with which the rival Churches meet at the Holy Sepulchre on Easter Saturday is greatly increased, and a disturbance of some kind is certain. In the year I speak of, though no lives were lost, there was, as it seems, a tough struggle in the church. I was amused at hearing of a taunt that was thrown that day upon an English traveller. He had taken his station in a convenient part of the church, and was no doubt displaying that peculiar air of serenity and gratification with which an English gentleman usually looks on at a row, when one of the Franciscans came by, all reeking from the fight, and was so disgusted at the coolness and placid contentment of the Englishman (who was a guest at the convent), that he forgot his monkish humility as well as the duties of hospitality, and plainly said, " You sleep under our roof, you eat our bread, you drink our wine, and then when Easter Saturday comes you don't fight for us ! "

Yet these rival Churches go on quietly enough till their blood is up. The terms on which they live remind one of the peculiar relation subsisting at Cambridge between "town and gown."

These contests and disturbances certainly do not originate with the lay-pilgrims, the great body of whom are, as I believe, quiet and inoffensive people. It is true, however, that their pious enterprise is believed by them to operate as a counterpoise for a multitude of sins, whether past or future, and perhaps they exert themselves in after life to restore the balance of good and evil. The Turks have a maxim which, like most cynical apophthegms, carries with it the buzzing trumpet of falsehood as well as the small, fine "sting of truth." " If your friend has made the pilgrimage once, distrust him ; if he has made the pilgrimage twice, cut him dead ! " The caution is said to be as applicable to the visitants of Jerusalem as to those of Mecca, but I cannot help believing that the frailties of all the hadjis,[1] whether Christian or Mahometan, are greatly exaggerated. I certainly regarded the pilgrims to Palestine as a well-disposed orderly body of people, not strongly enthusiastic, but desirous to comply with the ordinances of their religion, and to attain the great end of salvation as quietly and economically as possible.

[1] Hadji, a pilgrim.

When the solemnities of Easter are concluded the
pilgrims move off in a body to complete their good
work by visiting the sacred scenes in the neighbourhood of Jerusalem, including the wilderness of John
the Baptist, Bethlehem, and, above all, the Jordan,
for to bathe in those sacred waters is one of the chief
objects of the expedition. All the pilgrims—men,
women, and children—are submerged *en chemise*, and
the saturated linen is carefully wrapped up and pre-
served as a burial-dress that shall enure for salvation
in the realms of death.

I saw the burial of a pilgrim. He was a Greek,
miserably poor, and very old; he had just crawled
into the Holy City, and had reached at once the goal
of his pious journey and the end of his sufferings upon
earth. There was no coffin nor wrapper, and as I
looked full upon the face of the dead I saw how
deeply it was rutted with the ruts of age and misery.
The priest, strong and portly, fresh, fat, and alive
with the life of the animal kingdom, unpaid, or ill
paid for his work, would scarcely deign to mutter out
his forms, but hurried over the words with shocking
haste. Presently he called out impatiently, " Yalla !
Goor ! " (Come ! look sharp !), and then the dead
Greek was seized. His limbs yielded inertly to the
rude men that handled them, and down he went into
his grave, so roughly bundled in that his neck was
twisted by the fall, so twisted, that if the sharp
malady of life were still upon him the old man would
have shrieked and groaned, and the lines of his face
would have quivered with pain. The lines of his
face were not moved, and the old man lay still and
heedless, so well cured of that tedious life-ache, that
nothing could hurt him now. His clay was *itself
again*—cool, firm, and tough. The pilgrim had

found great rest. I threw the accustomed handful
of the holy soil upon his patient face, and then, and
in less than a minute, the earth closed coldly around
him.

I did not say "alas!" (nobody ever does that I
know of, though the word is so frequently written).
I thought the old man had got rather well out of the
scrape of being alive, and poor.

The destruction of the mere buildings in such a
place as Jerusalem would not involve the permanent
dispersion of the inhabitants, for the rocky neighbourhood in which the town is situate abounds in caves,
which would give an easy refuge to the people until
they gained an opportunity of rebuilding their
dwellings; therefore I could not help looking upon
the Jews of Jerusalem as being in some sort the
representatives, if not the actual descendants, of the
rascals who crucified our Saviour. Supposing this
to be the case, I felt that there would be some
interest in knowing how the events of the Gospel
history were regarded by the Israelites of modern
Jerusalem. The result of my inquiry upon this
subject was, so far as it went, entirely favourable to
the truth of Christianity. I understood that *the
performance of the miracles was not doubted by any of
the Jews in the place.* All of them concurred in
attributing the works of our Lord to the influence of
magic, but they were divided as to the species of
enchantment from which the power proceeded. The
great mass of the Jewish people believe, I fancy, that
the miracles had been wrought by aid of the powers
of darkness, but many, and those the more enlightened, would call Jesus " the good Magician."
To Europeans repudiating the notion of all magic,
good or bad, the opinion of the Jews as to the agency

by which the miracles were worked is a matter of no
importance ; but the circumstance of their admitting
that those miracles *were in fact performed*, is certainly
curious, and perhaps not quite immaterial.[1]

If you stay in the Holy City long enough to fall
into anything like regular habits of amusement and
occupation, and to become, in short, for a time " a
man about town " at Jerusalem, you will necessarily
lose the enthusiasm which you may have felt when
you trod the sacred soil for the first time, and it will
then seem almost strange to you to find yourself so
entirely surrounded in all your daily pursuits by the
designs and sounds of religion. Your hotel is a
monastery, your rooms are cells, the landlord is a
stately abbot, and the waiters are hooded monks. If
you walk out of the town you find yourself on the
Mount of Olives, or in the Valley of Jehoshaphat, or
on the Hill of Evil Counsel. If you mount your
horse and extend your rambles you will be guided to
the wilderness of St. John, or the birthplace of our
Saviour. Your club is the great Church of the Holy
Sepulchre, where everybody meets everybody every
day. If you lounge through the town, your Bond
Street is the Via Dolorosa, and the object of your
hopeless affections is some maid or matron all forlorn,
and sadly shrouded in her pilgrim's robe. If you
would hear music, it must be the chanting of friars ; if
you look at pictures, you see virgins with mis-fore-
shortened arms, or devils out of drawing, or angels
tumbling up the skies in impious perspective. If you
would make any purchases, you must go again to the

---

[1] [Kinglake might have added that Mohammedans admit
that Christ worked miracles and was miraculously born of
a virgin. They do not however believe that He was
crucified.]

church doors, and when you inquire for the manufactures of the place, you find that they consist of
double-blessed beads and sanctified shells. These
last are the favourite tokens which the pilgrims carry
off with them. The shell is graven, or rather
scratched, on the white side with a rude drawing of
the Blessed Virgin, or of the Crucifixion, or some other
scriptural subject. Having passed this stage it goes
into the hands of a priest. By him it is subjected to
some process for rendering it efficacious against the
schemes of our ghostly enemy. The manufacture is
then complete, and is deemed to be fit for use.

The village of Bethlehem lies prettily couched on
the slope of a hill. The sanctuary is a subterranean
grotto, and is committed to the joint-guardianship of
the Romans, Greeks, and Armenians, who vie with
each other in adorning it. Beneath an altar gorgeously
decorated, and lit with everlasting fires, there stands
the low slab of stone which marks the holy site of
the Nativity; and near to this is a hollow scooped
out of the living rock. Here the infant Jesus was
laid. Near the spot of the Nativity is the rock
against which the Blessed Virgin was leaning when
she presented her babe to the adoring shepherds.

Many of those Protestants who are accustomed to
despise tradition consider that this sanctuary is altogether unscriptural, that a grotto is not a stable, and
that mangers are made of wood. It is perfectly true,
however, that the many grottoes and caves which are
found among the rocks of Judea were formerly used
for the reception of cattle. They are so used at this
day. I have myself seen grottoes appropriated to this
purpose.

You know what a sad and sombre decorum it is
that outwardly reigns through the lands oppressed by

Moslem sway. Mahometans make beauty their
prisoner, and enforce such a stern and gloomy
morality, or at all events, such a frightfully close
semblance of it, that far and long the wearied
traveller may go without catching one glimpse of
outward happiness. By a strange chance in these
latter days it happened that, alone of all the places in
the land, this Bethlehem, the native village of our
Lord, escaped the moral yoke of the Mussulmans,
and heard again, after ages of dull oppression, the
cheering clatter of social freedom, and the voices of
laughing girls. It was after an insurrection, which
had been raised against the authority of Mehemet Ali,
that Bethlehem was freed from the hateful laws of
Asiatic decorum. The Mussulmans of the village
had taken an active part in the movement, and when
Ibrahim had quelled it, his wrath was still so hot,
that he put to death every one of the few Mahometans
of Bethlehem who had not already fled. The effect
produced upon the Christian inhabitants by the sudden
removal of this restraint was immense. The village
smiled once more. It is true that such sweet freedom
could not long endure. Even if the population of the
place should continue to be entirely Christian, the
sad decorum of the Mussulmans, or rather of the
Asiatics, would sooner or later be restored by the
force of opinion and custom. But for a while the
sunshine would last, and when I was at Bethlehem,
though long after the flight of the Mussulmans, the
cloud of Moslem propriety had not yet come back to
cast its cold shadow upon life. When you reach
that gladsome village, pray Heaven there still may be
heard there the voice of free, innocent girls. It will
sound so dearly welcome!

To a Christian, and thoroughbred Englishman,

not even the licentiousness which generally accom-
panies it can compensate for the oppressiveness of
that horrible outward decorum, which turns the cities
and the palaces of Asia into deserts and gaols. So,
I say, when you see and hear them, those romping
girls of Bethlehem will gladden your very soul.
Distant at first, and then nearer and nearer the timid
flock will gather around you, with their large burning eyes gravely fixed against yours, so that they see
into your brain; and if you imagine evil against
them, they will know of your ill thought before it is
yet well born, and will fly and be gone in the moment.
But presently, if you will only look virtuous enough
to prevent alarm, and vicious enough to avoid looking
silly, the blithe maidens will draw nearer and nearer
to you, and soon there will be one, the bravest of the
sisters, who will venture right up to your side and
touch the hem of your coat, in playful defiance of
the danger, and then the rest will follow the daring
of their youthful leader, and gather close round you,
and hold a shrill controversy on the wondrous formation that you call a hat, and the cunning of the hands
that clothed you with cloth so fine ; and then, growing
more profound in their researches, they will pass
from the study of your mere dress to a serious contemplation of your stately height, and your nut-brown
hair, and the ruddy glow of your English cheeks.
And if they catch a glimpse of your ungloved fingers,
then again will they make the air ring with their
sweet screams of wonder and amazement, as they
compare the fairness of your hand with their warmer
tints, and even with the hues of your own sunburnt
face. Instantly the ringleader of the gentle rioters
imagines a new sin; with tremulous boldness she
touches, then grasps your hand, and smoothes it

gently betwixt her own, and pries curiously into its make and colour, as though it were silk of Damascus, or shawl of Cashmere. And when they see you even then still sage and gentle, the joyous girls will suddenly and screamingly, and all at once, explain to each other that you are surely quite harmless and innocent, a lion that makes no spring, a bear that never hugs, and upon this faith, one after the other, they will take your passive hand, and strive to explain it, and make it a theme and a controversy. But the one, the fairest and the sweetest of all, is yet the most timid; she shrinks from the daring deeds of her playmates, and seeks shelter behind their sleeves, and strives to screen her glowing consciousness from the eyes that look upon her. But her laughing sisters will have none of this cowardice; they vow that the fair one *shall* be their 'complice, *shall* share their dangers, *shall* touch the hand of the stranger; they seize her small wrist, and drag her forward by force, and at last, whilst yet she strives to turn away, and to cover up her whole soul under the folds of downcast eyelids, they vanquish her utmost strength, they vanquish your utmost modesty, and marry her hand to yours. The quick pulse springs from her fingers, and throbs like a whisper upon your listening palm. For an instant her large timid eyes are upon you; in an instant they are shrouded again, and there comes a blush so burning, that the frightened girls stay their shrill laughter, as though they had played too perilously, and harmed their gentle sister. A moment, and all with a sudden intelligence turn away and fly like deer, yet soon again like deer they wheel round and return, and stand, and gaze upon the danger, until they grow brave once more.

" I regret to observe, that the removal of the moral restraint imposed by the presence of the Mahometan inhabitants has led to a certain degree of boisterous, though innocent, levity in the bearing of the Christians, and more especially in the demeanour of those who belong to the younger portion of the female population; but I feel assured that a more thorough knowledge of the principles of their own pure religion will speedily restore these young people to habits of propriety, even more strict than those which were imposed upon them by the authority of their Mahometan brethren."   Bah! thus you might chant, if you chose; but loving the truth, you will not so disown sweet Bethlehem; you will not disown or dissemble your right good hearty delight when you find, as though in a desert, this gushing spring of fresh and joyous girlhood.

CHAPTER XVII

THE DESERT

GAZA is upon the verge of the Desert, to which
it stands in the same relation as a seaport to
the sea. It is there that you *charter* your camels
("the ships of the Desert"), and lay in your stores
for the voyage.

These preparations kept me in the town for some
days. Disliking restraint, I declined making myself
the guest of the Governor (as it is usual and proper
to do), but took up my quarters at the caravanserai,
or "khan," as they call it in that part of Asia.

Dthemetri had to make the arrangements for my
journey, and in order to arm himself with sufficient
authority for doing all that was required, he found it
necessary to put himself in communication with the
Governor. The result of this diplomatic intercourse
was that the Governor, with his train of attendants,
came to me one day at my caravanserai, and formally
complained that Dthemetri had grossly insulted him.
I was shocked at this, for the man was always atten-
tive and civil to me, and I was disgusted at the idea
of his having been rewarded with insult. Dthemetri
was present when the complaint was made, and I
angrily asked him whether it was true that he had
really insulted the Governor, and what the deuce he

meant by it. This I asked with the full certainty
that Dthemetri, as a matter of course, would deny
the charge, would swear that a "wrong construction
had been put upon his words, and that nothing was
further from his thoughts," etc. etc., after the manner
of the parliamentary people, but to my surprise he
very plainly answered that he certainly *had* insulted
the Governor, and that rather grossly, but, he said,
it was quite necessary to do this in order to "strike
terror and inspire respect." "Terror and respect!
What on earth do you mean by that nonsense?"—
"Yes, but without striking terror and inspiring respect,
he (Dthemetri) would never be able to force on the
arrangements for my journey, and vossignoria would
be kept at Gaza for a month!" This would have
been awkward, and certainly I could not deny that
poor Dthemetri had succeeded in his odd plan of
inspiring respect, for at the very time that this explanation was going on in Italian the Governor
seemed more than ever, and more anxiously, disposed
to overwhelm me with assurances of goodwill, and
proffers of his best services. All this kindness, or
promise of kindness, I naturally received with courtesy
—a courtesy that greatly perturbed Dthemetri, for he
evidently feared that my civility would undo all the
good that his insults had achieved.

You will find, I think, that one of the greatest
drawbacks to the pleasure of travelling in Asia is the
being obliged, more or less, to make your way by
bullying. It is true that your own lips are not soiled
by the utterance of all the mean words that are spoken
for you, and that you don't even know of the sham
threats, and the false promises, and the vainglorious
boasts, put forth by your dragoman; but now and
then there happens some incident of the sort which

have just been mentioning, which forces you to believe, or suspect, that your dragoman is habitually fighting your battles for you in a way that you can hardly bear to think of.

A caravanserai is not ill adapted to the purposes for which it is meant. It forms the four sides of a large quadrangular court. The ground floor is used for warehouses, the first floor for guests, and the open court for the temporary reception of the camels, as well as for the loading and unloading of their burthens, and the transaction of mercantile business generally. The apartments used for the guests are small cells opening into a corridor, which runs round the four sides of the court.

Whilst I lay near the opening of my cell looking down into the court below, there arrived from the Desert a caravan, that is, a large assemblage of travellers. It consisted chiefly of Moldavian pilgrims, who to make their good work even more than complete had begun by visiting the shrine of the Virgin in Egypt, and were now going on to Jerusalem. They had been overtaken in the Desert by a gale of wind, which so drove the sand and raised up such mountains before them, that their journey had been terribly perplexed and obstructed, and their provisions including water, the most precious of all) had been exhausted long before they reached the end of their toilsome march. They were sadly wayworn. The arrival of the caravan drew many and various groups into the court. There was the Moldavian pilgrim with his sable dress and cap of fur and heavy masses of bushy hair; the Turk, with his various and brilliant garments; the Arab, superbly stalking under his striped blanket, that hung like royalty upon his stately form; the jetty Ethiopian in his slavish frock;

12

the sleek, smooth-faced scribe with his comely pelisse,
and his silver ink-box stuck in like a dagger at his
girdle. And mingled with these were the camels,
some standing, some kneeling and being unladen,
some twisting round their long necks and gently
stealing the straw from out of their own pack-
saddles.

In a couple of days I was ready to start. The
way of providing for the passage of the Desert is this :
there is an agent in the town who keeps himself in
communication with some of the desert Arabs that
are hovering within a day's journey of the place. A
party of these upon being guaranteed against seizure
or other ill-treatment at the hands of the Governor
come into the town, bringing with them the number
of camels which you require, and then they stipulate
for a certain sum to take you to the place of your
destination in a given time. The agreement which
they thus enter into includes a safe conduct through
their country as well as the hire of the camels.
According to the contract made with me I was to
reach Cairo within ten days from the commencement
of the journey. I had four camels, one for my
baggage, one for each of my servants, and one for
myself. Four Arabs, the owners of the camels, came
with me on foot. My stores were a small soldier's
tent, two bags of dried bread brought from the convent at Jerusalem, and a couple of bottles of wine
from the same source, two goatskins filled with
water, tea, sugar, a cold tongue, and (of all things in
the world) a jar of Irish butter which Mysseri had
purchased from some merchant. There was also a
small sack of charcoal, for the greater part of the
Desert through which we were to pass is destitute
of fuel.

The camel kneels to receive her load, and for a while she will allow the packing to go on with silent resignation; but when she begins to suspect that her master is putting more than a just burthen upon her poor hump she turns round her supple neck and looks sadly upon the increasing load, and then gently remonstrates against the wrong with the sigh of a patient wife. If sighs will not move you, she can weep. You soon learn to pity, and soon to love, her for the sake of her gentle and womanish ways.

You cannot, of course, put an English or any other riding saddle upon the back of a camel, but your quilt or carpet, or whatever you carry for the purpose of lying on at night, is folded and fastened on to the pack-saddle upon the top of the hump, and on this you ride, or rather sit. You sit as a man sits on a chair when he sits astride and faces the back of it. I made an improvement on this plan. I had my English stirrups strapped on to the cross-bars of the pack-saddle, and thus by gaining rest for my dangling legs, and gaining too the power of varying my position more easily than I could otherwise have done, I added very much to my comfort. Don't forget to do as I did.

The camel, like the elephant, is one of the old-fashioned sort of animals that still walk along upon the (now nearly exploded) plan of the ancient beasts that lived before the Flood. She moves forward both her near legs at the same time, and then awkwardly swings round her off shoulder and haunch so as to repeat the manœuvre on that side. Her pace, therefore, is an odd, disjointed and disjoining, sort of movement that is rather disagreeable at first, but you soon grow reconciled to it. The height to which you are raised is of great advantage to you in passing the burning sands of the Desert, for the air at such a distance from the ground is much cooler and more lively than that which circulates beneath.

For several miles beyond Gaza the land, which had been plentifully watered by the rains of the last week, was covered with rich verdure, and thickly jewelled with meadow flowers so fresh and fragrant that I began to grow almost uneasy, to fancy that the very Desert was receding before me, and that the long-desired adventure of passing its " burning sands " was to end in a mere ride across a field. But as I advanced the true character of the country began to display itself with sufficient clearness to dispel my apprehensions, and before the close of my first day's journey I had the gratification of finding that I was surrounded on all sides by a tract of real sand, and had nothing at all to complain of except that there peeped forth at intervals a few isolated blades of grass, and many of those stunted shrubs which are the accustomed food of the camel.

Before sunset I came up with an encampment of Arabs (the encampment from which my camels had been brought), and my tent was pitched amongst theirs. I was now amongst the true Bedouins. Almost every man of this race closely resembles his brethren. Almost every man has large and finely formed features; but his face is so thoroughly stripped of flesh, and the white folds from his headgear fall down by his haggard cheeks so much in the burial fashion, that he looks quite sad and ghastly. His large dark orbs roll slowly and solemnly over the white of his deep-set eyes; his countenance shows painful thought and long-suffering, the suffering of one fallen from a high estate. His gait is strangely majestic, and he marches along with his simple blanket as though he were wearing the purple. His common talk is a series of piercing screams and cries,[1] more painful to the ear than the most excruciating fine music that I ever endured.

The Bedouin women are not treasured up like the wives and daughters of other Orientals, and indeed they seemed almost entirely free from the restraints imposed by jealousy. The feint which they made of concealing their faces from me was always slight. They never, I think, wore the *yashmak* properly fixed. When they first saw me they used to hold up a part of their drapery with one hand across their faces, but they seldom persevered very steadily in subjecting me to this privation. Unhappy beings! they were sadly plain. The awful haggardness that gave something of character to the faces of the men was sheer ugliness in the poor women. It is a great shame, but the truth is 'that, except when we refer to the beautiful devotion of the mother to her child, all the fine things we say and think about women apply only to those who are tolerably good-looking or graceful. These Arab women were so plain and clumsy, that they seemed to me to be fit for nothing but another and a better world. They may have been good women enough so far as relates to the exercise of the minor virtues, but they had so grossly neglected the prime duty of looking pretty in this transitory life, that I could not at all forgive them. They seemed to feel the weight of their guilt, and to be truly and humbly penitent. I had the complete · command of their affections, for at any moment I could make their young hearts bound and their old

---

[1] Milnes cleverly goes to the French for the exact word which conveys the impression produced by the voice of the Arabs, and calls them " un peuple *criard*."

hearts jump by offering a handful of tobacco, and
yet, believe me, it was not in the first *soirée* that my
store of Latakia was exhausted.

The Bedouin women have no religion. This is
partly the cause of their clumsiness. Perhaps if from
Christian girls they would learn how to pray, their
souls might become more gentle, and their limbs be
clothed with grace.

You who are going into their country have a
direct personal interest in knowing something about
"Arab hospitality"; but the deuce of it is, that the
poor fellows with whom I have happened to pitch
my tent were scarcely ever in a condition to exercise
that magnanimous virtue with much *éclat*. Indeed,
Mysseri's canteen generally enabled me to outdo my
hosts in the matter of entertainment. They were
always courteous, however, and were never backward
in offering me the *youart*, a kind of whey, which is
the principal delicacy to be found amongst the
wandering tribes.

Practically, I think, Childe Harold would have
found it a dreadful bore to make "the Desert his
dwelling-place," for at all events, if he adopted the
life of the Arabs he would have tasted no solitude.
The tents are partitioned, not so as to divide the
Childe and the "fair spirit" who is his "minister"
from the rest of the world, but so as to separate the
twenty or thirty brown men that sit screaming in the
one compartment from the fifty or sixty brown
women and children that scream and squeak in the
other. If you adopt the Arab life for the sake of
seclusion you will be horribly disappointed, for you
will find yourself in perpetual contact with a mass of
hot fellow-creatures. It is true that all who are
inmates of the same tent are related to each other,

but I am not quite sure that that circumstance adds much to the charm of such a life. At all events, before you finally determine to become an Arab try a gentle experiment. Take one of those small, shabby houses in Mayfair, and shut yourself up in it with forty or fifty shrill cousins for a couple of weeks in July.

In passing the Desert you will find your Arabs wanting to start and to rest at all sorts of odd times. They like, for instance, to be off at one in the morning, and to rest during the whole of the afternoon. You must not give way to their wishes in this respect. I tried their plan once, and found it very harassing and unwholesome. An ordinary tent can give you very little protection against heat, for the fire strikes fiercely through single canvas, and you soon find that whilst you lie crouching and striving to hide yourself from the blazing face of the sun, his power is harder to bear than it is where you boldly defy him from the airy heights of your camel.

It had been arranged with my Arabs that they were to bring with them all the food which they would want for themselves during the passage of the Desert, but as we rested at the end of the first day's journey by the side of an Arab encampment, my camel men found all that they required for that night in the tents of their own brethren. On the evening of the second day, however, just before we encamped for the night, my four Arabs came to Dthemetri, and formally announced that they had not brought with them one atom of food, and that they looked entirely to my supplies for their daily bread. This was awkward intelligence. We were now just two days deep in the Desert, and I had brought with me no more bread than might be reasonably required for myself and my European attendants. I believed at the moment (for it seemed likely enough) that the men had really mistaken the terms of the arrangement, and feeling that the bore of being put upon half rations would be a less evil (and even to myself a less inconvenience) than the starvation of my Arabs, I at once told Dthemetri to assure them that my bread should be equally shared with all. Dthemetri, however, did not approve of this concession; he assured me quite positively that the Arabs thoroughly understood the agreement, and that if they were now without food they had wilfully brought themselves into this strait for the wretched purpose of bettering their bargain by the value of a few paras' worth of bread. This suggestion made me look at the affair in a new light. I should have been glad enough to put up with the slight privation to which my concession would subject me, and could have borne to witness the semi-starvation of poor Dthemetri with a fine, philosophical calm, but it seemed to me that the scheme, if scheme it were, had something of audacity in it, and was well enough calculated to try the extent of my softness. I well knew the danger of allowing such a trial to result in a conclusion that I was one who might be easily managed; and therefore, after thoroughly satisfying myself from Dthemetri's clear and repeated assertions that the Arabs had really understood the arrangement, I determined that they should not now violate it by taking advantage of my position in the midst of their big Desert, so I desired Dthemetri to tell them that they should touch no bread of mine. We stopped, and the tent was pitched. The Arabs came to me, and prayed loudly for bread. I refused them.

"Then we die!"

" God's will be done ! "

I gave the Arabs to understand that I regretted
their perishing by hunger, but that I should bear this
calmly, like any other misfortune not my own, that,
in short, I was happily resigned to *their* fate. The
men would have talked a great deal, but they were
under the disadvantage of addressing me through a
hostile interpreter; they looked hard upon my face,
but they found no hope there ; so at last they retired
as they pretended, to lay them down and die.

In about ten minutes from this time I found that
the Arabs were busily cooking their bread! Their
pretence of having brought no food was false, and
was only invented for the purpose of saving it. They
had a good bag of meal, which they had contrived
to stow away under the baggage upon one of the
camels in such a way as to escape notice. In Europe
the detection of a scheme like this would have occasioned a disagreeable feeling between the master and
the delinquent, but you would no more recoil from an
Oriental on account of a matter of this sort, than in
England you would reject a horse that had tried, and
failed, to throw you. Indeed, I felt quite good-
humouredly towards my Arabs, because they had so
woefully failed in their wretched attempt, and because, as it turned out, I had done what was right.
They too, poor fellows, evidently began to like me
immensely, on account of the hard-heartedness which
had enabled me to baffle their scheme.

The Arabs adhere to those ancestral principles of
bread-baking which have been sanctioned by the experience of ages. The very first baker of bread that
ever lived must have done his work exactly as the
Arab does at this day. He takes some meal and
holds it out in the hollow of his hands, whilst his

comrade pours over it a few drops of water ; he then mashes up the moistened flour into a paste, which he pulls into small pieces, and thrusts into the embers. His way of baking exactly resembles the craft or mystery of roasting chestnuts as practised by children; there is the same prudence and circumspection in choosing a good berth for the morsel, the same enterprise and self-sacrificing valour in pulling it out with the fingers.

The manner of my daily march was this. At about an hour before dawn I rose and made the most of about a pint of water, which I allowed myself for washing. Then I breakfasted upon tea and bread. As soon as the beasts were loaded I mounted my camel and pressed forward. My poor Arabs, being on foot, would sometimes moan with fatigue and pray for rest; but I was anxious to enable them to perform their contract for bringing me to Cairo within the stipulated time, and I did not therefore allow a halt until the evening came. About midday, or soon after, Mysseri used to bring up his camel alongside of mine, and supply me with a piece of bread softened in water (for it was dried hard like board), and also (as long as it lasted) with a piece of the tongue ; after this there came into my hand (how well I remember it) the little tin cup half-filled with wine and water.

As long as you are journeying in the interior of the Desert you have no particular point to make for as your resting-place. The endless sands yield nothing but small stunted shrubs ; even these fail after the first two or three days, and from that time you pass over broad plains, you pass over newly reared hills, you pass through valleys that the storm of the last week has dug, and the hills and the valleys are sand, sand, sand, still sand, and only sand, and sand and sand again. The earth is so samely that your eyes turn towards heaven—towards heaven, I mean, in the sense of sky. You look to the sun, for he is your taskmaster, and by him you know the measure of the work that you have done, and the measure of the work that remains for you to do. He comes when you strike your tent in the early morning, and then, for the first hour of the day as you move forward on your camel, he stands at your near side and makes you know that the whole day's toil is before you; then for a while, and a long while, you see him no more, for you are veiled and shrouded, and dare not look upon the greatness of his glory, but you know where he strides overhead by the touch of his flaming sword. No words are spoken, but your Arabs moan, your camels sigh, your skin glows, your shoulders ache, and for sights you see the pattern and the web of the silk that veils your eyes and the glare of the outer light. Time labours on; your skin glows and your shoulders ache, your Arabs moan, your camels sigh, and you see the same pattern in the silk, and the same glare of light beyond, but conquering Time marches on, and by and by the descending sun has compassed the heaven, and now softly touches your right arm, and throws your lank shadow over the sand right along on the way to Persia. Then again you look upon his face, for his power is all veiled in his beauty, and the redness of flames has become the redness of roses; the fair, wavy cloud that fled in the morning now comes to his sight once more, comes blushing, yet still comes on, comes burning with blushes, yet hastens and clings to his side.

Then arrives your time for resting. The world

about you is all your own, and there, where you will, you pitch your solitary tent; there is no living thing to dispute your choice. When at last the spot had been fixed upon and we came to a halt, one of the Arabs would touch the chest of my camel and utter at the same time a peculiar gurgling sound. The beast instantly understood and obeyed the sign, and slowly sunk under me till she brought her body to a level with the ground, then gladly enough I alighted. The rest of the camels were unloaded and turned loose to browse upon the shrubs of the desert, where shrubs there were, or where these failed, to wait for the small quantity of food that was allowed them out of our stores.

My servants, helped by the Arabs, busied themselves in pitching the tent and kindling the fire. Whilst this was doing I used to walk away towards the east, confiding in the print of my foot as a guide for my return. Apart from the cheering voices of my attendants I could better know and feel the loneliness of the Desert. The influence of such scenes, however, was not of a softening kind, but filled me rather with a sort of childish exultation in the self-sufficiency which enabled me to stand thus alone in the wideness of Asia — a shortlived pride, for wherever man wanders he still remains tethered by the chain that links him to his kind; and so when the night closed around me I began to return, to return, as it were, to my own gate. Reaching at last some high ground I could see, and see with delight, the fire of our small encampment, and when at last I regained the spot it seemed to me a very home that had sprung up for me in the midst of these solitudes. My Arabs were busy with their bread; Mysseri rattling teacups; the little kettle, with her odd old-maidish looks, sat humming away old songs about England; and two or three yards from the fire my tent stood prim and tight, with open portal, and with welcoming look, like " the old arm-chair " of our lyrist's " sweet Lady Anne."

At the beginning of my journey the night breeze blew coldly; when that happened, the dry sand was heaped up outside round the skirts of the tent, and so the wind, that everywhere else could sweep as he listed along those dreary plains, was forced to turn aside in his course and make way, as he ought, for the Englishman. Then within my tent there were heaps of luxuries — dining-rooms, dressing-rooms, libraries, bedrooms, drawing - rooms, oratories, all crowded into the space of a hearthrug. The first night, I remember, with my books and maps about me, I wanted light; they brought me a taper, and immediately from out of the silent Desert there rushed in a flood of life unseen before. Monsters of moths, of all shapes and hues, that never before perhaps had looked upon the shining of a flame, now madly thronged into my tent, and dashed through the fire of the candle till they fairly extinguished it with their burning limbs. Those who had failed in attaining this martyrdom suddenly became serious, and clung despondingly to the canvas.

By and by there was brought to me the fragrant tea and big masses of scorched and scorching toast, and the butter that had come all the way to me in this Desert of Asia from out of that poor, dear, starving Ireland. I feasted like a king, like four kings, like a boy in the fourth form.

When the cold, sullen morning dawned, and my people began to load the camels, I always felt loath to give back to the waste this little spot of ground that had glowed for a while with the cheerfulness of a human dwelling. One by one the cloaks, the saddles, the baggage, the hundred things that strewed the ground and made it look so familiar—all these were taken away and laid upon the camels. A speck in the broad tracts of Asia remained still impressed with the mark of patent portmanteaus and the heels of London boots; the embers of the fire lay black and cold upon the sand, and these were the signs we left.

My tent was spared to the last, but when all else was ready for the start then came its fall; the pegs were drawn, the canvas shivered, and in less than a minute there was nothing that remained of my genial home but only a pole and a bundle. The encroaching Englishman was off, and instant upon the fall of the canvas, like an owner who had waited and watched, the genius of the Desert stalked in.

To servants, as I suppose of any other Europeans not much accustomed to amuse themselves by fancy or memory, it often happens that after a few days journeying the loneliness of the Desert will become frightfully oppressive. Upon my poor fellows the access of melancholy came heavy, and all at once, as a blow from above ; they bent their necks, and bore it as best they could, but their joy was great on the fifth day when we came to an oasis called Gatieh, for here we found encamped a caravan (that is, an assemblage of travellers) from Cairo. The Orientals living in cities never pass the Desert except in this way ; many will wait for weeks, and even for months, until a sufficient number of persons can be found ready to undertake the journey at the same time— until the flock of sheep is big enough to fancy itself a match for wolves. They could not, I think,

really secure themselves against any serious danger by
this contrivance, for though they have arms, they are
so little accustomed to use them, and so utterly un-
organised, that they never could make good their
resistance to robbers of the slightest respectability.
It is not of the Bedouins that such travellers are
afraid, for the safe conduct granted by the chief of
the ruling tribe is never, I believe, violated, but it is
said that there are deserters and scamps of various
sorts who hover about the skirts of the Desert,
particularly on the Cairo side, and are anxious to
succeed to the property of any poor devils whom
they may find more weak and defenceless than
themselves.

These people from Cairo professed to be amazed
at the ludicrous disproportion between their numerical
forces and mine. They could not understand, and
they wanted to know, by what strange privilege it is
that an Englishman with a brace of pistols and a
couple of servants rides safely across the Desert,
whilst they, the natives of the neighbouring cities, are
forced to travel in troops, or rather in herds. One
of them got a few minutes of private conversation
with Dthemetri, and ventured to ask him anxiously
whether the English did not travel under the protection of evil demons. I had previously known
(from Methley, I think, who had travelled in
Persia) that this notion, so conducive to the safety
of our countrymen, is generally prevalent amongst
Orientals. It owes its origin, partly to the strong
wilfulness of the English gentleman (which not
being backed by any visible authority, either civil or
military, seems perfectly superhuman to the soft
Asiatic), but partly too to the magic of the banking
system, by force of which the wealthy traveller will

make all his journeys without carrying a handful of
coin, and yet when he arrives at a city will rain down
showers of gold. The theory is, that the English
traveller has committed some sin against God and
his conscience, and that for this the evil spirit has
hold of him, and drives him from his home like a
victim of the old Grecian furies, and forces him to
travel over countries far and strange, and most chiefly
over deserts and desolate places, and to stand upon
the sites of cities that once were and are now no
more, and to grope among the tombs of dead men.
Often enough there is something of truth in this
notion; often enough the wandering Englishman is
guilty (if guilt it be) of some pride or ambition, big
or small, imperial or parochial, which being offended
has made the lone place more tolerable than ballrooms to him, a sinner.

I can understand the sort of amazement of the
Orientals at the scantiness of the retinue with which
an Englishman passes the Desert, for I was somewhat struck myself when I saw one of my countrymen making his way across the wilderness in this
simple style. At first there was a mere moving
speck on the horizon. My party of course became all
alive with excitement, and there were many surmises.
Soon it appeared that three laden camels were
approaching, and that two of them carried riders.
In a little while we saw that one of the riders wore
European dress, and at last the travellers were pronounced to be an English gentleman and his servant.
By their side there were a couple, I think, of Arabs
on foot, and this was the whole party.

You, you love sailing; in returning from a cruise
to the English coast you see often enough a fisher-
man's humble boat far away from all shores, with an

ugly black sky above and an angry sea beneath. You watch the grizzly old man at the helm carrying his craft with strange skill through the turmoil of waters, and the boy, supple - limbed, yet weather - worn already, and with steady eyes that look through the blast, you see him understanding commandments from the jerk of his father's white eyebrow, now belaying and now letting go, now scrunching himself down into mere ballast, or baling out death with a pipkin. Stale enough is the sight, and yet when I see it I always stare anew, and with a kind of Titanic exultation, because that a poor boat with the brain of a man and the hands of a boy on board can match herself so bravely against black heaven and ocean. Well, so when you have travelled for days and days over an Eastern desert without meeting the likeness of a human being, and then at last see an English shooting-jacket and his servant come listlessly slouching along from out of the forward horizon, you stare at the wide unproportion between this slender company and the boundless plains of sand through which they are keeping their way.

This Englishman, as I afterwards found, was a military man returning to his country from India, and crossing the Desert at this part in order to go through Palestine. As for me, I had come pretty straight from England, and so here we met in the wilderness at about half-way from our respective starting-points. As we approached each other it became with me a question whether we should speak. I thought it likely that the stranger would accost me, and in the event of his doing so I was quite ready to be as sociable and chatty as I could be according to my nature ; but still I could not think of anything particular that I had to say to him. Of course, among civilised

people the not having anying to say is no excuse at all
for not speaking, but I was shy and indolent, and I felt
no great wish to stop and talk like a morning visitor
in the midst of those broad solitudes. The traveller
perhaps felt as I did, for except that we lifted our
hands to our caps and waved our arms in courtesy,
we passed each other as if we had passed in Bond
Street. Our attendants, however, were not to be
cheated of the delight that they felt in speaking to
new listeners and hearing fresh voices once more.
The masters, therefore, had no sooner passed each
other than their respective servants quietly stopped
and entered into conversation. As soon as my
camel found that her companions were not following
her she caught the social feeling and refused to go
on. I felt the absurdity of the situation, and determined to accost the stranger if only to avoid the
awkwardness of remaining stuck fast in the Desert
whilst our servants were amusing themselves. When
with this intent I turned round my camel I found
that the gallant officer who had passed me by about
thirty or forty yards was exactly in the same pre-
dicament as myself. I put my now willing camel in
motion and rode up towards the stranger, who seeing
this followed my example and came forward to meet
me. He was the first to speak. He was much too
courteous to address me as if he admitted the possibility of my wishing to accost him from any feeling
of mere sociability or civillian-like love of vain talk.
On the contrary, he at once attributed my advances
to a laudable wish of acquiring statistical information,
and accordingly, when we got within speaking
distance, he said, " I daresay you wish to know how
the plague is going on at Cairo ? " And then he
went on to say, he regretted that his information did

not enable him to give me in numbers a perfectly accurate statement of the daily deaths. He afterwards talked pleasantly enough upon other and less ghastly subjects. I thought him manly and intelligent, a worthy one of the few thousand strong Englishmen to whom the empire of India is committed.

The night after the meeting with the people of the caravan, Dthemetri, alarmed by their warnings, took upon himself to keep watch all night in the tent. No robbers came except a jackal, that poked his nose into my tent from some motive of rational curiosity. Dthemetri did not shoot him for fear of waking me. These brutes swarm in every part of Syria, and there were many of them even in the midst of the void sands that would seem to give such poor promise of food. I can hardly tell what prey they could be hoping for, unless it were that they might find now and then the carcass of some camel that had died on the journey. They do not marshal themselves into great packs like the wild dogs of Eastern cities, but follow their prey in families, like the place-hunters of Europe. Their voices are frightfully like to the shouts and cries of human beings. If you lie awake in your tent at night you are almost continually hearing some hungry family as it sweeps along in full cry. You hear the exulting scream with which the sagacious dam first winds the carrion, and the shrill response of the unanimous cubs as they sniff the tainted air, "Wha! wha! wha! wha! wha! wha! Whose gift is it in, mamma?"

Once during this passage my Arabs lost their way among the hills of loose sand that surrounded us, but after a while we were lucky enough to recover our right line of march. The same day we fell in with

a Sheik, the head of a family, that actually dwells at
no great distance from this part of the Desert during
nine months of the year. The man carried a match-
lock, of which he was very proud. We stopped and
sat down and rested a while for the sake of a little
talk. There was much that I should have liked to
ask this man, but he could not understand Dthemetri's
language, and the process of getting at his knowledge
by double interpretation through my Arabs was
unsatisfactory. I discovered, however (and my
Arabs knew of that fact), that this man and his
family lived habitually for nine months of the year
without touching or seeing either bread or water.
The stunted shrub growing at intervals through the
sand in this part of the Desert enables the camel
mares to yield a little milk, which furnishes the sole
food and drink of their owner and his people. During
the other three months (the hottest of the months, I
suppose) even this resource fails, and then the Sheik
and his people are forced to pass into another district.
You would ask me why the man should not remain
always in that district which supplies him with water
during three months of the year, but I don't know
enough of Arab politics to answer the question. The
Sheik was not a good specimen of the effect produced
by the diet to which he is subjected. He was very
small, very spare, and sadly shrivelled, a poor, over-
roasted snipe, a mere cinder of a man. I made him
sit down by my side, and gave him a piece of bread
and a cup of water from out of my goatskins. This
was not very tempting drink to look at, for it had
become turbid, and was deeply reddened by some
colouring matter contained in the skins, but it kept
its sweetness, and tasted like a strong decoction of
Russia leather. The Sheik sipped this, drop by drop,

with ineffable relish, and rolled his eyes solemnly round between every draught, as though the drink were the drink of the Prophet, and had come from the seventh heaven.

An inquiry about distances led to the discovery that this Sheik had never heard of the division of time into hours; my Arabs themselves, I think, were rather surprised at this.

About this part of my journey I saw the likeness of a fresh-water lake. I saw, as it seemed, a broad sheet of calm water, that stretched far and fair towards the south, stretching deep into winding creeks, and hemmed in by jutting promontories, and shelving smooth off towards the shallow side. On its bosom the reflected fire of the sun lay playing, and seeming to float upon waters deep and still.

Though I knew of the cheat, it was not till the spongy foot of my camel had almost trodden in the seeming waters that I could undeceive my eyes, for the shore-line was quite true and natural. I soon saw the cause of the phantasm. A sheet of water heavily impregnated with salts had filled this great hollow, and when dried up by evaporation had left a white saline deposit, that exactly marked the space which the waters had covered, and thus sketched a good shore-line. The minute crystals of the salt sparkled in the sun, and so looked like the face of a lake that is calm and smooth.

The pace of the camel is irksome, and makes your shoulders and loins ache from the peculiar way in which you are obliged to suit yourself to the movements of the beast, but you soon, of course, become inured to this, and after the first two days this way of travelling became so familiar to me, that (poor sleeper as I am) I now and then slumbered for some

moments together on the back of my camel. On the
fifth day of my journey the air above lay dead, and
all the whole earth that I could reach with my
utmost sight and keenest listening was still and
lifeless as some dispeopled and forgotten world that
rolls round and round in the heavens through wasted
floods of light. The sun, growing fiercer and fiercer,
shone down more mightily now than ever on me he
shone before, and as I dropped my head under his
fire, and closed my eyes against the glare that
surrounded me, I slowly fell asleep, for how many
minutes or moments I cannot tell, but after a while I
was gently awakened by a peal of church bells, my
native bells, the innocent bells of Marlen, that never
before sent forth their music beyond the Blaygon
hills! My first idea naturally was that I still
remained fast under the power of a dream. I roused
myself and drew aside the silk that covered my eyes,
and plunged my bare face into the light. Then at
least I was well enough wakened, but still those old
Marlen bells rung on, not ringing for joy, but properly,
prosily, steadily, merrily ringing "for church."
After a while the sound died away slowly. It
happened that neither I nor any of my party had a
watch by which to measure the exact time of its lasting, but it seemed to me that about ten minutes had
passed before the bells ceased. I attributed the
effect to the great heat of the sun, the perfect dryness
of the clear air through which I moved, and the deep
stillness of all around me. It seemed to me that
these causes, by occasioning a great tension, and
consequent susceptibility, of the hearing organs, had
rendered them liable to tingle under the passing touch
of some mere memory that must have swept across
my brain in a moment of sleep. Since my return to

England it has been told me that like sounds have been heard at sea, and that the sailor becalmed under a vertical sun in the midst of the wide ocean has listened in trembling wonder to the chime of his own village bells.

At this time I kept a poor shabby pretence of a journal, which just enabled me to know the day of the month and the week according to the European calendar, and when in my tent at night I got out my pocket-book I found that the day was Sunday, and roughly allowing for the difference of time in this longitude, I concluded that at the moment of my hearing that strange peal the church-going bells of Marlen must have been actually calling the prim congregation of the parish to morning prayer. The coincidence amused me faintly, but I could not pluck up the least hope that the effect which I had experienced was anything other than an illusion, an illusion liable to be explained (as every illusion is in these days) by some of the philosophers who guess at Nature's riddles. It would have been sweeter to believe that my kneeling mother by some pious enchantment had asked, and found, this spell to rouse me from my scandalous forgetfulness of God's holy day, but my fancy was too weak to carry a faith like that. Indeed, the vale through which the bells of Marlen send their song is a highly respectable vale, and its people (save one, two, or three) are wholly unaddicted to the practice of magical arts.

After the fifth day of my journey I no longer travelled over shifting hills, but came upon a dead level, a dead level bed of sand, quite hard, and studded with small shining pebbles.

The heat grew fierce; there was no valley nor hollow, no hill, no mound, no shadow of hill nor of mound, by which I could mark the way I was making. Hour by hour I advanced, and saw no change—I was still the very centre of a round horizon; hour by hour I advanced, and still there was the same, and the same, and the same—the same circle of flaming sky—the same circle of sand still glaring with light and fire. Over all the heaven above, over all the earth beneath, there was no visible power that could balk the fierce will of the sun: "he rejoiced as a strong man to run a race; his going forth was from the end of the heaven, and his circuit unto the ends of it; and there was nothing hid from the heat thereof." From pole to pole, and from the east to the west, he brandished his fiery sceptre as though he had usurped all heaven and earth. As he bid the soft Persian in ancient times, so now, and fiercely too, he bid me bow down and worship him; so now in his pride he seemed to command me, and say, "Thou shalt have none other gods but me." I was all alone before him. There were these two pitted together, and face to face—the mighty sun for one, and for the other this poor, pale, solitary self of mine, that I always carry about with me.

But on the eighth day, and before I had yet turned away from Jehovah for the glittering god of the Persians, there appeared a dark line upon the edge of the forward horizon, and soon the line deepened into a delicate fringe, that sparkled here and there as though it were sewn with diamonds. There, then, before me were the gardens and the minarets of Egypt and the mighty works of the Nile, and I (the eternal Ego that I am!)—I had lived to see, and I saw them.

When evening came I was still within the confines of the Desert, and my tent was pitched as usual; but one of my Arabs stalked away rapidly towards the west, without telling me of the errand on which he was bent. After a while he returned ; he had toiled on a graceful service ; he had travelled all the way on to the border of the living world, and brought me back for token an ear of rice, full, fresh, and green.

The next day I entered upon Egypt, and floated along (for the delight was as the delight of bathing) through green wavy fields of rice, and pastures fresh and plentiful, and dived into the cold verdure of groves and gardens, and quenched my hot eyes in shade, as though in deep, rushing waters.

CHAPTER XVIII

CAIRO AND THE PLAGUE [1]

CAIRO and plague ! During the whole time of my stay the plague was so master of the city, and showed itself so staringly in every street and every alley, that I can't now affect to dissociate the two ideas.

[1] There is some semblance of bravado in my manner of talking about the plague. I have been more careful to describe the terrors of other people than my own. The truth is, that during the whole period of my stay at Cairo I remained thoroughly impressed with a sense of my danger. I may almost say, that I lived in perpetual apprehension, for even in sleep, as I fancy, there remained with me some faint notion of the peril with which I was encompassed. But fear does not necessarily damp the spirits; on the contrary, it will often operate as an excitement, giving rise to unusual animation, and thus it affected me. If I had not been surrounded at this time by new faces, new scenes, and new sounds, the effect produced upon my mind by one unceasing cause of alarm might have been very different. As it was, the eagerness with which I pursued my rambles among the wonders of Egypt was sharpened and increased by the sting of the fear of death. Thus my account of the matter plainly conveys an impression that I remained at Cairo without losing my cheerfulness and buoyancy of spirits. And this is the truth, but it is also true, as I have freely confessed, that my sense of danger during the whole period was lively and continuous.

When coming from the Desert I rode through a village which lies near to the city on the eastern side, there approached me with busy face and earnest gestures a personage in the Turkish dress. His long flowing beard gave him rather a majestic look, but his briskness of manner, and his visible anxiety to accost me, seemed strange in an Oriental. The man in fact was French, or of French origin, and his object was to warn me of the plague, and prevent me from entering the city.

"Arrêtez-vous, monsieur, je vous en prie—arrêtez-vous; il ne faut pas entrer dans la ville; la peste y règne partout."

"Oui, je sais,[1] mais——"

"Mais monsieur, je dis la peste—la peste; c'est de LA PESTE qu'il est question."

"Oui, je sais, mais——"

"Mais monsieur, je dis encore LA PESTE—LA PESTE. Je vous conjure de ne pas entrer dans la ville—vous seriaz dans une ville empestée."

"Oui, je sais, mais——"

"Mais monsieur, je dois donc vous avertir tout bonnement que si vous entrez dans la ville, vous serez —enfin vous serez COMPROMIS!"[2]

"Oui, je sais, mais——"

---

[1] Anglicé for "je le sais." These answers of mine, as given above, are not meant as specimens of mere French, but of that fine, terse, nervous, *Continental English* with which I and my compatriots make our way through Europe. This language, by the by, is one possessing great force and energy, and is not without its literature, a literature of the very highest order. Where will you find more sturdy specimens of downright, honest, and noble English than in the Duke of Wellington's "French" despatches?

[2] The import of the word "compromised," when used in reference to contagion, is explained on page 18.

The Frenchman was at last convinced that it was
vain to reason with a mere Englishman, who could
not understand what it was to be "compromised."
I thanked him most sincerely for his kindly meant
warning; in hot countries it is very unusual indeed
for a man to go out in the glare of the sun and give
free advice to a stranger.

When I arrived at Cairo I summoned Osman
Effendi, who was, as I knew, the owner of several
houses, and would be able to provide me with apartments.   He had no difficulty in doing this, for there
was not one European traveller in Cairo besides
myself.   Poor Osman! he met me with a sorrowful
countenance, for the fear of the plague sat heavily on
his soul.   He seemed as if he felt that he was doing
wrong in lending me a resting-place, and he betrayed
such a listlessness about temporal matters, as one
might look for in a man who believed that his days
were numbered.   He caught me too soon after my
arrival coming out from the public baths,[1] and from
that time forward he was sadly afraid of me, for he
shared the opinions of Europeans with respect to the
effect of contagion.

Osman's history is a curious one.   He was a
Scotchman born, and when very young, being then a
drummer-boy, he landed in Egypt with Fraser's
force.   He was taken prisoner, and according to
Mahometan custom, the alternative of death or the
Koran was offered to him ; he did not choose death,

---

[1] It is said, that when a Mussulman finds himself
attacked by the plague he goes and takes a bath.   The
couches on which the bathers recline would carry infection,
according to the notions of the Europeans.   Whenever,
therefore, I took the bath at Cairo (except the first time of
my doing so) I avoided that part of the luxury which consists in being "put up to dry" upon a kind of bed.

and therefore went through the ceremonies which
were necessary for turning him into a good Mahometan.
But what amused me most in his history was this,
that very soon after having embraced Islam he was
obliged in practice to become curious and discriminat-
ing in his new faith, to make war upon Mahometan
dissenters, and follow the orthodox standard of the
Prophet in fierce campaigns against the Wahabees,[1]
who are the Unitarians of the Mussulman world.
The Wahabees were crushed, and Osman returning
home in triumph from his holy wars, began to flourish
in the world. He acquired property, and became
effendi, or gentleman. At the time of my visit to
Cairo he seemed to be much respected by his brother
Mahometans, and gave pledge of his sincere alienation
from Christianity by keeping a couple of wives. He
affected the same sort of reserve in mentioning them
as is generally shown by Orientals. He invited me,
indeed, to see his harem, but he made both his wives
bundle out before I was admitted. He felt, as it
seemed to me, that neither of them would bear
criticism, and I think that this idea, rather than any
motive of sincere jealousy, induced him to keep them
out of sight. The rooms of the harem reminded me
of an English nursery rather than of a Mahometan
paradise. One is apt to judge of a woman before
one sees her by the air of elegance or coarseness with
which she surrounds her home ; I judged Osman's
wives by this test, and condemned them both. But
the strangest feature in Osman's character was his
inextinguishable nationality. In vain they had
brought him over the seas in early boyhood ; in vain
had he suffered captivity, conversion, circumcision ;
in vain they had passed him through fire in their

[1] [See footnote, Introduction, p. xxi.]

Arabian campaigns, they could not cut away or burn out poor Osman's inborn love of all that was Scotch; in vain men called him Effendi; in vain he swept along in Eastern robes; in vain the rival wives adorned his harem: the joy of his heart still plainly lay in this, that he had three shelves of books, and that the books were thoroughbred Scotch — the Edinburgh this, the Edinburgh that, and above all, I recollect, he prided himself upon the "Edinburgh Cabinet Library."

The fear of the plague is its forerunner. It is likely enough that at the time of my seeing poor Osman the deadly taint was beginning to creep through his veins, but it was not till after I had left Cairo that he was visibly stricken. He died.

As soon as I had seen all that I wanted to see in Cairo and in the neighbourhood I wished to make my escape from a city that lay under the terrible curse of the plague, but Mysseri fell ill, in consequence, I believe, of the hardships which he had been suffering in my service. After a while he recovered sufficiently to undertake a journey, but then there was some difficulty in procuring beasts of burthen, and it was not till the nineteenth day of my sojourn that I quitted the city.

During all this time the power of the plague was rapidly increasing. When I first arrived, it was said that the daily number of "accidents" by plague, out of a population of about two hundred thousand, did not exceed four or five hundred, but before I went away the deaths were reckoned at twelve hundred a day. I had no means of knowing whether the numbers (given out, as I believe they were, by officials) were at all correct, but I could not help knowing that from day to day the number of the dead was increasing. My quarters were in a street which was one of the chief thoroughfares of the city. The funerals in Cairo take place between daybreak and noon, and as I was generally in my rooms during this part of the day, I could form some opinion as to the briskness of the plague. I don't mean this for a sly insinuation that I got up every morning with the sun. It was not so; but the funerals of most people in decent circumstances at Cairo are attended by singers and howlers, and the performances of these people woke me in the early morning, and prevented me from remaining in ignorance of what was going on in the street below.

These funerals were very simply conducted. The bier was a shallow wooden tray, carried upon a light and weak wooden frame. The tray had, in general, no lid, but the body was more or less hidden from view by a shawl or scarf. The whole was borne upon the shoulders of men, who contrived to cut along with their burthen at a great pace. Two or three singers generally preceded the bier; the howlers (who are paid for their vocal labours) followed after, and last of all came such of the dead man's friends and relations as could keep up with such a rapid procession; these, especially the women, would get terribly blown, and would straggle back into the rear; many were fairly " beaten off." I never observed any appearance of mourning in the mourners: the pace was too severe for any solemn affectation of grief.[1]

---

[1] [Mohammedans commonly believe that the souls of the dead do not rest in peace till their bodies are laid in the tomb. Hence they bury the corpse as quickly as possible, and run to the cemetery in order to shorten the interval during which the departed spirit is kept waiting. After

When first I arrived at Cairo the funerals that daily passed under my windows were many, but still there were frequent and long intervals without a single howl. Every day, however (except one, when I fancied that I observed a diminution of funerals), these intervals became less frequent and shorter, and at last, the passing of the howlers from morn till noon was almost incessant. I believe that about one-half of the whole people was carried off by this visitation. The Orientals, however, have more quiet fortitude than Europeans under afflictions of this sort, and they never allow the plague to interfere with their religious usages. I rode one day round the great burial-ground. The tombs are strewed over a great expanse, among the vast mountains of rubbish (the accumulations of many centuries) which surround the city. The ground, unlike the Turkish "cities of the dead," which are made so beautiful by their dark cypresses, has nothing to sweeten melancholy, nothing to mitigate the odiousness of death. Carnivorous beasts and birds possess the place by night, and now in the fair morning it was all alive with fresh comers—alive with dead. Yet at this very time, when the plague was raging so furiously, and on this very ground, which resounded so mournfully with the howls of arriving funerals, preparations were going on for the religious festival called the Kourban Bairam. Tents were pitched, and *swings hung for the amusement of children*—a

a few brief prayers at the graveside, the mourners retire forty paces, halt, and pray again. It is believed that at this moment two angels visit the deceased, inquire of his religious belief, and, if he replies in the words of the formula, that there is "no God but God, and Mohammed is the Prophet of God," admit him, not exactly to Paradise, but to a very tolerable section of Purgatory.]

ghastly holiday; but the Mahometans take a pride,
and a just pride, in following their ancient customs
undisturbed by the shadow of death.

I did not hear, whilst I was at Cairo, that any
prayer for a remission of the plague had been offered
up in the mosques. I believe that however frightful
the ravages of the disease may be, the Mahometans
refrain from approaching Heaven with their com-
plaints until the plague has endured for a long space,
and then at last they pray God, not that the plague
may cease, but that it may go to another city!

A good Mussulman seems to take pride in repudiating the European notion that the will of God can
be eluded by eluding the touch of a sleeve. When I
went to see the pyramids of Sakkara I was the guest
of a noble old fellow, an Osmanlee, whose soft rolling
language it was a luxury to hear after suffering, as I
had suffered of late, from the shrieking tongue of the
Arabs. This man was aware of the European ideas
about contagion, and his first care therefore was to
assure me that not a single instance of plague had
occurred in his village. He then inquired as to the
progress of the plague at Cairo. I had but a bad
account to give. Up to this time my host had carefully refrained from touching me out of respect to
the European theory of contagion, but as soon as
it was made plain that he, and not I, would be the
person endangered by contact, he gently laid his hand
upon my arm, in order to make me feel sure that the
circumstance of my coming from an infected city did
not occasion him the least uneasiness. In that touch
there was true hospitality.

Very different is the faith and the practice of
the Europeans, or rather, I mean of the Europeans
settled in the East, and commonly called Levantines.

14

When I came to the end of my journey over the Desert I had been so long alone, that the prospect of speaking to somebody at Cairo seemed almost a new excitement. I felt a sort of consciousness that I had a little of the wild beast about me, but I was quite in the humour to be charmingly tame, and to be quite engaging in my manners, if I should have an opportunity of holding communion with any of the human race whilst at Cairo. I knew no one in the place, and had no letters of introduction, but I carried letters of credit, and it often happens in places remote from England that those "advices" operate as a sort of introduction, and obtain for the bearer (if disposed to receive them) such ordinary civilities as it may be in the power of the banker to offer.

Very soon after my arrival I went to the house of the Levantine to whom my credentials were addressed. At his door several persons (all Arabs) were hanging about and keeping guard. It was not till after some delay, and the passing of some communications with those in the interior of the citadel, that I was admitted. At length, however, I was conducted through the court, and up a flight of stairs, and finally into the apartment where business was transacted. The room was divided by an excellent, substantial fence of iron bars, and behind this grille the banker had his station. The truth was, that from fear of the plague he had adopted the course usually taken by European residents, and had shut himself up "in strict quarantine"—that is to say, that he had, as he hoped, cut himself off from all communication with infecting substances. The Europeans long resident in the East, without any, or with scarcely any, exception, are firmly convinced that the plague is propagated by contact, and by

contact only; that if they can but avoid the touch
of an infecting substance they are safe, and that if
they cannot, they die. This belief induces them to
adopt the contrivance of putting themselves in that
state of siege which they call "quarantine." It is
a part of their faith that metals, and hempen rope,
and also, I fancy, one or two other substances, will
not carry the infection; and they likewise believe
that the germ of pestilence, which lies in an infected
substance, may be destroyed by submersion in water,
or by the action of smoke. They therefore guard
the doors of their houses with the utmost care
against intrusion, and condemn themselves, with all
the members of their family, including any European
servants, to a strict imprisonment within the walls
of their dwelling. Their native attendants are not
allowed to enter at all, but they make the necessary
purchases of provisions, which are hauled up through
one of the windows by means of a rope, and are then
soaked in water.

I knew nothing of these mysteries, and was not
therefore prepared for the sort of reception which I
met with. I advanced to the iron fence, and putting
my letter between the bars, politely proffered it to
Mr. Banker. Mr. Banker received me with a sad
and dejected look, and not "with open arms," or
with any arms at all, but with—a pair of tongs!
I placed my letter between the iron fingers, which
picked it up as if it were a viper, and conveyed it
away to be scorched and purified by fire and smoke.
I was disgusted at this reception, and at the idea
that anything of mine could carry infection to the
poor wretch who stood on the other side of the
grille, pale and trembling, and already meet for
death. I looked with something of the Mahometan's

feeling upon these little contrivances for eluding fate ; and in this instance, at least, they were vain. A few more days, and the poor money-changer, who had striven to guard the days of his life (as though they were coins) with bolts and bars of iron—he was seized by the plague, and he died.

To people entertaining such opinions as these respecting the fatal effect of contact, the narrow and crowded streets of Cairo were terrible as the easy slope that leads to Avernus. The roaring ocean and the beetling crags owe something of their sublimity to this—that if they be tempted, they can take the warm life of a man. To the contagionist, filled as he is with the dread of final causes, having no faith in destiny nor in the fixed will of God, and with none of the devil-may-care indifference which might stand him instead of creeds—to such one, every rag that shivers in the breeze of a plague-stricken city has this sort of sublimity. If by any terrible ordinance he be forced to venture forth, he sees death dangling from every sleeve, and as he creeps forward, he poises his shuddering limbs between the imminent jacket that is stabbing at his right elbow and the murderous pelisse that threatens to mow him clean down as it sweeps along on his left. But most of all, he dreads that which most of all he should love—the touch of a woman's dress ; for mothers and wives, hurrying forth on kindly errands from the bedsides of the dying, go slouching along through the streets more wilfully and less courteously than the men. For a while it may be that the caution of the poor Levantine may enable him to avoid contact, but sooner or later perhaps the dreaded chance arrives ; that bundle of linen, with the dark tearful eyes at the top of it, that labours along with the voluptuous clumsiness of Grisi

—she has touched the poor Levantine with the hem of her sleeve! From that dread moment his peace is gone; his mind, for ever hanging upon the fatal touch, invites the blow which he fears. He watches for the symptoms of plague so carefully, that sooner or later they come in truth. The parched mouth is a sign—his mouth *is* parched; the throbbing brain— his brain *does* throb; the rapid pulse—he touches his own wrist (for he dares not ask counsel of any man lest he be deserted), he touches his wrist, and feels how his frighted blood goes galloping out of his heart; there is nothing but the fatal swelling that is wanting to make his sad conviction complete; immediately he has an odd feel under the arm—no pain, but a little straining of the skin; he would to God it were his fancy that were strong enough to give him that sensation. This is the worst of all; it now seems to him that he could be happy and contented with his parched mouth and his throbbing brain and his rapid pulse, if only he could know that there were no swelling under the left arm; but dare he try?—In a moment of calmness and deliberation he dares not, but when for a while he has writhed under the torture of suspense, a sudden strength of will drives him to seek and know his fate. He touches the gland, and finds the skin sane and sound, but under the cuticle there lies a small lump like a pistol-bullet, that moves as he pushes it. Oh! but is this for all certainty, is this the sentence of death? Feel the gland of the other arm; there is not the same lump exactly, yet something a little like it: have not some people glands naturally enlarged?— would to Heaven he were one! So he does for himself the work of the plague, and when the Angel of Death, thus courted, does indeed and in truth come, he has only to finish that which has been so well begun; he passes his fiery hand over the brain of the victim, and lets him rave for a season, but all chance-wise, of people and things once dear, or of people and things indifferent. Once more the poor fellow is back at his home in fair Provence, and sees the sun-dial that stood in his childhood's garden; sees part of his mother, and the long-since-forgotten face of that little dead sister (he sees her, he says, on a Sunday morning, for all the church bells are ringing); he looks up and down through the universe, and owns it well piled with bales upon bales of cotton, and cotton eternal—so much so that he feels, he knows, he swears he could make that winning hazard, if the billiard table would not slant upwards, and if the cue were a cue worth playing with; but it is not—it's a cue that won't move—his own arm won't move—in short, there's the devil to pay in the brain of the poor Levantine, and perhaps the next night but one he becomes the " life and the soul " of some squalling jackal family who fish him out by the foot from his shallow and sandy grave.

Better fate was mine. By some happy perverseness (occasioned perhaps by my disgust at the notion of being received with a pair of tongs) I took it into my pleasant head that all the European notions about contagion were thoroughly unfounded; that the plague might be providential or " epidemic " (as they phrase it), but was not contagious; and that I could not be killed by the touch of a woman's sleeve, nor yet by her blessed breath. I therefore determined that the plague should not alter my habits and amusements in any one respect. Though I came to this resolve from impulse, I think that I took the course which was in effect the most prudent, for the cheer-

fulness of spirits which I was thus enabled to retain
discouraged the yellow-winged angel, and prevented
him from taking a shot at me. I, however, so far
respected the opinion of the Europeans, that I
avoided touching when I could do so without privation or inconvenience. This endeavour furnished
me with a sort of amusement as I passed through
the streets. The usual mode of moving from place
to place in the city of Cairo is upon donkeys, of
which great numbers are always in readiness, with
donkey-boys attached. I had two who constantly
(until one of them died of the plague) waited at my
door upon the chance of being wanted. I found this
way of moving about exceedingly pleasant, and never
attempted any other. I had only to mount my beast,
and tell my donkey-boy the point for which I was
bound, and instantly I began to glide on at a capital
pace. The streets of Cairo are not paved in any
way, but strewed with a dry sandy soil, so deadening
to sound, that the footfall of my donkey could
scarcely be heard. There is no *trottoir*, and as you
ride through the streets you mingle with the people
on foot. Those who are in your way, upon being
warned by the shouts of the donkey-boy, move very
slightly aside, so as to leave you a narrow lane,
through which you pass at a gallop. In this way
you glide on delightfully in the very midst of crowds,
without being inconvenienced or stopped for a
moment. It seems to you that it is not the donkey
but the donkey-boy who wafts you on with his
shouts through pleasant groups, and air that feels
thick with the fragrance of burial spice. "Eh!
Sheik, Eh! Bint,—reggalek,—shumalek," etc.
etc.—O old man, O virgin, get out of the way on the
right—O virgin, O old man, get out of way on the

left—this Englishman comes, he comes, he comes ! "
The narrow alley which these shouts cleared for my
passage made it possible, though difficult, to go on
for a long way without touching a single person, and
my endeavours to avoid such contact were a sort of
game for me in my loneliness, which was not without
interest. If I got through a street without being
touched, I won ; if I was touched, I lost—lost a
deuce of stake, according to the theory of the
Europeans ; but that I deemed to be all nonsense—
I only lost that game, and would certainly win the
next.

There is not much in the way of public buildings
to admire at Cairo, but I saw one handsome mosque,
to which an instructive history is attached. A
Hindustanee merchant having amassed an immense
fortune settled in Cairo, and soon found that his
riches in the then state of the political world gave
him vast power in the city—power, however, the
exercise of which was much restrained by the
counteracting influence of other wealthy men. With
a view to extinguish every attempt at rivalry the
Hindustanee merchant built this magnificent mosque
at his own expense. When the work was complete,
he invited all the leading men of the city to join him
in prayer within the walls of the newly built temple,
and he then caused to be massacred all those who
were sufficiently influential to cause him any jealousy
or uneasiness—in short, all "the respectable men" of
the place ; after this he possessed undisputed power
in the city and was greatly revered—he is revered to
this day. It seemed to me that there was a touching
simplicity in the mode which this man so successfully
adopted for gaining the confidence and goodwill of
his fellow-citizens. There seems to be some im-

probability in the story (though not nearly so gross as it might appear to an European ignorant of the East, for witness Mehemet Ali's destruction of the Mamelukes, a closely similar act, and attended with the like brilliant success [1]), but even if the story be false as a mere fact, it is perfectly true as an illustration —it is a true exposition of the means by which the respect and affection of Orientals may be conciliated.

I ascended one day to the citadel, which commands a superb view of the town. The fanciful and elaborate gilt-work of the many minarets gives a light and florid grace to the city as seen from this height, but before you can look for many seconds at such things your eyes are drawn westward — drawn westward and over the Nile, till they rest upon the massive enormities of the Ghizeh Pyramids.

I saw within the fortress many yoke of men all haggard and woebegone, and a kennel of very fine lions well fed and flourishing : I say *yoke* of men, for the poor fellows were working together in bonds ; I say a *kennel* of lions, for the beasts were not enclosed in cages, but simply chained up like dogs.

I went round the bazaars : it seemed to me that pipes and arms were cheaper here than at Constantinople, and I should advise you therefore if you go to both places to prefer the market of Cairo. I had previously bought several of such things at Constantinople, and did not choose to encumber myself, or to speak more honestly, I did not choose to disencumber my purse by making any more purchases. In the open slave-market I saw about

[1] Mehemet Ali invited the Mamelukes. to a feast, and murdered them whilst preparing to enter the banquet hall.

fifty girls exposed for sale, but all of them black, or
"invisible" brown. A slave agent took me to
some rooms in the upper storey of the building, and
also into several obscure houses in the neigbourhood,
with a view to show me some white women. The
owners raised various objections to the display of
their ware, and well they might, for I had not
the least notion of purchasing; some refused on
account of the illegality of the proceeding,[1] and
others declared that all transactions of this sort were
completely out of the question as long as the plague
was raging. I only succeeded in seeing one white
slave who was for sale, but on this one the owner
affected to set an immense value, and raised my
expectations to a high pitch by saying that the girl
was Circassian, and was "fair as the full moon."
After a good deal of delay I was at last led into
a room, at the farther end of which was that mass of
white linen which indicates an Eastern woman. She
was bid to uncover her face, and I presently saw
that, though very far from being good-looking,
according to my notion of beauty, she had not been
inaptly described by the man who compared her
to the full moon, for her large face was perfectly
round and perfectly white. Though very young,
she was nevertheless extremely fat. She gave me
the idea of having been got up for sale, of having
been fattened and whitened by medicines or by some
peculiar diet. I was firmly determined not to see
any more of her than the face. She was perhaps
disgusted at this my virtuous resolve, as well as
with my personal appearance ; perhaps she saw my
distaste and disappointment ; perhaps she wished to
gain favour with her owner by showing her attachment

[1] It is not strictly lawful to sell *white* slaves to a Christian.

to his faith : at all events, she holloaed out very lustily and very decidedly that " she would not be bought by the infidel."

Whilst I remained at Cairo I thought it worth while to see something of the magicians, because I considered that these men were in some sort the descendants of those who contended so stoutly against the superior power of Aaron. I therefore sent for an old man who was held to be the chief of the magicians, and desired him to show me the wonders of his art. The old man looked and dressed his character exceedingly well ; the vast turban, the flowing beard, and the ample robes were all that one could wish in the way of appearance. The first experiment (a very stale one) which he attempted to perform for me was that of showing the forms and faces of my absent friends, not to me, but to a boy brought in from the streets for the purpose, and said to be chosen at random. A *mangale* (pan of burning charcoal) was brought into my room, and the magician bending over it, sprinkled upon the fire some substances which must have consisted partly of spices or sweetly burning woods, for immediately a fragrant smoke arose that curled around the bending form of the wizard, the while that he pronounced his first incantations. When these were over the boy was made to sit down, and a common green shade was bound over his brow ; then the wizard took ink, and still continuing his incantations, wrote certain mysterious figures upon the boy's palm, and directed him to rivet his attention to these marks without looking aside for an instant. Again the incantations proceeded, and after a while the boy, being seemingly a little agitated, was asked whether he saw anything on the palm of his hand. He declared that he saw a kind of military procession, with flags and banners, which he described rather minutely. I was then called upon to name the absent person whose form was to be made visible. I named Keate. You were not at Eton, and I must tell you, therefore, what manner of man it was that I named, though I think you must have some idea of him already, for wherever from utmost Canada to Bundelcund — wherever there was the whitewashed wall of an officer's room, or of any other apartment in which English gentlemen are forced to kick their heels, there likely enough (in the days of his reign) the head of Keate would be seen scratched or drawn with those various degrees of skill which one observes in the representations of saints. Anybody without the least notion of drawing could still draw a speaking, nay scolding, likeness of Keate. If you had no pencil, you could draw him well enough with a poker, or the leg of a chair, or the smoke of a candle. He was little more (if more at all) than five feet in height, and was not very great in girth, but in this space was concentrated the pluck of ten battalions. He had a really noble voice, which he could modulate with great skill, but he had also the power of quacking like an angry duck, and he almost always adopted this mode of communication in order to inspire respect. He was a capital scholar, but his ingenuous learning had *not* " softened his manners " and *had* " permitted them to be fierce " —tremendously fierce ; he had the most complete command over his temper — I mean over his *good* temper, which he scarcely ever allowed to appear : you could not put him out of humour— that is, out of the *ill*-humour which he thought to be fitting for a headmaster. His red shaggy

eyebrows were so prominent, that he habitually used
them as arms and hands for the purpose of pointing
out any object towards which he wished to direct
attention; the rest of his features were equally
striking in their way, and were all and all his own;
he wore a fancy-dress partly resembling the costume
of Napoleon, and partly that of a widow-woman. I
could not by any possibility have named anybody
more decidedly differing in appearance from the rest
of the human race.

"Whom do you name?" — "I name John
Keate."—"Now, what do you see?" said the
wizard to the boy.—"I see," answered the boy,
"I see a fair girl with golden hair, blue eyes, pallid
face, rosy lips." *There* was a shot! I shouted out
my laughter to the horror of the wizard, who perceiving the grossness of his failure, declared that
the boy must have known sin (for none but the
innocent can see truth), and accordingly kicked him
downstairs.

One or two other boys were tried, but none could
"see truth"; they all made sadly "bad shots."

Notwithstanding the failure of these experiments,
I wished to see what sort of mummery my magician
would practise if I called upon him to show me some
performances of a higher order than those which had
been attempted. I therefore entered into a treaty
with him, in virtue of which he was to descend with
me into the tombs near the Pyramids, and there
evoke the devil. The negotiation lasted some time,
for Dthemetri, as in duty bound, tried to beat down
the wizard as much as he could, and the wizard, on
his part, manfully stuck up for his price, declaring
that to raise the devil was really no joke, and insinuating that to do so was an awesome crime. I let

Dthemetri have his way in the negotiation, but I felt in reality very indifferent about the sum to be paid, and for this reason, namely, that the payment (except a very small present which I might make or not, as I chose) was to be *contingent on success.* At length the bargain was made, and it was arranged that after a few days, to be allowed for preparation, the wizard should raise the devil for two pounds ten, play or pay —no devil, no piastres.

The wizard failed to keep his appointment. I sent to know why the deuce he had not come to raise the devil. The truth was, that my Mahomet had gone to the mountain. The plague had seized him, and he died.

Although the plague had now spread terrible havoc around me, I did not see very plainly any corresponding change in the looks of the streets until the seventh day after my arrival. I then first observed that the city was *silenced.* There were no outward signs of despair nor of violent terror, but many of the voices that had swelled the busy hum of men were already hushed in death, and the survivors, so used to scream and screech in their earnestness whenever they bought or sold, now showed an unwonted indifference about the affairs of this world : it was less worth while for men to haggle and haggle, and crack the sky with noisy bargains, when the great commander was there, who could " pay all their debts with the roll of his drum."

At this time I was informed that of twenty-five thousand people at Alexandria, twelve thousand had died already ; the destroyer had come rather later to Cairo, but there was nothing of weariness in his strides. The deaths came faster than ever they befell in the plague of London ; but the calmness of

Orientals under such visitations, and the habit of using biers for interment, instead of burying coffins along with the bodies, rendered it practicable to dispose of the dead in the usual way, without shocking the people by any unaccustomed spectacle of horror. There was no tumbling of bodies into carts, as in the plague of Florence and the plague of London. Every man, according to his station, was properly buried, and that in the usual way, except that he went to his grave in a more hurried pace than might have been adopted under ordinary circumstances.

The funerals which poured through the streets were not the only public evidence of deaths. In Cairo this custom prevails: At the instant of a man's death (if his property is sufficient to justify the expense) professional howlers are employed. I believe that these persons are brought near to the dying man when his end appears to be approaching, and the moment that life is gone they lift up their voices and send forth a loud wail from the chamber of death. Thus I knew when my near neighbours died; sometimes the howls were near, sometimes more distant. Once I was awakened in the night by the wail of death in the next house, and another time by a like howl from the house opposite; and there were two or three minutes, I recollect, during which the howl seemed to be actually *running* along the street.

I happened to be rather teased at this time by a sore throat, and I thought it would be well to get it cured if I could before I again started on my travels. I therefore inquired for a Frank doctor, and was informed that the only one then at Cairo was a young Bolognese refugee, who was so poor that he had not

been able to take flight, as the other medical men
had done. At such a time as this it was out of the
question to *send* for a European physician ; a person
thus summoned would be sure to suppose that the
patient was ill of the plague, and would decline to
come. I therefore rode to the young doctor's
residence. After experiencing some little difficulty
in finding where to look for him, I ascended a flight
or two of stairs and knocked at his door. No one
came immediately, but after some little delay the
medico himself opened the door, and admitted me.
I of course made him understand that I had come to
consult him, but before entering upon my throat
grievance I accepted a chair, and exchanged a
sentence or two of commonplace conversation. Now
the natural commonplace of the city at this season
was of a gloomy sort, "Come va la peste?"
(how goes the plague?) and this was precisely the
question I put. A deep sigh, and the words, " Sette
cento per giorno, signor " (seven hundred a day),
pronounced in a tone of the deepest sadness and
dejection, were the answer I received. The day
was not oppressively hot, yet I saw that the doctor
was perspiring profusely, and even the outside surface
of the thick shawl dressing-gown, in which he had
wrapped himself, appeared to be moist. He was a
handsome, pleasant - looking young fellow, but the
deep melancholy of his tone did not tempt me to
prolong the conversation, and without further delay I
requested that my throat might be looked at. The
medico held my chin in the usual way, and examined
my throat. He then wrote me a prescription, and
almost immediately afterwards I bade him farewell,
but as he conducted me towards the door I observed
an expression of strange and unhappy watchfulness in

his rolling eyes. It was not the next day, but the next day but one, if I rightly remember, that I sent to request another interview with my doctor. In due time Dthemetri, who was my messenger, returned, looking sadly aghast—he had "*met* the medico," for so he phrased it, "coming out from his house—in a bier!"

It was of course plain that when the poor Bolognese was looking at my throat, and almost mingling his breath with mine, he was stricken of the plague. I suppose that the violent sweat in which I found him had been produced by some medicine, which he must have taken in the hope of curing himself. The peculiar rolling of the eyes which I had remarked is, I believe, to experienced observers, a pretty sure test of the plague. A Russian acquaintance of mine, speaking from the information of men who had made the Turkish campaigns of 1828 and 1829, told me that by this sign the officers of Sabalkansky's force were able to make out the plague-stricken soldiers with a good deal of certainty.

It so happened that most of the people with whom I had anything to do during my stay at Cairo were seized with plague, and all these died. Since I had been for a long time *en route* before I reached Egypt, and was about to start again for another long journey over the Desert, there were of course many little matters touching my wardrobe and my travelling equipments which required to be attended to whilst I remained in the city. It happened so many times that Dthemetri's orders in respect to these matters were frustrated by the deaths of the tradespeople and others whom he employed, that at last I became quite accustomed to the peculiar manner which he assumed when he prepared to announce a new death

15

to me. The poor fellow naturally supposed that I
should feel some uneasiness at hearing of the
" accidents " which happened to persons employed
by me, and he therefore communicated their deaths
as though they were the deaths of friends. He
would cast down his eyes and look like a man
abashed, and then gently, and with a mournful
gesture, allow the words, " Morto, signor," to come
through his lips. I don't know how many of such
instances occurred, but they were several, and besides
these (as I told you before), my banker, my doctor,
my landlord, and my magician all died of the plague.
A lad who acted as a helper in the house which I
occupied lost a brother and a sister within a few
hours. Out of my two established donkey-boys,
one died. I did not hear of any instance in which a
plague-stricken patient had recovered.

Going out one morning I met unexpectedly the
scorching breath of the kamsin wind, and fearing that I
should faint under the horrible sensations which it
caused, I returned to my rooms. Reflecting, however, that I might have to encounter this wind in the
Desert, where there would be no possibility of
avoiding it, I thought it would be better to brave it
once more in the city, and to try whether I could
really bear it or not. I therefore mounted my ass
and rode to old Cairo, and along the gardens by the
banks of the Nile. The wind was hot to the touch
as though it came from a furnace. It blew strongly,
but yet with such perfect steadiness, that the trees
bending under its force remained fixed in the same
curves without perceptibly waving. The whole sky
was obscured by a veil of yellowish grey, that shut
out the face of the sun. The streets were utterly
silent, being indeed almost entirely deserted; and

not without cause, for the scorching blast, whilst it
fevers the blood, closes up the pores of the skin, and
is terribly distressing, therefore, to every animal that
encounters it. I returned to my rooms dreadfully ill.
My head ached with a burning pain, and my pulse
bounded quick and fitfully, but perhaps (as in the
instance of the poor Levantine, whose death I was
mentioning) the fear and excitement which I felt in
trying my own wrist may have made my blood flutter
the faster.

It is a thoroughly well believed theory, that during
the continuance of the plague you can't be ill of any
other febrile malady—an unpleasant privilege that!
for ill I was, and ill of fever, and I anxiously wished
that the ailment might turn out to be anything rather
than plague. I had some right to surmise that my
illness may have been merely the effect of the hot
wind; and this notion was encouraged by the
elasticity of my spirits, and by a strong forefeeling
that much of my destined life in this world was yet
to come, and yet to be fulfilled. That was my
instinctive belief, but when I carefully weighed the
probabilities on the one side and on the other, I
could not help seeing that the strength of argument
was all against me. There was a strong antecedent
likelihood in *favour* of my being struck by the same
blow as the rest of the people who had been dying
around me. Besides, it occurred to me that, after
all, the universal opinion of the Europeans upon a
medical question, such as that of contagion, might
probably be correct, and *if it were*, I was so
thoroughly "compromised," and especially by the
touch and breath of the dying medico, that I had no
right to expect any other fate than that which now
seemed to have overtaken me. Balancing as well as

I could all the considerations which hope and fear suggested, I slowly and reluctantly came to the conclusion that, according to all merely reasonable probability, the plague had come upon me.

You would suppose that this conviction would have induced me to write a few farewell lines to those who were dearest, and that having done that, I should have turned my thoughts towards the world to come. Such, however, was not the case. I believe that the prospect of death often brings with it strong anxieties about matters of comparatively trivial import, and certainly with me the whole energy of the mind was directed towards the one petty object of concealing my illness until the latest possible moment—until the delirious stage. I did not believe that either Mysseri or Dthemetri, who had served me so faithfully in all trials, would have deserted me (as most Europeans are wont to do) when they knew that I was stricken by plague, but I shrank from the idea of putting them to this test, and I dreaded the consternation which the knowledge of my illness would be sure to occasion.

I was very ill indeed at the moment when my dinner was served, and my soul sickened at the sight of the food; but I had luckily the habit of dispensing with the attendance of servants during my meal, and as soon as I was left alone I made a melancholy calculation of the quantity of food which I should have eaten if I had been in my usual health, and filled my plates accordingly, and gave myself salt, and so on, as though I were going to dine. I then transferred the viands to a piece of the omnipresent *Times* newspaper, and hid them away in a cupboard, for it was not yet night, and I dared not throw the food into the street until darkness came. I did not at all relish this process of fictitious dining, but at length the cloth was removed, and I gladly reclined on my divan (I would not lie down) with the *Arabian Nights* in my hand.

I had a feeling that tea would be a capital thing for me, but I would not order it until the usual hour. When at last the time came, I drank deep draughts from the fragrant cup. The effect was almost instantaneous. A plenteous sweat burst through my skin, and watered my clothes through and through. I kept myself thickly covered. The hot, tormenting weight which had been loading my brain was slowly heaved away. The fever was extinguished. I felt a new buoyancy of spirits, and an unusual activity of mind. I went into my bed under a load of thick covering, and when the morning came, and I asked myself how I was, I found that I was thoroughly well.

I was very anxious to procure, if possible, some medical advice for Mysseri, whose illness prevented my departure. Every one of the European practising doctors, of whom there had been many, had either died or fled. It was said, however, that there was an Englishman in the medical service of the Pasha who quietly remained at his post, but that he never engaged in private practice. I determined to try if I could obtain assistance in this quarter. I did not venture at first, and at such a time as this, to ask him to visit a servant who was prostrate on the bed of sickness, but thinking that I might thus gain an opportunity of persuading him to attend Mysseri, I wrote a note mentioning my own affair of the sore throat, and asking for the benefit of his medical advice. He instantly followed back my messenger, and was at once shown up into my room. I entreated him to stand off, telling him fairly how deeply I was " compromised," and especially by my contact with a person actually ill and since dead of plague. The generous fellow, with a good-humoured laugh at the terrors of the contagionists, marched straight up to me, and forcibly seized my hand, and shook it with manly violence. I felt grateful indeed, and swelled with fresh pride of race because that my countryman could carry himself so nobly. He soon cured Mysseri as well as me, and all this he did from no other motives than the pleasure of doing a kindness and the delight of braving a danger.

At length the great difficulty [1] which I had had in procuring beasts for my departure was overcome, and now, too, I was to have the new excitement of travelling on dromedaries. With two of these beasts and three camels I gladly wound my way from out of the pest-stricken city. As I passed through the streets I observed a fanatical - looking elder, who stretched forth his arms, and lifted up his voice in a speech which seemed to have some reference to me. Requiring an interpretation, I found that the man had said, " The Pasha seeks camels, and he finds them not ; the Englishman says, ' Let camels be brought,' and behold, there they are ! "

I no sooner breathed the free, wholesome air of the Desert than I felt that a great burden which I had been scarcely conscious of bearing was lifted away from my mind. For nearly three weeks I had lived under peril of death ; the peril ceased, and not till then did I know how much alarm and anxiety I had really been suffering.

[1] The difficulty was occasioned by the immense exertions which the Pasha was making to collect camels for military purposes.

CHAPTER XIX

THE PYRAMIDS

I WENT to see and to explore the Pyramids.

Familiar to one from the days of early childhood are the forms of the Egyptian Pyramids, and now, as I approached them from the banks of the Nile, I had no print, no picture before me, and yet the old shapes were there; there was no change; they were just as I had always known them. I straightened myself in my stirrups, and strived to persuade my understanding that this was real Egypt, and that those angles which stood up between me and the West were of harder stuff, and more ancient than the paper pyramids of the green portfolio. Yet it was not till I came to the base of the great Pyramid that reality began to weigh upon my mind. Strange to say, the bigness of the distinct blocks of stones was the first sign by which I attained to feel the immensity of the whole pile. When I came, and trod, and touched with my hands, and climbed, in order that by climbing I might come to the top of one single stone, then, and almost suddenly, a cold sense and understanding of the Pyramid's enormity came down, overcasting my brain.

Now try to endure this homely, sick-nursish illustration of the effect produced upon one's mind by the mere vastness of the great Pyramid. When I was very young (between the ages, I believe, of three and five years old), being then of delicate health, I was often in time of night the victim of a strange kind of mental oppression. I lay in my bed perfectly conscious, and with open eyes, but without power to speak or to move, and all the while my brain was oppressed to distraction by the presence of a single and abstract idea, the idea of solid immensity. It seemed to me in my agonies that the horror of this visitation arose from its coming upon me without form or shape, that the close presence of the direst monster ever bred in hell would have been a thousand times more tolerable than that simple idea of solid size. My aching mind was fixed and riveted down upon the mere quality of vastness, vastness, vastness, and was not permitted to invest with it any particular object. If I could have done so, the torment would have ceased. When at last I was roused from this state of suffering, I could not of course in those days (knowing no verbal metaphysics, and no metaphysics at all, except by the dreadful experience of an abstract idea)—I could not of course find words to describe the nature of my sensations, and even now I cannot explain why it is that the forced contemplation of a mere quality, distinct from matter, should be so terrible. Well, now my eyes saw and knew, and my hands and my feet informed my understanding that there was nothing at all abstract about the great Pyramid—it·was a big triangle, sufficiently concrete, easy to see, and rough to the touch; it could not, of course, affect me with the peculiar sensation which I have been talking of, but yet there was something akin to that old nightmare agony in the terrible completeness with which a mere mass of masonry could fill and load my mind.

And Time too; the remoteness of its origin, no less than the enormity of its proportions, screens an Egyptian Pyramid from the easy and familiar contact of our modern minds; at its base the common earth ends, and all above is a world—one not created of God, not seeming to be made by men's hands, but rather the sheer giant-work of some old dismal age weighing down this younger planet.

Fine sayings! but the truth seems to be after all, that the Pyramids are quite of this world; that they were piled up into the air for the realisation of some kingly crotchets about immortality, some priestly longing for burial fees; and that as for the building, they were built like coral rocks by swarms of insects —by swarms of poor Egyptians, who were not only the abject tools and slaves of power, but who also ate onions for the reward of their immortal labours! [1] The Pyramids are quite of this world.

I of course ascended to the summit of the great Pyramid, and also explored its chambers, but these I need not describe. The first time that I went to the Pyramids of Ghizeh there were a number of Arabs hanging about in its neighbourhood, and wanting to receive presents on various pretences; their Sheik was with them. There was also present an ill-looking fellow in soldier's uniform. This man on my departure claimed a reward, on the ground that he had maintained order and decorum amongst the Arabs. His claim was not considered valid by my dragoman, and was rejected accordingly. My

[1] Herodotus, in an after age, stood by with his note-book, and got, as he thought, the exact returns of all the rations served out.

donkey-boys afterwards said they had overheard this fellow propose to the Sheik to put me to death whilst I was in the interior of the great Pyramid, and to share with him the booty. Fancy a struggle for life in one of those burial chambers, with acres and acres of solid masonry between one's self and the daylight! I felt exceedingly glad that I had not made the rascal a present.

I visited the very ancient Pyramids of Aboukir and Sakkara. There are many of these, and of various shapes and sizes, and it struck me that, taken together, they might be considered as showing the progress and perfection (such as it is) of pyramidical architecture. One of the Pyramids at Sakkara is almost a rival for the full-grown monster at Ghizeh; others are scarcely more than vast heaps of brick and stone : these last suggested to me the idea that after all the Pyramid is nothing more nor less than a variety of the sepulchral mound so common in most countries (including, I believe, Hindustan, from whence the Egyptians are supposed to have come). Men accustomed to raise these structures for their dead kings or conquerors would carry the usage with them in their migrations, but arriving in Egypt, and seeing the impossibility of finding earth sufficiently tenacious for a mound, they would approximate as nearly as might be to their ancient custom by raising up a round heap of stones—in short, conical pyramids. Of these there are several at Sakkara, and the materials of some are thrown together without any order or regularity. The transition from this simple form to that of the square angular pyramid was easy and natural, and it seemed to me that the gradations through which the style passed from infancy up to its mature enormity could plainly be traced at Sakkara.

CHAPTER XX

THE SPHINX

AND near the Pyramids, more wondrous and more awful than all else in the land of Egypt, there sits the lonely Sphinx. Comely the creature is, but the comeliness is not of this world. The once worshipped beast is a deformity and a monster to this generation; and yet you can see that those lips, so thick and heavy, were fashioned according to some ancient mould of beauty—some mould of beauty now forgotten—forgotten because that Greece drew forth Cytherea from the flashing foam of the Ægean, and in her image created new forms of beauty, and made it a law among men that the short and proudly wreathed lip should stand for the sign and the main condition of loveliness through all generations to come. Yet still there lives on the race of those who were beautiful in the fashion of the elder world, and Christian girls of Coptic blood will look on you with the sad, serious gaze, and kiss you your charitable hand with the big pouting lips of the very Sphinx.

Laugh and mock if you will at the worship of stone idols, but mark ye this, ye breakers of images, that in one regard the stone idol bears awful semblance of Deity—unchangefulness in the midst of change; the same seeming will, and intent for ever, and ever inexorable! Upon ancient dynasties of Ethiopian and Egyptian kings; upon Greek, and Roman; upon Arab and Ottoman conquerors; upon Napoleon dreaming of an Eastern Empire; upon battle and pestilence; upon the ceaseless misery of the Egyptian race; upon keen-eyed travellers—Herodotus yesterday, and Warburton[1] to-day: upon all and more, this unworldly Sphinx has watched, and watched like a Providence with the same earnest eyes, and the same sad, tranquil mien. And we, we shall die, and Islam will wither away, and the Englishman, leaning far over to hold his loved India, will plant a firm foot on the banks of the Nile, and sit in the seats of the Faithful, and still that sleepless rock will lie watching, and watching the works of the new, busy race with those same sad, earnest eyes, and the same tranquil mien everlasting. You dare not mock at the Sphinx.

[1] [The author of the *Crescent and the Cross*, which appeared the same year as *Eothen*.]

CHAPTER XXI

THE "dromedary" of Egypt and Syria is not the two - humped animal described by that name in books of natural history, but is, in fact, of the same family as the camel, to which it stands in about the same relation as a racer to a cart-horse. The fleetness and endurance of this creature are extraordinary. It is not usual to force him into a gallop, and I fancy from his make that it would be quite impossible for him to maintain that pace for any length of time ; but the animal is on so large a scale, that the jogtrot at which he is generally ridden implies a progress of perhaps ten or twelve miles an hour, and this pace, it is said, he can keep up incessantly, without food, or water, or rest, for three whole days and nights.

Of the two dromedaries which I had obtained for this journey, I mounted one myself, and put Dthemetri on the other. My plan was to ride on with Dthemetri to Suez as rapidly as the fleetness of the beasts would allow, and to let Mysseri (who was still weak from the effects of his late illness) come quietly on with the camels and baggage.

The trot of the dromedary is a pace terribly disagreeeble to the rider, until he becomes a little accustomed to it ; but after the first half-hour I so far schooled myself to this new exercise, that I felt capable of keeping it up (though not without aching limbs) for several hours together. Now, therefore, I was anxious to dart forward, and annihilate at once the whole space that divided me from the Red Sea. Dthemetri, however, could not get on at all. Every attempt which he made to trot seemed to threaten the utter dislocation of his whole frame, and indeed I doubt whether anyone of Dthemetri's age (nearly forty, I think), and unaccustomed to such exercise, could have borne it at all easily; besides, the dromedary which fell to his lot was evidently a very bad one ; he every now and then came to a dead stop, and coolly knelt down, at though suggesting that the rider had better get off at once and abandon the attempt as one that was utterly hopeless.

When for the third or fourth time I saw Dthemetri thus planted, I lost my patience, and went on without him. For about two hours, I think, I advanced without once looking behind me. I then paused, and cast my eyes back to the western horizon. There was no sign of Dthemetri, nor of any other living creature. This I expected, for I knew that I must have far out-distanced all my followers. I had ridden away from my party merely by way of gratifying my impatience, and with the intention of stopping as soon as I felt tired, until I was overtaken. I now observed, however (this I had not been able to do whilst advancing so rapidly), that the track which I had been following was seemingly the track of only one or two camels. I did not fear that I had diverged very largely from the true route, but still I could not feel any reasonable certainty that my party would follow any line of march within sight of me.

I had to consider, therefore, whether I should remain where I was, upon the chance of seeing my people come up, or whether I would push on alone, and find my way to Suez. I had now learned that I could not rely upon the continued guidance of any track, but I knew that (if maps were right) the point for which I was bound bore just due east of Cairo, and I thought that, although I might miss the line leading most directly to Suez, I could not well fail to find my way sooner or later to the Red Sea. The worst of it was that I had no provision of food or water with me, and already I was beginning to feel thirst. I deliberated for a minute, and then determined that I would abandon all hope of seeing my party again in the Desert, and would push forward as rapidly as possible towards Suez.

It was not, I confess, without a sensation of awe that I swept with my sight the vacant round of the horizon, and remembered that I was all alone, and unprovisioned in the midst of the arid waste; but this very awe gave tone and zest to the exultation with which I felt myself launched. Hitherto, in all my wandering, I had been under the care of other people—sailors, Tatars, guides, and dragomen had watched over my welfare, but now at last I was here in this African desert, and I *myself, and no other, had charge of my life.* I liked the office well. I had the greatest part of the day before me, a very fair dromedary, a fur pelisse, and a brace of pistols, but no bread and no water; for that I must ride—and ride I did.

For several hours I urged forward my beast at a rapid though steady pace, but now the pangs of thirst began to torment me. I did not relax my pace, however, and I had not suffered long when a moving object appeared in the distance before me. The intervening space was soon traversed, and I found myself approaching a Bedouin Arab mounted on a camel, attended by another Bedouin on foot. They stopped. I saw that, as usual, there hung from the pack-saddle of the camel a large skin water-flask, which seemed to be well filled. I steered my dromedary close up alongside of the mounted Bedouin, caused my beast to kneel down, then alighted, and keeping the end of the halter in my hand, went up to the mounted Bedouin without speaking, took hold of his water-flask, opened it, and drank long and deep from its leathern lips. Both of the Bedouins stood fast in amazement and mute horror; and really, if they had never happened to see a European before, the apparition was enough to startle them. To see for the first time a coat and a waistcoat, with the semblance of a white human head at the top, and for this ghastly figure to come swiftly out of the horizon upon a fleet dromedary, approach them silently and with a demoniacal smile, and drink a deep draught from their water-flask—this was enough to make the Bedouins stare a little; they, in fact, stared a great deal—not as Europeans stare, with a restless and puzzled expression of countenance, but with features all fixed and rigid, and with still, glassy eyes. Before they had time to get decomposed from their state of petrifaction I had remounted my dromedary, and was darting away towards the east.

Without pause or remission of pace I continued to press forward, but after a while I found to my confusion that the slight track which had hitherto guided me now failed altogether. I began to fear that I must have been all along following the course of some wandering Bedouins, and I felt that if this were the case, my fate was a little uncertain.

I had no compass with me, but I determined upon the eastern point of the horizon as accurately as I could by reference to the sun, and so laid down for myself a way over the pathless sands.

But now my poor dromedary, by whose life and strength I held my own, began to show signs of distress; a thick, clammy, and glutinous kind of foam gathered about her lips, and piteous sobs burst from her bosom in the tones of human misery. I doubted for a moment whether I would give her a little rest, a relaxation of pace, but I decided that I would not, and continued to push forward as steadily as before.

The character of the country became changed. I had ridden away from the level tracts, and before me now, and on either side, there were vast hills of sand and calcined rocks, that interrupted my progress and baffled my doubtful road, but I did my best. With rapid steps I swept round the base of the hills, threaded the winding hollows, and at last, as I rose in my swift course to the crest of a lofty ridge, Thalatta! Thalatta! by Jove! I saw the sea!

My tongue can tell where to find a clue to many an old pagan creed, because that (distinctly from all mere admiration of the beauty belonging to Nature's works) I acknowledge a sense of mystical reverence when first I look, to see some illustrious feature of the globe—some coastline of ocean, some mighty river or dreary mountain range, the ancient barrier of kingdoms. But the Red Sea! It might well claim my earnest gaze by force of the great Jewish migration which connects it with the history of our

16

own religion. From this very ridge, it is likely enough, the panting Israelites first saw that shining inlet of the sea. Ay! ay! but moreover, and best of all, that beckoning sea assured my eyes, and proved how well I had marked out the east for my path, and gave me good promise that sooner or later the time would come for me to rest and drink. It was distant, the sea, but I felt my own strength, and I had *heard* of the strength of dromedaries. I pushed forward as eagerly as though I had spoiled the Egyptians and were flying from Pharaoh's police.

I had not yet been able to discover any symptoms of Suez, but after a while I descried in the distance a large, blank, isolated building. I made towards this, and in time got down to it. The building was a fort, and had been built there for the protection of a well which it contained within its precincts. A cluster of small huts adhered to the fort, and in a short time I was receiving the hospitality of the inhabitants, who were grouped upon the sands near their hamlet. To quench the fires of my throat with about a gallon of muddy water, and to swallow a little of the food placed before me, was the work of a few minutes, and before the astonishment of my hosts had even begun to subside, I was pursuing my onward journey. Suez, I found, was still three hours distant, and the sun going down in the west warned me that I must find some other guide to keep me in the right direction. This guide I found in the most fickle and uncertain of the elements. For some hours the wind had been freshening, and it now blew a violent gale; it blew not fitfully and in squalls, but with such remarkable steadiness that I felt convinced it would blow from the same quarter for several hours. When the sun set, therefore, I carefully looked for the point from which the wind was blowing, and found that it came from the very west, and was blowing exactly in the direction of my route. I had nothing to do, therefore, but to go straight to leeward; and this was not difficult, for the gale blew with such immense force, that if I diverged at all from its line I instantly felt the pressure of the blast on the side towards which I was deviating. Very soon after sunset there came on complete darkness, but the strong wind guided me well, and sped me, too, on my way.

I had pushed on for about, I think, a couple of hours after nightfall, when I saw the glimmer of a light in the distance, and this I ventured to hope must be Suez. Upon approaching it, however, I found that it was only a solitary fort, and I passed on without stopping.

On I went, still riding down the wind, when an unlucky accident occurred, for which, if you like, you can have your laugh against me. I have told you already what sort of lodging it is that you have upon the back of a camel. You ride the dromedary in the same fashion; you are perched rather than seated on a bunch of carpets or quilts upon the summit of the hump. It happened that my dromedary veered rather suddenly from her onward course. Meeting the movement, I mechanically turned my left wrist as though I were holding a bridle-rein, for the complete darkness prevented my eyes from reminding me that I had nothing but a halter in my hand. The expected resistance failed, for the halter was hanging upon that side of the dromedary's neck towards which I was slightly leaning. I toppled over, head foremost, and then went falling and falling through air, till my crown came whang against the ground. And the ground too was perfectly hard (compacted sand), but the thickly-wadded headgear which I wore for protection against the sun saved my life. The notion of my being able to get up again after falling head-foremost from such an immense height seemed to me at first too paradoxical to be acted upon, but I soon found that I was not a bit hurt. My dromedary utterly vanished. I looked round me, and saw the glimmer of a light in the fort which I had lately passed, and I began to work my way back in that direction. The violence of the gale made it hard for me to force my way towards the west, but I succeeded at last in regaining the fort. To this, as to the other fort which I had passed, there was attached a cluster of huts, and I soon found myself surrounded by a group of villainous, gloomy - looking fellows. It was a horrid bore for me to have to swagger and look big at a time when I felt so particularly small on account of my tumble and my lost dromedary ; but there was no help for it, I had no Dthemetri now to " strike terror " for me. I knew hardly one word of Arabic, but somehow or other I contrived to announce it as my absolute will and pleasure that these fellows should find me the means of gaining Suez. They acceded, and having a donkey, they saddled it for me, and appointed one of their number to attend me on foot.

I afterwards found that these fellows were not Arabs, but Algerine refugees, and that they bore the character of being sad scoundrels. They justified this imputation to some extent on the following day. They allowed Mysseri with my baggage and the camels to pass unmolested, but an Arab lad belonging to the party happened to lag a little way in the rear, and him (if they were not maligned) these rascals stripped and robbed. Low indeed is the state of bandit morality when men will allow the sleek traveller with well-laden camels to pass in quiet, reserving their spirit of enterprise for the tattered turban of a miserable boy.

I reached Suez at last. The British agent, though roused from his midnight sleep, received me in his home with the utmost kindness and hospitality. Oh! by Jove, how delightful it was to lie on fair sheets, and to dally with sleep, and to wake, and to sleep, and to wake once more, for the sake of sleeping again!

CHAPTER XXII

I WAS hospitably entertained by the British consul, or agent, as he is there styled. He is the *employé* of the East India Company, and not of the Home Government. Napoleon during his stay of five days at Suez had been the guest of the consul's father, and I was told that the divan in my apartment had been the bed of the great commander.

There are two opinions as to the point at which the Israelites passed the Red Sea. One is, that they traversed only the very small creek at the northern extremity of the inlet, and that they entered the bed of the water at the spot on which Suez now stands; the other, that they crossed the sea from a point eighteen miles down the coast. The Oxford theologians, who, with Milman their professor,[1] believe that Jehovah conducted His chosen people without disturbing the order of nature, adopt the first view, and suppose that the Israelites passed during an ebb-tide, aided by a violent wind. One among many objections to this supposition is, that the time of a single ebb would not have been sufficient for the passage of that vast multitude of men and beasts, or even for a small fraction of it. Moreover, the

[1] See Milman's *History of the Jews*, first edition.

246

creek to the north of this point can be compassed in an hour, and in two hours you can make the circuit of the salt marsh over which the sea may have extended in former times. If, therefore, the Israelites crossed so high up as Suez, the Egyptians, unless infatuated by Divine interference, might easily have recovered their stolen goods from the encumbered fugitives by making a slight detour. The opinion which fixes the point of passage at eighteen miles' distance, and from thence right across the ocean depths to the eastern side of the sea, is supported by the unanimous tradition of the people, whether Christians or Mussulmans, and is consistent with Holy Writ: "the waters were a wall unto them on their right hand, *and on their left.*" The Cambridge mathematicians seem to think that the Israelites were enabled to pass over dry land by adopting a route not usually subjected to the influx of the sea. This notion is plausible in a merely hydrostatical point of view, and is supposed to have been adopted by most of the Fellows of Trinity, but certainly not by Thorp, who is one of the most amiable of their number. It is difficult to reconcile this theory with the account given in Exodus, unless we can suppose that the words " sea " and " waters " are there used in a sense implying dry land.

Napoleon when at Suez made an attempt to follow the supposed steps of Moses by passing the creek at this point, but it seems, according to the testimony of the people at Suez, that he and his horsemen managed the matter in a way more resembling the failure of the Egyptians than the success of the Israelites. According to the French account, Napoleon got out of the difficulty by that warrior-like presence of mind which served him so well when the fate of nations depended on the decision of a moment—he ordered his horsemen to disperse in all directions, in order to multiply the chances of finding shallow water, and was thus enabled to discover a line by which he and his people were extricated. The story told by the people of Suez is very different: they declare that Napoleon parted from his horse, got thoroughly submerged, and was only fished out by the assistance of the people on shore.

I bathed twice at the point assigned to the passage of the Israelites, and the second time that I did so I chose the time of low water and tried to walk across, but I soon found myself out of my depth, or at least in water so deep that I could only advance by swimming.

The dromedary, which had bolted in the Desert, was brought into Suez the day after my arrival, but my pelisse and my pistols, which had been attached to the saddle, had disappeared. These articles were treasures of great importance to me at that time, and I moved the Governor of the town to make all possible exertions for their recovery. He acceded to my wishes as well as he could, and very obligingly imprisoned the first seven poor fellows he could lay his hands on.

At first the Governor acted in the matter from no other motive than that of courtesy to an English traveller, but afterwards, and when he saw the value which I set upon the lost property, he pushed his measures with a degree of alacrity and heat which seemed to show that he felt a personal interest in the matter. It was supposed either that he expected a large present in the event of succeeding, or that he was striving by all means to trace the property, in order that he might lay his hands on it after my departure.

I went out sailing for some hours, and when I

returned I was horrified to find that two men had been bastinadoed by order of the Governor, with a view to force them to a confession of their theft. It appeared, however, that there really was good ground for supposing them guilty, since one of the holsters was actually found in their possession. It was said, too (but I could hardly believe it), that whilst one of the men was undergoing the bastinado, his comrade was overhead encouraging him to bear the torment without peaching. Both men, if they had the secret, were resolute in keeping it, and were sent back to their dungeon. I of course took care that there should be no repetition of the torture, at least so long as I remained at Suez.

The Governor was a thorough Oriental, and until a comparatively recent period had shared in the old Mahometan feeling of contempt for Europeans. It happened, however, one day that an English gun-brig had appeared off Suez, and sent her boats ashore to take in fresh water. Now fresh water at Suez is a somewhat scarce and precious com-modity : it is kept in tanks, the chief of which is at some distance from the place. Under these circum-stances the request for fresh water was refused, or, at all events, was not complied with. The captain of the brig was a simple-minded man with a strongish will, and he at once declared that if his casks were not filled in three hours he would destroy the whole place. " A great people indeed ! " said the Governor ; " a wonderful people, the English ! " He instantly caused every cask to be filled to the brim from his own tank, and ever afterwards enter-tained for the English a degree of affection and respect, for which I felt infinitely indebted to the gallant captain.

The day after the abortive attempt to extract a
confession from the prisoners, the Governor, the
consul, and I sat in council, I know not how long,
with a view of prosecuting the search for the stolen
goods. The sitting, considered in the light of a
criminal investigation, was characteristic of the East.
The proceedings began as a matter of course by the
prosecutor's smoking a pipe and drinking coffee with
the Governor, who was judge, jury, and sheriff. I
got on very well with him (this was not my first
interview), and he gave me the pipe from his lips in
testimony of his friendship. I recollect, however,
that my prime adviser, thinking me, I suppose, a great
deal too shy and retiring in my manner, entreated me
to put up my boots and to soil the Governor's divan,
in order to inspire respect and strike terror. I
thought it would be as well for me to retain the right
of respecting myself, and that it was not quite
necessary for a well-received guest to strike any terror
at all.

Our deliberations were assisted by the numerous
attendants who lined the three sides of the room not
occupied by the divan. Any one of these who took
it into his head to offer a suggestion would stand
forward and humble himself before the Governor
and then state his views; every man thus giving
counsel was listened to with some attention.

After a great deal of fruitless planning the Governor
directed that the prisoners should be brought in. I
was shocked when they entered, for I was not
prepared to see them come *carried* into the room
upon the shoulders of others. It had not occurred to
me that their battered feet would be too sore to bear
the contact of the floor. They persisted in asserting their innocence. The Governor wanted to recur

to the torture, but that I prevented, and the men were carried back to their dungeon.

A scheme was now suggested by one of the attendants which seemed to me childishly absurd, but it was nevertheless tried. The plan was to send a man to the prisoners, who was to make them believe that he had obtained entrance into their dungeon upon some other pretence, but that he had in reality come to treat with them for the purchase of the stolen goods. This shallow expedient of course failed.

The Governor himself had not nominally the power of life and death over the people in his district, but he could if he chose send them to Cairo, and have them hanged there. I proposed, therefore, that the prisoners should be *threatened* with this fate. The answer of the Governor made me feel rather ashamed of my effeminate suggestion. He said that if I wished it he would willingly threaten them with death, but he also said that if he threatened *he should execute the threat.*

Thinking at last that nothing was to be gained by keeping the prisoners any longer in confinement, I requested that they might be set free. To this the Governor acceded, though only, as he said, out of favour to me, for he had a strong impression that the men were guilty. I went down to see the prisoners let out with my own eyes. They were very grateful, and fell down to the earth, kissing my boots. I gave them a present to console them for their wounds, and they seemed to be highly delighted.

Although the matter terminated in a manner so satisfactory to the principal sufferers, there were symptoms of some angry excitement in the place: it was said that public opinion was much shocked at the fact that Mahometans had been beaten on account of a loss sustained by a Christian. My journey was to recommence the next day, and it was hinted that if I persevered in my intention of proceeding, the people would have an easy and profitable opportunity of wreaking their vengeance on me. If ever they formed any scheme of the kind, they at all events refrained from any attempt to carry it into effect.

One of the evenings during my stay at Suez was enlivened by a triple wedding. There was a long and slow procession. Some carried torches, and others were thumping drums and firing pistols. The bridegrooms came last, all walking abreast. My only reason for mentioning the ceremony (which was otherwise uninteresting) is, that I scarcely ever in all my life saw any phenomena so ridiculous as the meekness and gravity of those three young men whilst being " led to the altar."

CHAPTER XXIII

THE route over the Desert from Suez to Gaza is not frequented by merchants, and is seldom passed by a traveller. This part of the country is less uniformly barren than the tracts of shifting sand that lie on the El Arish route. The shrubs on which the camel feeds are more frequent, and in many spots the sand is mingled with so much of productive soil as to admit the growth of corn. The Bedouins are driven out of this district during the summer by the total want of water, but before the time for their forced departure arrives they succeed in raising little crops of barley from these comparatively fertile patches of ground. They bury the fruit of their labours, leaving marks by which, upon their return, they may be able to recognise the spot. The warm, dry sand stands them for a safe granary. The country at the time I passed it (in the month of April) was pretty thickly sprinkled with Bedouins expecting their harvest. Several times my tent was pitched alongside of their encampments. I have told you already what the impressions were which these people produced upon my mind.

I saw several creatures of the antelope kind in this part of the Desert, and one day my Arabs surprised in her sleep a young gazelle (for so I called her), and took the darling prisoner. I carried her before me on my camel for the rest of the day, and kept her in my tent all night. I did all I could to coax her, but the trembling beauty refused to touch food, and would not be comforted. Whenever she had a seeming opportunity of escaping she struggled with a violence so painfully disproportioned to her fine, delicate limbs, that I could not continue the cruel attempt to make her my own. In the morning, therefore, I set her free, anticipating some pleasure from seeing the joyous bound with which, as I thought, she would return to her native freedom. She had been so stupefied, however, by the exciting events of the preceding day and night, and was so puzzled as to the road she should take, that she went off very deliberately, and with an uncertain step. She went away quite sound in limb, but her intellect may have been upset. Never in all likelihood had she seen the form of a human being until the dreadful moment when she woke from her sleep and found herself in the grip of an Arab. Then her pitching and tossing journey on the back of a camel, and lastly, a *soirée* with me by candlelight! I should have been glad to know, if I could, that her heart was not utterly broken.

My Arabs were somewhat excited one day by discovering the fresh print of a foot—the foot, as they said, of a lion. I had no conception that the lord of the forest (better known as a crest) ever stalked away from his jungles to make inglorious war in these smooth plains against antelopes and gazelles. I supposed that there must have been some error of interpretation, and that the Arabs meant to speak of a tiger. It appeared, however, that this was not the

ase. Either the Arabs were mistaken, or the noble
rute, uncooped and unchained, had but lately
rossed my path.

The camels with which I traversed this part of the
Desert were very different in their ways and habits
om those that you get on a frequented route. They
ere never led. There was not the slightest sign of
track in this part of the Desert, but the camels
ever failed to choose the right line. By the
irection taken at starting they knew, I suppose, the
oint (some encampment) for which they were to
ake. There is always a leading camel (generally,
believe, the eldest), who marches foremost, and
etermines the path for the whole party. If it
appens that no one of the camels has been accustomed
o lead the others, there is very great difficulty in
aking a start. If you force your beast forward for
moment, he will contrive to wheel and draw back,
t the same time looking at one of the other camels
ith an expression and gesture exactly equivalent to
près vous. The responsibility of finding the way
evidently assumed very unwillingly. After some
me, however, it becomes understood that one of the
easts has reluctantly consented to take the lead, and
e accordingly advances for that purpose. For a
inute or two he goes on with much indecision,
king first one line and then another, but soon by the
d of some mysterious sense he discovers the true
irection, and follows it steadily from morning to
ght. When once the leadership is established, you
annot by any persuasion, and can scarcely by any
rce, induce a junior camel to walk one single step
advance of the chosen guide.

On the fifth day I came to an oasis, called the
Vady el Arish, a ravine, or rather a gully, through

which during a part of the year there runs a stream of water. On the sides of the gully there were a number of those graceful trees which the Arabs call *tarfa*. The channel of the stream was quite dry in the part at which we arrived, but at about half a mile off some water was found, which, though very muddy, was tolerably sweet. This was a happy discovery, for all the water that we had brought from the neighbourhood of Suez was rapidly putrefying.

The want of foresight is an anomalous part of the Bedouin's character, for it does not result either from recklessness or stupidity. I know of no human being whose body is so thoroughly the slave of mind as that of the Arab. His mental anxieties seem to be for ever torturing every nerve and fibre of his body, and yet with all this exquisite sensitiveness to the suggestions of the mind, he is grossly improvident. I recollect, for instance, that when setting out upon this passage of the Desert, my Arabs, in order to lighten the burthen of their camels, were most anxious that we should take with us only two days' supply of water. They said that by the time that supply was exhausted we should arrive at a spring which would furnish us for the rest of the journey. My servants very wisely, and with much pertinacity, resisted the adoption of this plan, and took care to have both the large skins well filled. We proceeded, and found no water at all, either at the expected spring or for many days afterwards, so that nothing but the precaution of my own people saved us from the very severe suffering which we should have endured if we had entered upon the Desert with only a two days' supply. The Arabs themselves being on foot would have suffered much more than I from the consequences of their improvidence.

This unaccountable want of foresight prevents the Bedouin from appreciating at a distance of eight or ten days the amount of the misery which he entails upon himself at the end of that period. His dread of a city is one of the most painful mental affections that I have ever observed, and yet when the whole breadth of the Desert lies between him and the town to which you are going, he will freely enter into an agreement to *land* you in the city for which you are bound. When, however, after many a day of toil the distant minarets at length appear, the poor Bedouin relaxes the vigour of his pace, his steps become faltering and undecided, every moment his uneasiness increases, and at length he fairly sobs aloud, and embracing your knees, implores with the most piteous cries and gestures that you will dispense with him and his camels, and find some other means of entering the city. This, of course, one can't agree to, and the consequence is that one is obliged to witness and resist the most moving expressions of grief and fond entreaty. I had to go through a most painful scene of this kind when I entered Cairo, and now the horror which these wilder Arabs felt at the notion of entering Gaza led to consequences still more distressing. The dread of cities results partly from a kind of wild instinct which has always characterised the descendants of Ishmael, but partly too from a well-founded apprehension of ill-treatment. So often it happens that the poor Bedouin, when once jammed in between walls, is seized by the Government authorities for the sake of his camels, that his innate horror of cities becomes really justified by results.

The Bedouins with whom I performed this journey were wild fellows of the Desert, quite unaccustomed to let out themselves or their beasts for hire, and when

17

they found that by the natural ascendency of
Europeans they were gradually brought down to a
state of subserviency to me, or rather to my attendants, they bitterly repented, I believe, of having
placed themselves under our control. They were
rather difficult fellows to manage, and gave Dthemetri
a good deal of trouble, but I liked them all the better
for that.

Selim, the chief of the party, and the man to
whom all our camels belonged, was a fine, savage,
stately fellow. There were, I think, five other
Arabs of the party, but when we approached the end
of the journey they one by one began to make off
towards the neighbouring encampments, and by the
time that the minarets of Gaza were in sight, Selim
the owner of the camels, was the only one who
remained. He, poor fellow, as we neared the town
began to discover the same terrors that my Arabs
had shown when I entered Cairo. I could not
possibly accede to his entreaties and consent to let
my baggage be laid down on the bare sands, without
any means of having it brought on into the city. So
at length, when poor Selim had exhausted all his
rhetoric of voice and action and tears, he fixed his
despairing eyes for a minute upon the cherished beasts
that were his only wealth, and then suddenly and
madly dashed away into the farther Desert. I continued my course and reached the city at last, but it
was not without immense difficulty that we could
constrain the poor camels to pass under the hated
shadow of its walls. They were the genuine beasts
of the Desert, and it was sad and painful to witness
the agony they suffered when thus they were forced
to encounter the fixed habitations of men. They
shrank from the beginning of every high, narrow

street as though from the entrance of some horrible
cave or bottomless pit; they sighed and wept like
women. When at last we got them within the
courtyard of the khan they seemed to be quite
broken-hearted, and looked round piteously for their
loving master; but no Selim came. I had imagined
that he would enter the town secretly by night in
order to carry off those five fine camels, his only
wealth in this world, and seemingly the main objects
of his affection. But no; his dread of civilisation
was too strong. During the whole of the three days
that I remained at Gaza he failed to show himself,
and thus sacrificed in all probability not only his
camels, but the money which I had stipulated to pay
him for the passage of the Desert. In order, however, to do all I could towards saving him from this
last misfortune I resorted to a contrivance frequently
adopted by the Asiatics: I assembled a group of
grave and worthy Mussulmans in the courtyard of
the khan, and in their presence paid over the gold to
a Sheik who was accustomed to communicate with
the Arabs of the Desert. All present solemnly promised that if ever Selim should come to claim his
rights, they would bear true witness in his favour.

I saw a great deal of my old friend the Governor
of Gaza. He had received orders to send back all
persons coming from Egypt, and force them to perform quarantine at El Arish. He knew so little of
quarantine regulations, however, that his dress was
actually in contact with mine whilst he insisted upon
the stringency of the orders which he had received.
He was induced to make an exception in my favour,
and I rewarded him with a musical snuff-box which
I had bought at Smyrna for the purpose of presenting
it to any man in authority who might happen to

do me an important service. The Governor was delighted with his toy, and took it off to his harem with great exultation. He soon, however, returned with an altered countenance; his wives, he said, had got hold of the box and put it out of order. So shortlived is human happiness in this frail world!

The Governor fancied that he should incur less risk if I remained at Gaza for two or three days more, and he wanted me to become his guest. I persuaded him, however, that it would be better for him to let me depart at once. He wanted to add to my baggage a roast lamb and a quantity of other cumbrous viands, but I escaped with half a horse-load of leaven bread, which was very good of its kind, and proved a most useful present. The air with which the Governor's slaves affected to be almost breaking down under the weight of the gifts which they bore on their shoulders, reminded me of the figures one sees in some of the old pictures.

CHAPTER XXIV

PASSING now once again through Palestine and Syria I retained the tent which I had used in the Desert, and found that it added very much to my comfort in travelling. Instead of turning out a family from some wretched dwelling, and depriving them of a repose which I was sure not to find for myself, I now, when evening came, pitched my tent upon some smiling spot within a few hundred yards of the village to which I looked for my supplies, that is, for milk and bread if I had it not with me, and sometimes also for eggs. The worst of it is, that the needful viands are not to be obtained by coin, but only by intimidation. I at first tried the usual agent, money. Dthemetri, with one or two of my Arabs, went into the village near which I was encamped and tried to buy the required provisions, offering liberal payment, but he came back empty-handed. I sent him again, but this time he held different language. He required to see the elders of the place, and threatening dreadful vengeance, directed them upon their responsibility to take care that my tent should be immediately and abundantly supplied. He was obeyed at once, and the provisions refused to me as a purchaser soon arrived, trebled or quadrupled, when demanded by way of a forced contribution. I quickly found (I think it required two experiments to convince me) that this peremptory method was the only one which could be adopted with success. It never failed. Of course, however, when the provisions have been actually obtained you can, if you choose, give money exceeding the value of the provisions to *somebody*. An English, a thoroughbred English, traveller will always do this (though it is contrary to the custom of the country) for the quiet (false quiet though it be) of his own conscience, but so to order the matter that the poor fellows who have been forced to contribute should be the persons to receive the value of their supplies, is not possible. For a traveller to attempt anything so grossly just as that would be too outrageous. The truth is, that the usage of the East, in old times, required the people of the village, at their own cost, to supply the wants of travellers, and the ancient custom is now adhered to, not in favour of travellers generally, but in favour of those who are deemed sufficiently powerful to enforce its observance. If the villagers therefore find a man waiving this right to oppress them, and offering coin for that which he is entitled to take without payment, they suppose at once that he is actuated by fear (fear of *them*, poor fellows!), and it is so delightful to them to act upon this flattering assumption, that they will forego the advantage of a good price for their provisions rather than the rare luxury of refusing for once in their lives to part with their own possessions.

The practice of intimidation thus rendered necessary is utterly hateful to an Englishman. He finds himself forced to conquer his daily bread by the pompous threats of the dragoman, his very subsistence, as well

as his dignity and personal safety, being made to
depend upon his servant's assuming a tone of authority
which does not at all belong to him. Besides, he
can scarcely fail to see that as he passes through the
country he becomes the innocent cause of much extra
injustice, many supernumerary wrongs. This he
feels to be especially the case when he travels with
relays. To be the owner of a horse or a mule within
reach of an Asiatic potentate, is to lead the life of the
hare and the rabbit, hunted down and ferreted out.
Too often it happens that the works of the field
are stopped in the daytime, that the inmates of the
cottage are roused from their midnight sleep by the
sudden coming of a Government officer, and the poor
husbandman, driven by threats and rewarded by
curses, if he would not lose sight for ever of his
captured beasts, must quit all and follow them. This
is done that the Englishman may travel. He would
make his way more harmless if he could, but horses or
mules he *must* have, and these are his ways and means.

The town of Nablus is beautiful; it lies in a valley
hemmed in with olive groves, and its buildings are
interspersed with frequent palm-trees. It is said to
occupy the site of the ancient Sychem. I know not
whether it was there indeed that the father of the
Jews was accustomed to feed his flocks, but the valley
is green and smiling, and is held at this day by a race
more brave and beautiful than Jacob's unhappy
descendants.

Nablus is the very furnace of Mahometan bigotry;[1]
and I believe that only a few months before the time
of my going there it would have been quite unsafe
for a man, unless strongly guarded, to show himself
to the people of the town in a Frank costume; but

[1] [Nablus still maintains its reputation for bigotry.]

since their last insurrection the Mahometans of the
place had been so far subdued by the severity of
Ibrahim Pasha, that they dared not now offer the
slightest insult to a European. It was quite plain,
however, that the effort with which the men of the
old school refrained from expressing their opinion of
a hat and a coat was horribly painful to them. As
I walked through the streets and bazaars a dead
silence prevailed; every man suspended his employ-
ment, and gazed on me with a fixed, glassy look,
which seemed to say, "God is good, but how
marvellous and inscrutable are His ways that thus
He permits this white-faced dog of a Christian to
hunt through the paths of the faithful."

The insurrection of these people had been more
formidable than any other that Ibrahim Pasha had to
contend with. He was only able to crush them at
last by the assistance of a fellow renowned for his
resources in the way of stratagem and cunning, as
well as for his knowledge of the country. This
personage was no other than Aboo Goosh ("the
father of lies"[1]), who was taken out of prison for
the purpose. The "father of lies" enabled Ibrahim
to hem in the insurrection and extinguish it. He
was rewarded with the Governorship of Jerusalem,
which he held when I was there. I recollect, by
the by, that he tried one of his stratagems upon me.
I did not go to see him, as I ought in courtesy to
have done, during my stay at Jerusalem; but I
happened to be the owner of a rather handsome

---

[1] This is an appellation not implying blame, but merit;
the "lies" which it purports to affiliate are feints and
cunning stratagems, rather than the baser kind of false-
hoods. The expression, in short, has nearly the same
meaning as the English word "Yorkshireman."

amber *tchibouque* piece, which the Governor heard of, and by some means contrived to see. He sent to me, and dressed up a statement that he would give me a price immensely exceeding the sum which I had given for it. He did not add my *tchibouque* to the rest of his trophies.

There was a small number of Greek Christians resident in Nablus, and over these the Mussulmans held a high hand, not even permitting them to speak to each other in the open streets ; but if the Moslems thus set themselves above the poor Christians of the place, I, or rather my servants, soon took the ascendant over *them*. I recollect that just as we were starting from the place, and at a time when a number of people had gathered together in the main street to see our preparations, Mysseri, being provoked at some piece of perverseness on the part of a true believer, coolly thrashed him with his horsewhip before the assembled crowd of fanatics. I was much annoyed at the time, for I thought that the people would probably rise against us. They turned rather pale, but stood still.

The day of my arrival at Nablus was a fête—the new-year's day of the Mussulmans.[1][2] Most of the

---

[1] The 29th of April.

[2] [This was no doubt the case in this particular, but it must not be supposed that April 29 is the Mohammedan New Year's Day. The Moslem religious year consists of twelve lunar months, and is eleven days shorter than the Christian year. Hence, if in one year Muharrem (the first month) falls on April 29, it would fall on April 18 the next. In consequence of the great inconveniences of this mode of reckoning, Turks adopt for secular matters another ra called the Financial year, which starts from the Hijra, but has solar months. But feasts and fasts are fixed by the lunar year, so that the month of Ramazan rotates through all the seasons.]

people were amusing themselves in the beautiful lawns and shady groves without the city. The men (except myself) were all remotely apart from the other sex. The women in groups were diverting themselves and their children with swings. They were so handsome, that they could not keep up their yashmaks. I believe that they had never before looked upon a man in the European dress, and when they now saw in me that strange phenomenon, and saw, too, how they could please the creature by showing him a glimpse of beauty, they seemed to think it was better fun to do this than to go on playing with swings. It was always, however, with a sort of zoological expression of countenance that they looked on the horrible monster from Europe, and whenever one of them gave me to see for one sweet instant the blushing of her unveiled face, it was with the same kind of air as that with which a young, timid girl will edge her way up to an elephant and tremblingly give him a nut from the tips of her rosy fingers.

CHAPTER XXV[1]

MARIAM

THERE is no spirit of propagandism in the Mussulmans of the Ottoman dominions. True it is that a prisoner of war, or a Christian condemned

[1] [The statements at the beginning of this chapter are altogether inaccurate. From the religious point of view a good Mohammedan is as much, and more, bound than a Christian to encourage any form of missionary enterprise, seeing that all non - Moslems are destined to inevitable damnation. From the legal and practical point of view, the exercise of all religions is nominally free in Turkey, and it is therefore illegal to convert a Christian at the point of the sword, but it will be sufficient to remind the reader that during the massacres of 1895–96 many thousands of Armenians turned Mohammedans, and that those who wished to subsequently return to their old religion found great difficulty in doing so.

As a rule Turks despise the Christian races too much to take any trouble about converting them, but it is absurd to say that conversions are illegal. On the contrary, they are fairly frequent, and it is only necessary that the person converted should state publicly that his change of religion is due to his own free will. Cases of young girls embracing Islam are not rare. According to the law, minors wishing to become Moslems must be taken to the house of a respectable person, where a priest of their own religion can have access to them, and their change of faith is not legal until they are of age (which means in the case of a girl twelve or thirteen), but in practice every effort is made to isolate them in such cases from their friends and surround them with Mohammedans.]

to death, may on some occasions save his life by adopting the religion of Mahomet, but instances of this kind are now exceedingly rare, and are quite at variance with the general system. Many Europeans, I think, would be surprised to learn that which is nevertheless quite true, namely, that an attempt to disturb the religious repose of the empire by the conversion of a Christian to the Mahometan faith is positively illegal. The event which now I am going to mention shows plainly enough that the unlawfulness of such interference is distinctly recognised even in the most bigoted stronghold of Islam.

During my stay at Nablus I took up my quarters at the house of the Greek "papa" as he is called, that is, the Greek priest. The priest himself had gone to Jerusalem upon the business I am going to tell you of, but his wife remained at Nablus, and did the honours of her home.

Soon after my arrival a deputation from the Greek Christians of the place came to request my interference in a matter which had occasioned vast excitement.

And now I must tell you how it came to happen, as it did continually, that people thought it worth while to claim the assistance of a mere traveller, who was totally devoid of all just pretensions to authority or influence of even the humblest description, and especially I must explain to you how it was that the power thus attributed did really belong to me, or rather to my dragoman. Successive political convulsions had at length fairly loosed the people of Syria from their former rules of conduct, and from all their old habits of reliance. The violence and success with which Mehemet Ali

crushed the insurrection of the Mahometan population
had utterly beaten down the head of Islam, and
extinguished, for the time at least, those virtues and
vices which had sprung from the Mahometan faith.
Success so complete as Mehemet Ali's, if it had
been attained by an ordinary Asiatic potentate,
would have induced a notion of stability. The
readily bowing mind of the Oriental would have
bowed low and long under the feet of a conqueror
whom God had thus strengthened. But Syria was
no field for contests strictly Asiatic. Europe was
involved, and though the heavy masses of Egyptian
troops, clinging with strong grip to the land, might
seem to hold it fast, yet every peasant practically
felt, and knew, that in Vienna or Petersburg or
London there were four or five pale-looking men who
could pull down the star of the Pasha with shreds of
paper and ink. The people of the country knew, too,
that Mehemet Ali was strong with the strength of
the Europeans—strong by his French general, his
French tactics, and his English engines. Moreover,
they saw that the person, the property, and even the
dignity of the humblest European was guarded with
the most careful solicitude. The consequence of
all this was, that the people of Syria looked vaguely,
but confidently, to Europe for fresh changes.
Many would fix upon some nation, France or
England, and steadfastly regard it as the arriving
sovereign of Syria. Those whose minds remained
in doubt equally contributed to this new state of
public opinion, which no longer depended upon
religion and ancient habits, but upon bare hopes
and fears. Every man wanted to know, not who
was his neighbour, but who was to be his ruler ;
whose feet he was to kiss, and by whom *his* feet

were to be ultimately beaten. Treat your friend,
says the proverb, as though he were one day to
become your enemy, and your enemy as though he
were one day to become your friend. The Syrians
went further, and seemed inclined to treat every
stranger as though he might one day become their
Pasha. Such was the state of circumstances and of
feeling which now for the first time had thoroughly
opened the mind of Western Asia for the reception
of Europeans and European ideas. The credit of
the English especially was so great, that a good
Mussulman flying from the conscription, or any other
persecution, would come to seek from the formerly
despised hat that protection which the turban could
no longer afford ; and a man high in authority (as,
for instance, the Governor in command of Gaza)
would think that he had won a prize, or, at all
events, a valuable lottery ticket, if he obtained
a written approval of his conduct from a simple
traveller.

Still, in order that any immediate result should
follow from all this unwonted readiness in the Asiatic
to succumb to the European, it was necessary that
someone should be at hand who could see and would
push the advantage. I myself had neither the inclination nor the power to do so, but it happened that
Dthemetri, who, as my dragoman, represented me on
all occasions, was the very person of all others best
fitted to avail himself with success of this yielding
tendency in the Oriental mind. If the chance or
birth and fortune had made poor Dthemetri a tailor
during some part of his life, yet religion and the
literature of the Church which he served had made
him · a man, and a brave man too. The lives of
saints with which he was familiar were full of heroic

actions provoking imitation, and since faith in a creed involves a faith in its ultimate triumph, Dthemetri was bold from a sense of true strength. His education too, though not very general in its character, had been carried quite far enough to justify him in pluming himself upon a very decided advantage over the great bulk of the Mahometan population, including the men in authority. With all this consciousness of religious and intellectual superiority Dthemetri had lived for the most part in countries lying under Mussulman governments, and had witnessed (perhaps too had suffered from) their revolting cruelties; the result was that he abhorred and despised the Mahometan faith and all who clung to it. And this hate was not of the dry, dull, and inactive sort. Dthemetri was in his sphere a true Crusader, and whenever there appeared a fair opening in the defences of Islam, he was ready and eager to make the assault. These sentiments, backed by a consciousness of understanding the people with whom he had to do, made Dthemetri not only firm and resolute in his constant interviews with men in authority, but sometimes also (as you may know already) very violent and even insulting. This tone, which I always disliked, though I was fain to profit by it, invariably succeeded. It swept away all resistance; there was nothing in the then depressed and succumbing mind of the Mussulman that could oppose a zeal so warm and fierce.

As for me, I of course stood aloof from Dthemetri's crusades, and did not even render him any active assistance when he was striving (as he almost always was, poor fellow) on my behalf; I was only the death's head and white sheet with which he scared the enemy. I think, however, that I played this spectral part exceedingly well, for I seldom appeared at all in any discussion, and whenever I did, I was sure to be white and calm.

The event which induced the Christians of Nablus to seek for my assistance was this. A beautiful young Christian, between fifteen and sixteen years old, had lately been married to a man of her own creed. About the same time (probably on the occasion of her wedding) she was accidently seen by a Mussulman Sheik of great wealth and local influence, who instantly became madly enamoured of her. The strict morality which so generally prevails where the Mussulmans have complete ascendency prevented the Sheik from entertaining any such sinful hopes as a European might have ventured to cherish under the like circumstances, and he saw no chance of gratifying his love excpt by inducing the girl to embrace his own creed. If he could induce her to take this step, her marriage with the Christian would be dissolved, and then there would be nothing to prevent him from making her the last and brightest of his wives. The Sheik was a practical man, and quickly began his attack upon the theological opinions of the bride. He did not assail her with the eloquence of any imaums or Mussulman saints; he did not press upon her the eternal truths of the "Cow," [1] or the beautiful morality of "the Table"; [1] he sent her no tracts, not even a copy of the holy Koran. An old woman acted as missionary. She brought with her a whole basketful of arguments— jewels and shawls and scarfs, and all kinds of persuasive finery. Poor Mariam! she put on the jewels and took a calm view of the Mahometan religion in a little hand-mirror; she could not be

---

[1] These are the names given by the Prophet to certain chapters of the Koran.

leaf to such eloquent earrings, and the great truths of Islam came home to her young bosom in the delicate folds of the cashmere; she was ready to abandon her faith.

The Sheik knew very well that his attempt to convert an infidel was illegal, and that his proceedings would not bear investigation, so he took care to pay a large sum to the Governor of Nablus in order to obtain his connivance.

At length Mariam quitted her home and placed herself under the protection of the Mahometan authorities, who, however, refrained from delivering her into the arms of her lover, and detained her in a mosque until the fact of her real conversion (which had been indignantly denied by her relatives) should be established. For two or three days the mother of the young convert was prevented from communicating with her child by various evasive contrivances, but not, it would seem, by a flat refusal. At length it was announced that the young lady's profession of faith might be heard from her own lips. At an hour appointed the friends of the Sheik and the relatives of the damsel met in the mosque. The young convert addressed her mother in a loud voice, and said, " God is God, and Mahomet is the Prophet of God, and thou, oh my mother, art an infidel, feminine dog ! "

You would suppose that this declaration, so clearly nounced, and that, too, in a place where Mahometnism is perhaps more supreme than in any other part of the empire, would have sufficed to have confirmed the pretensions of the lover. This, however, was not the case. The Greek priest of the place was despatched on a mission to the Governor of Jerusalem (Aboo Goosh), in order to complain

against the proceedings of the Sheik and obtain a
restitution of the bride.   Meanwhile the Mahometan
authorities at Nablus were so conscious of having
acted unlawfully in conspiring to disturb the faith of
the beautiful infidel, that they hesitated to take any
further steps, and the girl was still detained in the
mosque.

Thus matters stood when the Christians of the
place came and sought to obtain my assistance.

I felt (with regret) that I had no personal interest
in the matter, and I also thought that there was no
pretence for my interfering with the conflicting claim
of the Christian husband and the Mahometan lover
and I therefore declined to take any step.

My speaking of the husband, by the bye, remind
me that he was extremely backward about the great
work of recovering his youthful bride.   The relation
of the girl, who felt themselves disgraced by her
conduct, were vehement and excited to a high pitch
but the Menelaus of Nablus was exceedingly calm
and composed.

The fact that it was not technically my duty to
interfere in a matter of this kind was a very sufficient
and yet a very unsatisfactory, reason for my refusal
of all assistance.   Until you are placed in situation
of this kind you can hardly tell how painful it is to
refrain from intermeddling in other people's affairs—
to refrain from intermeddling when you feel that you
can do so with happy effect, and can remove a load
of distress by the use of a few small phrases.   Upon
this occasion, however, an expression fell from one
of the girl's kinsmen which not only determined me
against the idea of interfering, but made me hope
that all attempts to recover the proselyte would fail
This person, speaking with the most savage bitterness

and with the cordial approval of all the other relatives, said that the girl ought to be beaten to death. I could not fail to see that if the poor child were ever restored to her family she would be treated with the most frightful barbarity. I heartily wished, therefore, that the Mussulmans might be firm, and preserve their young prize from any fate so dreadful as that of a return to her own relations.

The next day the Greek priest returned from his mission to Aboo Goosh, but the " father of lies," it would seem, had been well plied with the gold of the enamoured Sheik, and contrived to put off the prayers of the Christians by cunning feints. Now, therefore, a second and more numerous deputation than the first waited upon me, and implored my intervention with the Governor. I informed the assembled Christians that since their last application I had carefully considered the matter. The religious question I thought might be put aside at once, for the excessive levity which the girl had displayed proved clearly that in adopting Mahometanism she was not quitting any other faith. Her mind must have been thoroughly blank upon religious questions, and she was not, therefore, to be treated as a Christian that had strayed from the flock, but rather as a child without any religion at all, who was willing to conform to the usages of those who would deck her with jewels, and clothe her with cashmere shawls.

So much for the religious part of the question. Well, then, in a mere temporal sense, it appeared to me that (looking merely to the interests of the damsel, for I rather unjustly put poor Menelaus quite out of the question) the advantages were all on the side of the Mahometan match. The Sheik was in a much higher station of life than the superseded husband, and had given the best possible proof of his ardent affection by the sacrifices he had made, and the risks he had incurred, for the sake of the beloved object. I therefore stated fairly, to the horror and amazement of all my hearers, that the Sheik, in my view, was likely to make a most capital husband, and that I entirely " approved of the match."

I left Nablus under the impression that Mariam would soon be delivered to her Mussulman lover. I afterwards found, however, that the result was very different. Dthemetri's religious zeal and hate had been so much excited by the account of these events, and by the grief and mortification of his co-religionists, that when he found me firmly determined to decline all interference in the matter, he secretly appealed to the Governor in my name, and (using, I suppose, many violent threats, and telling no doubt many lies about my station and influence) extorted a promise that the proselyte should be restored to her relatives. I did not understand that the girl had been actually given up whilst I remained at Nablus, but Dthemetri certainly did not desist from his instances until he had satisfied himself by some means or other (for mere words amounted to nothing) that the promise would be actually performed. It was not till I had quitted Syria, and when Dthemetri was no longer in my service, that this villainous, though well-motived trick, of his came to my knowledge. Mysseri, who had informed me of the step which had been taken, did not know it himself until some time after we had quitted Nablus, when Dthemetri exultingly confessed his successful enterprise. I know not whether the engagement which my zealous dragoman extorted from the Governor was ever complied with. I shudder to think of the fate which must have befallen poor Mariam if she fell into the hands of the Christians.

CHAPTER XXVI

THE PROPHET DAMOOR

FOR some hours I passed along the shores of the fair lake of Galilee ; then turning a little to the westward, I struck into a mountainous tract, and as I advanced thenceforward, the lie of the country kept growing more and more bold. At length I drew near to the city of Safed. It sits as proud as a fortress upon the summit of a craggy height ; yet because of its minarets and stately trees, the place looks happy and beautiful. It is one of the holy cities of the Talmud, and according to this authority, the Messiah will reign there for forty years before He takes possession of Sion. The sanctity and historical importance thus attributed to the city by anticipation render it a favourite place of retirement for Israelites, of whom it contains, they say, about four thousand, a number nearly balancing that of the Mahometan inhabitants. I knew by my experience of Tabarieh that a "holy city" was sure to have a population of vermin somewhat proportionate to the number of its Israelites, and I therefore caused my tent to be pitched upon a green spot of ground at a respectful distance from the walls of the town.

When it had become quite dark (for there was no moon that night) I was informed that several Jews had secretly come from the city in the hope of obtaining some assistance from me in circumstances of imminent danger; I was also informed that they claimed my aid upon the ground that some of their number were British subjects. It was arranged that the two principal men of the party should speak for the rest, and these were accordingly admitted into my tent. One of the two called himself the British vice-consul, and he had with him his consular cap, but he frankly said that he could not have dared to assume this emblem of his dignity in the daytime, and that nothing but the extreme darkness of the night rendered it safe for him to put it on upon this occasion. The other of the spokesmen was a Jew of Gibraltar, a tolerably well-bred person, who spoke English very fluently.

These men informed me that the Jews of the place, who were exceedingly wealthy, had lived peaceably in their retirement until the insurrection which took place in 1834, but about the beginning of that year a highly religious Mussulman called Mohammed Damoor went forth into the market-place, crying with a loud voice, and prophesying that on the fifteenth of the following June the true Believers would rise up in just wrath against the Jews, and despoil them of their gold and their silver and their jewels. The earnestness of the prophet produced some impression at the time, but all went on as usual, until at last the fifteenth of June arrived. When that day dawned the whole Mussulman population of the place assembled in the streets that they might see the result of the prophecy. Suddenly Mohammed Damoor rushed furious into the crowd, and the fierce shout of the prophet soon ensured the fulfilment of his prophecy. Some of the Jews fled, and some remained, but they who fled and they who remained, alike, and unresistingly, left their property to the hands of the spoilers.   The most odious of all outrages, that of searching the women for the base purpose of discovering such things as gold and silver concealed about their persons, was perpetrated without shame.   The poor Jews were so stricken with terror, that they submitted to their fate even where resistance would have been easy.   In several instances a young Mussulman boy, not more than ten or twelve years of age, walked straight into the house of a Jew and stripped him of his property before his face, and in the presence of his whole family.[1]   When the insurrection was put down some of the Mussulmans (most probably those who had got no spoil wherewith they might buy immunity) were punished, but the greater part of them escaped.   None of the booty was restored, and the pecuniary redress which the Pasha had undertaken to enforce for them had been hitherto so carefully delayed, that the hope of ever obtaining it had grown very faint.   A new Governor had been appointed to the command of the place, with stringent orders to ascertain the real extent of the losses, and to discover the spoilers, with a view of compelling them to make restitution.   It was found that, notwithstanding the urgency of the instructions which the Governor had received, he did not push on the affair with the vigour that had been expected.   The Jews complained, and either by the protection of the British consul at Damascus, or by some other means, had influence enough to induce the appointment of a special commissioner—they called him "the Modeer"—whose duty it was to watch

---

[1] It was after the interview which I am talking of, and not from the Jews themselves, that I learnt this fact.

for and prevent anything like connivance on the part of the Governor, and to push on the investigation with vigour and impartiality.

Such were the instructions with which some few weeks since the Modeer came charged. The result was that the investigation had made no practical advance, and that the Modeer as well as the Governor was living upon terms of affectionate friendship with Mohammed Damoor and the rest of the principal spoilers.

Thus stood the chance of redress for the past, but the cause of the agonising excitement under which the Jews of the place now laboured was recent and justly alarming. Mohammed Damoor had again gone forth into the market-place, and lifted up his voice and prophesied a second spoliation of the Israelites. This was grave matter; the words of such a practical man as Mohammed Damoor were not to be despised. I fear I must have smiled visibly, for I was greatly amused, and even, I think, gratified at the account of this second prophecy. Nevertheless, my heart warmed towards the poor oppressed Israelites, and I was flattered, too, in the point of my national vanity at the notion of the far-reaching link by which a Jew in Syria, who had been born on the rock of Gibraltar, was able to claim me as his fellow-countryman. If I hesitated at all between the "impropriety" of interfering in a matter which was no business of mine and the "infernal shame" of refusing my aid at such a conjecture, I soon came to a very ungentlemanly decision, namely, that I would be guilty of the "impropriety," and not of the "infernal shame." It seemed to me that the immediate arrest of Mohammed Damoor was the one thing needful to the safety of the Jews, and I felt confident (for reasons which I have already mentioned in speaking of the Nablus affair) that I should be able to obtain this result by making a formal application to the Governor. I told my applicants that I would take this step on the following morning. They were very grateful, and were, for a moment, much pleased at the prospect of safety which might thus be opened to them, but the deliberation of a minute entirely altered their views, and filled them with new terror. They declared that any attempt, or pretended attempt, on the part of the Governor to arrest Mohammed Damoor would certainly produce an immediate movement of the whole Mussulman population, and a consequent massacre and robbery of the Israelites. My visitors went out, and remained I know not how long consulting with their brethren, but all at last agreed that their present perilous and painful position was better than a certain and immediate attack, and that if Mohammed Damoor was seized, their second estate would be worse than their first. I myself did not think that this would be the case, but I could not of course force my aid upon the people against their will; and, moreover, the day fixed for the fulfilment of this second prophecy was not very close at hand. A little delay, therefore, in providing against the impending danger would not necessarily be fatal. The men now confessed that although they had come with so much mystery and, as they thought, at so great a risk to ask my assistance, they were unable to suggest any mode in which I could aid them, except indeed by mentioning their grievances to the consul-general at Damascus. This I promised to do, and this I did.

My visitors were very thankful to me for the

readiness which I had shown to intermeddle in their affairs, and the grateful wives of the principal Jews sent to me many compliments, with choice wines and elaborate sweetmeats.

The course of my travels soon drew me so far from Safed, that I never heard how the dreadful day passed off which had been fixed for the accomplishment of the second prophecy. If the predicted spoliation was prevented, poor Mohammed Damoor must have been forced, I suppose, to say that he had prophesied in a metaphorical sense. This would be a sad falling off from the brilliant and substantial success of the first experiment.

CHAPTER XXVII

FOR a part of two days I wound under the base of the snow-crowned Djibel el Sheik, and then entered upon a vast and desolate plain, rarely pierced at intervals by some sort of withered stem.· The earth in its length and its breadth and all the deep universe of sky was steeped in light and heat. On I rode through the fire, but long before evening came there were straining eyes that saw, and joyful voices that announced, the sight of Shaum Shereef—the " holy," the " blessed " Damascus.

But that which at last I reached with my longing eyes was not a speck in the horizon, gradually expanding to a group of roofs and walls, but a long, low line of blackest green, that ran right across in the distance from east to west. And this, as I approached, grew deeper, grew wavy in its outline. Soon forest trees shot up before my eyes, and robed their broad shoulders so freshly, that all the throngs of olives as they rose into view looked sad in their proper dimness. There were even now no houses to see, but only the minarets peered out from the midst of shade into the glowing sky, and bravely touched the sun. There seemed to be here no

284

mere city, but rather a province wide and rich, that bounded the torrid waste.

Until about a year, or two years, before the time of my going there Damascus had kept up so much of the old bigot zeal against Christians, or rather, against Europeans, that no one dressed as a Frank could have dared to show himself in the streets; but the firmness and temper of Mr. Farren, who hoisted his flag in the city as consul-general for the district, had soon put an end to all intolerance of Englishmen. Damascus was safer than Oxford.[1] When I entered the city in my usual dress there was but one poor fellow that wagged his tongue, and him, in the open streets, Dthemetri horsewhipped. During my stay I went wherever I chose, and attended the public baths without molestation. Indeed, my relations with the pleasanter portion of the Mahometan population were upon a much better footing here than at most other places.

In the principal streets of Damascus there is a path for foot-passengers, which is raised, I think, a foot or two above the bridle-road. Until the arrival of the British consul-general none but a Mussulman

[1] An enterprising American traveller, Mr. Everett, lately conceived the bold project of penetrating to the University of Oxford, and this notwithstanding that he had been in his infancy (they begin very young those Americans) a Unitarian preacher. Having a notion, it seems, that the ambassadorial character would protect him from insult, he adopted the stratagem of procuring credentials from his Government as Minister Pleni-potentiary at the Court of her Britannic Majesty; he also wore the exact costume of a Trinitarian. But all his contrivances were vain; Oxford disdained, and rejected, and insulted him (not because he represented a swindling community, but) because that his infantine sermons were strictly remembered against him; the enterprise failed.

had been permitted to walk upon the upper way.
Mr. Farren would not, of course, suffer that the
humiliation of any such exclusion should be
submitted to by an Englishman, and I always
walked upon the raised path as free and unmolested
as if I had been in Pall Mall. The old usage was,
however, maintained with as much strictness as ever
against the Christian Rayahs and Jews : not one of
them could have set his foot upon the privileged
path without endangering his life.

I was lounging one day, I remember, along " the
paths of the faithful," when a Christian Rayah from
the bridle-road below saluted me with such earnestness, and craved so anxiously to speak and be spoken
to, that he soon brought me to a halt. He had nothing
to tell, except only the glory and exultation with
which he saw a fellow-Christian stand level with the
imperious Mussulmans. Perhaps he had been absent
from the place for some time, for otherwise I hardly
know how it could have happened that my exaltation
was the first instance he had seen. His joy was
great. So strong and strenuous was England (Lord
Palmerston reigned in those days), that it was a
pride and delight for a Syrian Christian to look up
and say that the Englishman's faith was his too. If
I was vexed at all that I could not give the man a
lift and shake hands with him on level ground, there
was no alloy to *his* pleasure. He followed me on,
not looking to his own path, but keeping his eyes on
me. He saw, as he thought, and said (for he came
with me on to my quarters), the period of the
Mahometan's absolute ascendency, the beginning of
the Christian's. He had so closely associated the
insulting privilege of the path with actual dominion,
that seeing it now in one instance abandoned, he

looked for the quick coming of European troops. His lips only whispered, and that tremulously, but his fiery eyes spoke out their triumph in long and loud hurrahs: "I, too, am a Christian. My foes are the foes of the English. We are all one people, and Christ is our King."

If I poorly deserved, yet I liked this claim of brotherhood. Not all the warnings which I heard against their rascality could hinder me from feeling kindly towards my fellow-Christians in the East. English travellers, from a habit perhaps of depreciating sectarians in their own country, are apt to look down upon the Oriental Christians as being "dissenters" from the established religion of a Mahometan empire. I never did thus. By a natural perversity of disposition, which my nursemaids called contrairiness, I felt the more strongly for my creed when I saw it despised among men. I quite tolerated the Christianity of Mahometan countries, notwithstanding its humble aspect and the damaged character of its followers. I went further, and extended some sympathy towards those who, with all the claims of superior intellect, learning, and industry, were kept down under the heel of the Mussulmans by reason of their having *our* faith. I heard, as I fancied, the faint echo of an old Crusader's conscience, that whispered and said, "Common cause!" The impulse was, as you may suppose, much too feeble to bring me into trouble; it merely influenced my actions in a way thoroughly characteristic of this poor sluggish century, that is, by making me speak almost as civilly to the followers of Christ as I did to their Mahometan foes.

This " holy " Damascus, this " earthly paradise "

of the Prophet, so fair to the eyes that he dared not trust himself to tarry in her blissful shades, she is a city of hidden palaces, of copses and gardens, and fountains and bubbling streams. The juice of her life is the gushing and ice-cold torrent that tumbles from the snowy sides of Anti - Lebanon. Close along on the river's edge, through seven sweet miles of rustling boughs and deepest shade, the city spreads out her whole length. As a man falls flat, face forward on the brook, that he may drink and drink again, so Damascus, thirsting for ever, lies down with her lips to the stream and clings to its rushing waters.

The chief places of public amusement, or rather, of public relaxation, are the baths and the great café ; this last, which is frequented at night by most of the wealthy men, and by many of the humbler sort, consists of a number of sheds, very simply framed and built in a labyrinth of running streams, which foam and roar on every side. The place is lit up in the simplest manner by numbers of small pale lamps strung upon loose cords, and so suspended from branch to branch, that the light, though it looks so quiet amongst the darkening foliage, yet leaps and brightly flashes as it falls upon the troubled waters. All around, and chiefly upon the very edge of the torrents, groups of people are tranquilly seated. They all drink coffee, and inhale the cold fumes of the *narghile* ; they talk rather gently the one to the other, or else are silent. A father will sometimes have two or three of his boys around him ; but the joyousness of an Oriental child is all of the sober sort, and never disturbs the reigning calm of the land.

It has been generally understood, I believe, that

the houses of Damascus are more sumptuous than those of any other city in the East. Some of these, said to be the most magnificent in the place, I had an opportunity of seeing.

Every rich man's house stands detached from its neighbours at the side of a garden, and it is from this cause no doubt that the city (severely menaced by prophecy) has hitherto escaped destruction. You know some parts of Spain, but you have never, I think, been in Andalusia : if you had, I could easily show you the interior of a Damascene house by referring you to the Alhambra or Alcanzar of Seville. The lofty rooms are adorned with a rich inlaying of many colours and illuminated writing on the walls. The floors are of marble. One side of any room intended for noonday retirement is generally laid open to a quadrangle, in the centre of which there dances the jet of a fountain. There is no furniture that can interfere with the cool, palace-like emptiness of the apartments. A divan (which is a low and doubly broad sofa) runs round the three walled sides of the room. A few Persian carpets (which ought to be called Persian rugs, for that is the word which indicates their shape and dimensions) are sometimes thrown about near the divan; they are placed without order, the one partly lapping over the other, and thus disposed, they give to the room an appearance of uncaring luxury; except these (of which I saw few, for the time was summer, and fiercely hot), there is nothing to obstruct the welcome air, and the whole of the marble floor from one divan to the other, and from the head of the chamber across to the murmuring fountain, is thoroughly open and free.

So simple as this is Asiatic luxury ! The Oriental

is not a contriving animal; there is nothing intricate
in his magnificence. The impossibility of handing
down property from father to son for any long period
consecutively seems to prevent the existence of those
traditions by which, with us, the refined modes of
applying wealth are made known to its inheritors.
We know that in England a newly-made rich man
cannot, by taking thought and spending money,
obtain even the same-looking furniture as a gentleman.
The complicated character of an English establishment allows room for subtle distinctions between that
which is *comme il faut*, and that which is not. All
such refinements are unknown in the East; the Pasha
and the peasant have the same tastes. The broad
cold marble floor, the simple couch, the air freshly
waving through a shady chamber, a verse of the
Koran emblazoned on the wall, the sight and the
sound of falling water, the cold fragrant smoke of
the *narghile*, and a small collection of wives and
children in the inner apartments — all these, the
utmost enjoyments of the grandee, are yet such as to
be appreciable by the humblest Mussulman in the
empire.

But its gardens are the delight, the delight and
the pride of Damascus. They are not the formal
parterres which you might expect from the Oriental
taste; they rather bring back to your mind the
memory of some dark old shrubbery in our northern
isle, that has been charmingly *un-* "kept up" for
many and many a day. When you see a rich
wilderness of wood in decent England, it is like
enough that you see it with some soft regrets. The
puzzled old woman at the lodge can give small
account of "the family." She thinks it is "Italy"
that has made the whole circle of her world so

gloomy and sad. You avoid the house in lively dread of a lone housekeeper, but you make your way on by the stables; you remember that gable with all its neatly nailed trophies of fitchets and hawks and owls, now slowly falling to pieces; you remember that stable, and that—but the doors are all fastened that used to be standing ajar, the paint of things painted is blistered and cracked, grass grows in the yard; just there, in October mornings, the keeper would wait with the dogs and the guns—no keeper now; you hurry away, and gain the small wicket that used to open to the touch of a lightsome hand— it is fastened with a padlock (the only new looking thing), and is stained with thick, green damp; you climb it, and bury yourself in the deep shade, and strive but lazily with the tangling briars, and stop for long minutes to judge and determine whether you will creep beneath the long boughs and make them your archway, or whether perhaps you will lift your heel and tread them down under foot. Long doubt, and scarcely to be ended till you wake from the memory of those days when the path was clear, and chase that phantom of a muslin sleeve that once weighed warm upon your arm.

Wild as that, the nighest woodland of a deserted home in England, but without its sweet sadness, is the sumptuous garden of Damascus. Forest trees, tall and stately enough if you could see their lofty crests, yet lead a tussling life of it below, with their branches struggling against strong numbers of bushes and wilful shrubs. The shade upon the earth is black as night. High, high above your head, and on every side all down to the ground, the thicket is hemmed in and choked up by the interlacing boughs that droop with the weight of roses, and load the

slow air with their damask breath.[1] There are no
other flowers. Here and there, there are patches of
ground made clear from the cover, and these are
either carelessly planted with some common and
useful vegetable, or else are left free to the wayward
ways of Nature, and bear rank weeds, moist-looking
and cool to the eyes, and freshening the sense with
their earthy and bitter fragrance. There is a lane
opened through the thicket, so broad in some places
that you can pass along side by side; in some so
narrow (the shrubs are for ever encroaching) that
you ought, if you can, to go on the first and hold
back the bough of the rose-tree. And through this
wilderness there tumbles a loud rushing stream, which
is halted at last in the lowest corner of the garden,
and there tossed up in a fountain by the side of the
simple alcove. This is all.

Never for an instant will the people of Damascus
attempt to separate the idea of bliss from these wild
gardens and rushing waters. Even where your best
affections are concerned, and you, prudent preachers,
" hold hard " and turn aside when they come near
the mysteries of the happy state, and we (prudent
preachers too), we will hush our voices, and never
reveal to finite beings the joys of the " earthly
paradise."

[1] The rose-trees which I saw were all of the kind we
call " damask "; they grow to an immense height and size.

CHAPTER XXVIII

"THE ruins of Baalbec!" Shall I scatter the vague, solemn thoughts and all the airy phantasies which gather together when once those words are spoken, that I may give you instead tall columns and measurements true, and phrases built with ink? No, no; the glorious sounds shall still float on as of yore, and still hold fast upon your brain with their own dim and infinite meaning.

Come! Baalbec is over; I got "rather well" out of that.

The path by which I crossed the Lebanon is like, I think, in its features to one which you must know, namely, that of the Foorca in the Bernese Oberland. For a great part of the way I toiled rather painfully through the dazzling snow, but the labour of ascending added to the excitement with which I looked for the summit of the pass. The time came. There was a minute in the which I saw nothing but the steep, white shoulder of the mountain, and there was another minute, and that the next, which showed me a nether heaven of fleecy clouds that floated along far down in the air beneath me, and showed me beyond the breadth of all Syria west of the Lebanon. But chiefly I clung with my eyes to the dim, steadfast

293

line of the sea which closed my utmost view. I had
grown well used of late to the people and the scenes
of forlorn Asia—well used to tombs and ruins, to
silent cities and deserted plains, to tranquil men and
women sadly veiled; and now that I saw the-even
plain of the sea, I leapt with an easy leap to its
yonder shores, and saw all the kingdoms of the West
in that fair path that could lead me from out of this
silent land straight on into shrill Marseilles, or round
by the pillars of Hercules to the crash and roar of
London. My place upon this dividing barrier was
as a man's puzzling station in eternity, between the
birthless past and the future that has no end.
Behind me I left an old, decrepit world; religions
dead and dying; calm tyrannies expiring in silence;
women hushed and swathed, and turned into waxen
dolls; love flown, and in its stead mere royal and
"paradise" pleasures. Before me there waited glad
bustle and strife; love itself, an emulous game;
religion, a cause and a controversy, well smitten and
well defended; men governed by reasons and suasion
of speech; wheels going, steam buzzing—a mortal
race, and a slashing pace, and the devil taking the
hindmost—taking *me*, by Jove! (for that was my
inner care), if I lingered too long upon the difficult
pass that leads from thought to action.

I descended and went towards the west.

The group of cedars remaining on this part of the
Lebanon is held sacred by the Greek Church on
account of a prevailing notion that the trees were
standing at a time when the temple of Jerusalem was
built. They occupy three or four acres on the
mountain's side, and many of them are gnarled in a
way that implies great age, but except these signs I
saw nothing in their appearance or conduct that

tended to prove them contemporaries of the cedars employed in Solomon's Temple. The final cause to which these aged survivors owed their preservation was explained to me in the evening by a glorious old fellow (a Christian chief), who made me welcome in the valley of Eden. In ancient times the whole range of the Lebanon had been covered with cedars, and as the fertile plains beneath became more and more infested by Government officers and tyrants of high and low degree, the people by degrees abandoned them and flocked to the rugged mountains, which were less accessible to their indolent oppressors. The cedar forests gradually shrank under the axe of the encroaching multitudes, and seemed at last to be on the point of disappearing entirely, when an aged chief who ruled in this district, and who had witnessed the great change effected even in his own lifetime, chose to say that some sign or memorial should be left of the vast woods with which the mountains had formerly been clad, and commanded accordingly that this group of trees (which was probably situated at the highest point to which the forest had reached) should remain untouched. The chief, it seems, was not moved by the notion I have mentioned as prevailing in the Greek Church, but rather by some sentiment of veneration for a great natural feature—a sentiment akin, perhaps, to that old and earthborn religion, which made men bow down to creation before they had yet learnt how to know and worship the Creator.

The chief of the valley in which I passed the night was a man of large possessions, and he entertained me very sumptuously. He was highly intelligent, and had had the sagacity to foresee that Europe would intervene authoritatively in the affairs

of Syria. Bearing this idea in mind, and with a
view to give his son an advantageous start in the
ambitious career, for which he was destined, he had
hired for him a teacher of the Italian language, the
only accessible European tongue. The tutor, however, who was a native of Syria, either did not know
or did not choose to teach the European forms of
address, but contented himself with instructing his
pupil in the mere language of Italy. This circumstance gave me an opportunity (the only one I ever
had, or was likely to have [1]) of hearing the phrases
of Oriental courtesy in a European tongue. The
boy was about twelve or thirteen years old, and
having the advantage of being able to speak to me
without the aid of an interpreter, he took a prominent
part in doing the honours of his father's house. He
went through his duties with untiring assiduity, and
with a kind of gracefulness which by mere description can scarcely be made intelligible to those who
are unacquainted with the manners of the Asiatics.
The boy's address resembled a little that of a highly
polished and insinuating Roman Catholic priest, but
had more of girlish gentleness. It was strange to
hear him gravely and slowly enunciating the common
and extravagant compliments of the East in good
Italian, and in soft, persuasive tones. I recollect
that I was particularly amused at the gracious
obstinacy with which he maintained that the house in
which I was so hospitably entertained belonged not
to his father, but to me. To say this once was only
to use the common form of speech, signifying no
more than our sweet word "welcome," but the
amusing part of the matter was that, whenever in the

[1] A dragoman never interprets in terms the courteous
language of the East.

course of conversation I happened to speak of his father's house or the surrounding domàin, the boy invariably interfered to correct my pretended mistake, and to assure me once again with a gentle decisiveness of manner that the whole property was really and exclusively mine, and that his father had not the most distant pretensions to its ownership.

I received from my host much, and (as I now know) most true, information respecting the people of the mountains, and their power of resisting Mehemet Ali. The chief gave me very plainly to understand that the mountaineers, being dependent upon others for bread and gunpowder (the two great necessaries of martial life), could not long hold out against a power which occupied the plains and commanded the sea ; but he also assured me, and that very significantly, that if this source of weakness were provided against, *the mountaineers were to be depended upon ;* he told me that in ten or fifteen days the chiefs could bring together some fifty thousand fighting men.

CHAPTER XXIX

SURPRISE OF SATALIEH [1]

WHILST I was remaining upon the coast of Syria I had the good fortune to become acquainted with the Russian Sataliefsky,[2] a general officer, who in his youth had fought and bled at Borodino, but was now better known among diplomats by the important trust committed to him at a period highly critical for the affairs of Eastern Europe. I must not tell you his family name ; my mention of his title can do him no harm, for it is I, and I only, who have conferred it, in consideration of the

[1] [This place, which is commonly called Adalia (Antalia in Turkish), is now a port in the province of Konia.

In the time of the Crusades the name varied between Attalie (or Attalia) and Sattalie (Sattalia). As it seems clear that it is derived from the founder, King Attalus, the S must be a later addition, and is perhaps to be identified with the Greek preposition εἰς, which is responsible for such forms as Istambol (εἰς τὴν πόλιν).]

[2] A title signifying transcender or conqueror of Satalieh. *

* [Sataliefsky is merely an adjective derived from Satalieh, and means " the Satalian," just as Zabalkansky (p. 24) means " the Trans-Balkanic one." I mention this because in both cases Kinglake gives the translation "Transcender " of the Balkans or Satalieh.]

military and diplomatic services performed under my
own eyes.

The General as well as I was bound for Smyrna,
and we agreed to sail together in an Ionian brigantine.
We did not charter the vessel, but we made our
arrangement with the captain upon such terms that
we could be put ashore upon any part of the coast
that we might choose. We sailed, and day after day
the vessel lay dawdling on the sea with calms and
feeble breezes for her portion. I myself was well re-
paid for the painful restlessness which such weather
occasions, because I gained from my companion a
little of that vast fund of interesting knowledge with
which he was stored, knowledge a thousand times
the more highly to be prized since it was not of the
sort that is to be gathered from books, but only
from the lips of those who have acted a part in
the world.

When after nine days of sailing, or trying to sail,
we found ourselves still hanging by the mainland
to the north of the isle of Cyprus, we determined
to disembark at Satalieh, and to go on thence by
land. A light breeze favoured our purpose, and
it was with great delight that we neared the
fragrant land, and saw our anchor go down in the
bay of Satalieh, within two or three hundred yards
of the shore.

The town of Satalieh [1] is the chief place of the
Pashalic in which it is situate, and its citadel is the
residence of the Pasha. We had scarcely dropped
our anchor when a boat from the shore came
alongside with officers on board, who announced that
the strictest orders had been received for maintaining

[1] Spelt " Attalia " and sometimes " Adalia " in English
books and maps.

a quarantine of three weeks against all vessels coming from Syria, and directed accordingly that no one from the vessel should disembark. In reply we sent a message to the Pasha, setting forth the rank and titles of the General, and requiring permission to go ashore. After a while the boat came again alongside, and the officers declaring that the orders received from Constantinople were imperative and unexceptional, formally enjoined us in the name of the Pasha to abstain from any attempt to land.

I had been hitherto much less impatient of our slow voyage than my gallant friend, but this opposition made the smooth sea seem to me like a prison, from which I must and would break out. I had an unbounded faith in the feebleness of Asiatic potentates, and I proposed that we should set the Pasha at defiance. The General had been worked up to a state of a most painful agitation by the idea of being driven from the shore which smiled so pleasantly before his eyes, and he adopted my suggestion with rapture.

We determined to land.

To approach the sweet shore after a tedious voyage, and then to be suddenly and unexpectedly prohibited from landing—this is so maddening to the temper, that no one who had ever experienced the trial would say that even the most violent impatience of such restraint is wholly inexcusable. I am not going to pretend, however, that the course which we chose to adopt on the occasion can be perfectly justified. The impropriety of a traveller's setting at naught the regulations of a foreign State is clear enough, and the bad taste of compassing such a purpose by mere gasconading is still more glaringly plain. I knew perfectly well that if the

Pasha understood his duty, and had energy enough to perform it, he would order out a file of soldiers the moment we landed, and cause us both to be shot upon the beach, without allowing more contact than might be absolutely necessary for the purpose of making us stand fire ; but I also firmly believed that the Pasha would not see the befitting line of conduct nearly so well as I did, and that even if he did know his duty, he would hardly succeed in finding resolution enough to perform it.

We ordered the boat to be got in readiness, and the officers on shore seeing these preparations, gathered together a number of guards, who assembled upon the sands. We saw that great excitement prevailed, and that messengers were continually going to and fro between the shore and the citadel. Our captain, out of compliment to his Excellency, had provided the vessel with a Russian war-flag, which he had hoisted alternately with the Union Jack, and we agreed that we would attempt our disembarkation under this, the Russian standard ! I was glad when we came to that resolution, for I should have been sorry to engage the honoured flag of England in such an affair as that which we were undertaking. The Russian ensign was therefore committed to one of the sailors, who took his station at the stern of the boat. We gave particular instructions to the captain of the brigantine, and when all was ready, the General and I, with our respective servants, got into the boat, and were slowly rowed towards the shore. The guards gathered together at the point for which we were making, but when they saw that our boat went on without altering her course, *they ceased to stand very still ;* none of them ran away, or even shrank back, but they looked as if *the pack were being shuffled,*

every man seeming desirous to change places with
his neighbour. They were still at their post, however,
when our oars went in, and the bow of our boat ran
up—well up upon the beach.

The General was lame by an honourable wound
received at Borodino, and could not without some
assistance get out of the boat; I, therefore, landed
the first. My instructions to the captain were
attended to with the most perfect accuracy, for
scarcely had my foot indented the sand when the
four six-pounders of the brigantine quite gravely
rolled out their brute thunder. Precisely as I had
expected, the guards and all the people who had
gathered about them gave way under the shock
produced by the mere sound of guns, and we were all
allowed to disembark with the least molestation.

We immediately formed a little column, or rather,
as I should have called it, a procession, for we had
no fighting aptitude in us, and were only trying, as it
were, how far we could go in frightening full-grown
children. First marched the sailor with the Russian
flag of war bravely flying in the breeze, then came
the General and I, then our servants, and lastly, if
I rightly recollect, two more of the brigantine's
crew. Our flag-bearer so exulted in his honourable
office, and bore the colours aloft with so much of
pomp and dignity, that I found it exceedingly hard
to keep a grave countenance. We advanced towards
the castle, but the people had now had time to
recover from the effect of the six-pounders (only of
course loaded with powder), and they could not help
seeing not only the numerical weakness of our party,
but the very slight amount of wealth and resource
which it seemed to imply. They began to hang round
us more closely, and just as this reaction was begin-

ning, the General, who was perfectly unacquainted with the Asiatic character, thoughtlessly turned round in order to speak to one of the servants. The effect of this slight move was magical. The people thought we were going to give way, and instantly closed round us. In two words, and with one touch, I showed my comrade the danger he was running, and in the next instant we were both advancing more pompously than ever. Some minutes afterwards there was a second appearance of reaction, followed again by wavering and indecision on the part of the Pasha's people, but at length it seemed to be understood that we should go unmolested into the audience hall.

Constant communication had been going on between the receding crowd and the Pasha, and so when we reached the gates of the citadel we saw that preparations were made for giving us an awe-striking reception. Parting at once from the sailors and our servants, the General and I were conducted into the audience hall ; and there at least I suppose the Pasha hoped that he would confound us by his greatness. The hall was nothing more than a large whitewashed room. Oriental potentates have a pride in that sort of simplicity, when they can contrast it with the exhibition of power, and this the Pasha was able to do, for the lower end of the hall was filled with his officers. These men, of whom I thought there were about fifty or sixty, were all handsomely, though plainly, dressed in the military frockcoats of Europe ; they stood in mass, and so as to present a hollow semicircular front towards the upper end of the hall at which the Pasha sat ; they opened a narrow lane for us when we entered, and as soon as we had passed they again closed up their ranks. An attempt was made to induce us to remain at a respect-

ful distance from his mightiness. To have yielded
in this point would have been fatal to our success,
perhaps to our lives; but the General and I had
already determined upon the place which we should
take, and we rudely pushed on towards the upper
end of the hall.

Upon the divan, and close up against the right
hand corner of the room, there sat the Pasha, his
limbs gathered in, the whole creature coiled up like
an adder. His cheeks were deadly pale, and his lips
perhaps had turned white, for without moving a
muscle the man impressed me with an immense idea
of the wrath within him. He kept his eyes inexorably fixed as if upon vacancy, and with the look of a
man accustomed to refuse the prayers of those who
sue for life. We soon discomposed him, however,
from this studied fixity of feature, for we marched
straight up to the divan and sat down, the Russian
close to the Pasha, and I by the side of the Russian.
This act astonished the attendants, and plainly
disconcerted the Pasha. He could no longer maintain the glassy stillness of the eyes which he had
affected, and evidently became much agitated. At
the feet of the satrap there stood a trembling Italian.
This man was a sort of medico in the potentate's
service, and now in the absence of our attendants he
was to act as interpreter. The Pasha caused him to
tell us that we had openly defied his authority, and
had forced our way on shore in the teeth of his own
officers.

Up to this time I had been the planner of the
enterprise, but now that the moment had come when
all would depend upon able and earnest speechifying,
I felt at once the immense superiority of my gallant
friend, and gladly left to him the whole conduct of

this discussion. Indeed he had vast advantages over
me, not only by his superior command of language
and his far more spirited style of address, but also in
his consciousness of a good cause ; for whilst I felt
myself completely in the wrong, his Excellency had
really worked himself up to believe that the Pasha's
refusal to permit our landing was a gross outrage and
insult. Therefore, without deigning to defend our
conduct, he at once commenced a spirited attack upon
the Pasha. The poor Italian doctor translated one
or two sentences to the Pasha, but he evidently
mitigated their import. The Russian, growing
warm, insisted upon his attack with redoubled energy
and spirit ; but the medico, instead of translating,
began to shake violently with terror, and at last he
came out with his *non ardisco*, and fairly confessed
that he dared not interpret fierce words to his master.

Now then, at a time when everything seemed to
depend upon the effect of speech, we were left without an interpreter.

But this very circumstance, which at first appeared
so unfavourable, turned out to be advantageous. The
General, finding that he could not have his words
translated, ceased to speak in Italian, and recurred to
his accustomed French ; he became eloquent. No
one present except myself understood one syllable of
what he was saying, but he had drawn forth his
passport, and the energy and violence with which, as
he spoke, he pointed to the graven Eagle of all the
Russias, began to make an impression. The Pasha
saw at his side a man not only free from every the
least pang of fear, but raging, as it seemed, with just
indignation, and thenceforward he plainly began to
think that, in some way or other (he could not tell
how) he must certainly have been in the wrong. In

20

a little time he was so much shaken that the Italian
ventured to resume his interpretation, and my
comrade had again the opportunity of pressing his
attack upon the Pasha. His argument, if I rightly
recollect its import, was to this effect: " If the vilest
Jews were to come into the harbour, you would but
forbid them to land, and force them to perform
quarantine; yet this is the very course, O Pasha,
which your rash officers dared to think of adopting
with *us* !—those mad and reckless men would have
actually dealt towards a Russian general officer and
an English gentleman as if they had been wretched
Israelites ! Never—never will we submit to such an
indignity. His Imperial Majesty knows how to
protect his nobles from insult, and would never endure
that a general of his army should be treated in
matter of quarantine as though he were a mere
Eastern Jew ! This argument told with great
effect. The Pasha fairly admitted that he felt its
weight, and he now only struggled to obtain such a
compromise as might partly save his dignity. He
wanted us to perform a quarantine of one day for
form's sake, and in order to show his people that he
was not utterly defied ; but finding that we were
inexorable, he not only abandoned his attempt, but
promised to supply us with horses.

When the discussion had arrived at this happy
conclusion, *tchibouques* and coffee were brought, and
we passed, I think, nearly an hour in friendly
conversation. The Pasha, it now appeared, had
once been a prisoner of war in Russia, and a conviction of the Emperor's vast power, necessarily acquired
during this captivity, made him perhaps more alive
than an untravelled Turk would have been to the
force of my comrade's eloquence.

The Pasha now gave us a generous feast. Our promised horses were brought without much delay. I gained my loved saddle once more, and when the moon got up and touched the heights of Taurus, we were joyfully winding our way through the first of his rugged defiles.

APPENDIX

THE HOME OF LADY HESTER
STANHOPE

IT was late when we came in sight of two high conical hills, on one of which stands the village of Djouni, on the other a circular wall, over which dark trees were waving; and this was the place in which Lady Hester Stanhope had finished her strange and eventful career. It had formerly been a convent, but the Pasha of Sidon had given it to the "prophet-lady," who converted its naked walls into a palace, and its wilderness into gardens.

The sun was setting as we entered the enclosure, and we were soon scattered about the outer court, picketing our horses, rubbing down their foaming flanks, and washing out their wounds. The buildings that constituted the palace were of a very scattered and complicated description, covering a wide space, but only one storey in height: courts and gardens, stables and sleeping-rooms, halls of audience and ladies' bowers, were strangely intermingled. Heavy weeds were growing everywhere among the open portals, and we forced our way with difficulty through a tangle of roses and jasmine to the inner court; here choice flowers once bloomed, and fountains played in

marble basins, but now was presented a scene of the most melancholy desolation. As the watchfire blazed up, its gleam fell upon masses of honeysuckle and woodbine, on white, mouldering walls beneath, and dark, waving trees above; while the group of mountaineers who gathered round its light, with their long beards and vivid dresses, completed the strange picture.

The clang of sword and spear resounded through the long galleries; horses neighed among bowers and boudoirs; strange figures hurried to and fro among the colonnades, shouting in Arabic, English, and Italian; the fire crackled, the startled bats flapped their heavy wings, and the growl of distant thunder filled up the pauses in the rough symphony.

Our dinner was spread on the floor in Lady Hester's favourite apartment; her deathbed was our sideboard, her furniture our fuel, her name our conversation. Almost before the meal was ended two of our party had dropped asleep over their trenchers from fatigue; the Druses had retired from the haunted precincts to their village; and W——, L——, and I went out into the garden to smoke our pipes by Lady Hester's lonely tomb. About midnight we fell asleep upon the ground, wrapped in our capotes, and dreamed of ladies and tombs and prophets till the neighing of our horses announced the dawn.

After a hurried breakfast on fragments of the last night's repast we strolled out over the extensive gardens. Here many a broken arbour and trellis, bending under masses of jasmine and honeysuckle, show the care and taste that were once lavished on this wild but beautiful hermitage; a garden-house, surrounded by an enclosure of roses run wild, lies in

the midst of a grove of myrtle and bay trees. This was Lady Hester's favourite resort during her lifetime; and now, within its silent enclosure,

> "After life's fitful fevers he sleeps well."

The hand of ruin has dealt very sparingly with all these interesting relics; the Pasha's power by day, and the fear of spirits by night, keep off marauders; and though *we* made free with broken benches and fallen doorposts for fuel, we reverently abstained from displacing anything in the establishment except a few roses, which there was no living thing but bees and nightingales to regret. It was one of the most striking and interesting spots I ever witnessed: its silence and beauty, its richness and desolation, lent to it a touching and mysterious character, that suited well the memory of that strange hermit-lady who has made it a place of pilgrimage, even in Palestine.[1]

The Pasha of Sidon presented Lady Hester with the deserted convent of Mar Elias on her arrival in his country, and this she soon converted into a fortress, garrisoned by a band of Albanians: her only attendants besides were her doctor, her secretary, and some female slaves. Public rumour soon busied

---

[1] While Lady Hester Stanhope lived, although numbers visited the convent, she almost invariably refused admittance to strangers. She assigned as a reason the use which M. de Lamartine had made of his interview. Mrs. T., who passed some weeks at Djouni, told me, that when Lady Hester read his account of this interview, she exclaimed, "It is all false; we did not converse together for more than five minutes; but no matter, no traveller hereafter shall betray or forge my conversation." The author of *Eothen*, however, was her guest, and has given us an interesting account of his visit in his brilliant volume.

itself with such a personage, and exaggerated her influence and power. It is even said that she was crowned Queen of the East at Palmyra by fifty thousand Arabs. She certainly exercised almost despotic power in her neighbourhood on the mountain; and what was perhaps the most remarkable proof of her talents, she prevailed on some Jews to advance large sums of money to her on her note of hand. She lived for many years, beset with difficulties and anxieties, but to the last she held on gallantly; even when confined to her bed and dying she sought for no companionship or comfort but such as she could find in her own powerful, though unmanageable, mind.

Mr. Moore, our consul at Beyrout, hearing she was ill, rode over the mountains to visit her, accompanied by Mr. Thomson, the American missionary. It was evening when they arrived, and a profound silence was over all the palace. No one met them; they lighted their own lamps in the outer court, and passed unquestioned through court and gallery until they came to where *she* lay. A corpse was the only inhabitant of the palace, and the isolation from her kind which she had sought so long was indeed complete. That morning thirty-seven servants had watched every motion of her eye: its spell once darkened by death, every one fled with such plunder as they could secure. A little girl, adopted by her and maintained for years, took her watch and some papers on which she had set peculiar value. Neither the child nor the property were ever seen again. Not a single thing was left in the room where she lay dead, except the ornaments upon her person. No one had ventured to touch these; even in death she seemed able to protect herself. At midnight her countryman and the missionary carried her out by torchlight to a spot in the garden that had been formerly her favourite resort, and here they buried the self-exiled lady.—*From* "THE CRESCENT AND THE CROSS," *by Eliot Warburton.*

THE END

PRINTED BY MORRISON AND GIBB LIMITED, EDINBURGH